Correspondence and Chronicles

from the
Convent

He will not break a bruised reed,
neither will He quench a smoldering wick.
Is 42:3

Do Not Be afraid of those
who kill the body
but can not kill
the soul

Matthew 10:28

Events, locales and conversations from my
memories have been recreated to maintain anonymity.
Have also changed the names of individuals
and any identifying characteristics.

For Annie
my real sister
who always has my
best interest
at
Heart

Clicking Down the Corridor

I. A New Purpose

I did not realize that I was visiting every convent in New England
and as far North as Quebec City in a constant state of flux until my
brother-in-law said that I could make a living doing this. It then
occurred to me that I must choose one and settle down. How does
the romantic idealist do this? I was considering all the wrong
criteria. You see, I liked the old-fashioned traditional habits. Most
of the Religious orders were dispensing with those. Then I was
looking for a bucolic setting and preferably, one not too far from
home – so much for giving up my will! I enjoyed traveling to all the
different convents if only I could find one that wore blue like the nun
on the bottle of "Blue Nun" wine! I guess I figured all the rest
would fall into place. There was an order in Worcester,
Massachusetts and they wore burgundy. They would set up their
coffee maker the night before so that a button merely had to be

pressed before Matins began and then, after Mass, voila, fresh coffee. I was also looking at an order where the Sisters did not have to rise until 7 a.m. That was a tough one, but you see, I have always been more of a night person. Food was another consideration for me too – did they have good meals. I wanted to serve Our Lord but I guess I wanted to do it my way.

I loved the nuns in Quebec. The Chapel was way up on the seventh floor. It always smelled so clean there. They made their own soap.
I went with one of the Sisters when she went to purchase new winter boots. Her name was Sister Marcelle. She took me to The Plains of Abraham afterwards. It was a cold, windy biting day in February.
These were the Grey Nuns. However, they wore brown. I liked the idea that Grampa's family hailed from Quebec and he was always talking about the Chateau Frontenac and how he and Gramma would stay there.

One day, my Pastor told me about a Sister who was starting a new order up in Ottawa. She was working closely with Father Paul Marx. Her plan was to raise up an order to protect the unborn. I went there to see if maybe this was where God wanted me. Sister Lucille was domineering and frankly, very manipulative. Here Father Salmon dropped me off, hat boxes and my stereo – and this Sister, who had a deep voice – much like the actress Patricia Neal, was very overbearing. It was as though she was putting all her angst from the previous order which she had left into this effort. It was her strong will and ambitious ways that just put me off. There were a couple of lay people there who worked in the office in the day time. They did not like it there either. I left my beautiful Saint Therese portrait and my Saint Anthony portrait – both of which were huge, along with my stereo – to the gal who was working in the office. Afterall, she made a mean lemon meringue pie. Then, when Father Salmon came to visit, it did not take him long to realize that something was awry. He arranged for me to go back home by way of Brushton. There, I stayed with Miss Catherine Sullivan. She was a cute older Irish lady who played the piano. She was one of the "pillars of the Church" at Saint Mary's in Brushton. Miss Sullivan had a neighbor who was Native American Indian. He would check on her and do odd jobs. He was stealthy and quiet. He would just appear. You never heard him coming. Miss Sullivan made her coffee in an unusual manner. She would perk it and she had this set up where she lined a filter with tin foil. The coffee was very good. Miss Sullivan lived across the street from the church. She had this huge mural that hung at the foot of the stairs. My friend Nancy was very taken with this mural. It was the scene of a girl on a swing. There was something rather mystical about it. My friend Nancy and her son Christopher, a second cousin to me, came to pick me up the following day. I suppose that I was so relieved that I acted a bit crazy as I ran over to the water pump and made a motion reminiscent of Helen Keller. Incidentally, my great Aunt Mary had Helen Keller's autograph, but, as Chris Plante says, "I digress".

In the interim, I had written to Gramma Farleigh. I was fearful of disappointing her. She understood more than I gave her credit for.

Then, within the year, Father Salmon had told me of another order that was starting up. It was Cardinal O'Malley's order – The Sisters of Hope. Again, it was an order necessary for the times – to protect and enhance the sanctity of life from the moment of conception to natural death. I was on board. I wrote to His Eminence and I was thrilled when I received a personal reply. I was invited to the next retreat in New York. All the paperwork was completed and then another trip ensued where I had to take Psychological testing. I was to go to the seminary in Yonkers. The train got stuck on the tracks due to an accident and I did not get into Yonkers until two in the morning. I had my interview with the Pycholigist the next morning. Another prospective candidate was there too. I got back on the Amtak later that day and returned home to Grampa's. Within a week, I learned that I had been accepted to be received as a postulant in the coming February.

I thought I had better get caught up on correspondence so I wrote to many of my friends to let them know of my plans. I received a letter written on January 21st, 1992 from Sloan Wilson. It was written from his yacht Ketch "Pretty Betty III":

Dear Virginia,

Betty and I were much moved by your letter. We are not people who are devoted to any formal religion, but we know that the churches have helped many people to live useful and purposeful lives. The main thing is to be devoted to someone or something more important than oneself, whether it is an art, a science, a family, a government or a religious order. And nothing is set in concrete – people can go from one form of self-consecration to another as thy mature and change if they want to. In any case, you obviously are a wise, moral and loving person. I feel sure that whatever you do will be right for you and that you will help many people. No matter what path or paths you choose. May God, (as I fail to understand Him), be with you!

Affectionately,
Sloan
Then his lovely wife Betty writes on the same page:

Dear Virginia,

Your convent in Riverdale is neary Tenafly, N.J. where my step-daughter Becka livs. We visit her, her husband and four children. We would love to meet you again. So when we are up there sometime, could we get together for lunch or something? Her phone number is: -------- and Jessica's number is -------------- and ours is - ----------------------.
Thanks for filling us in about Lynn. Glad she is okay. Sorry her mother died. Anything else about Ti?

Best Love,

Betty

****

I needed to reply to another letter written from a most beautiful Poor Clare nun who is from Port Henry.

She writes:
Christmastide 1991 -92

Dear Virginia,

From the Heart of the Holy Child, pulsing with Divine Love in that tiny Breast, may the grace of this Christmas season flow like a river of peace through all your days in the New Year before us. In joys, or sorrows, good health or illness, success or failure, difficulties, or smooth going, we can have that peace only He can give. He has come to share our whole life, to be our strength, our consolation, our joy, our peace. All our hopes are in this Little One Who invites us to come to Him, give Him our trust, our love, our adoration. Then all we need, He gives us everything, and infinitely more than we could imagine. We know that those little arms extended now will so endearingly be outstretched in another fashion at the end of His life to prove the depths of His love and mercy. No wonder we decorate, celebrate, sing, dance and jubilate over His Birth and want to share the good news that God is truly with us, our Emmanuel! Thank you warmly for adding to the joy and festivities of our Christmas with your thoughtfulness and gracious remembrance. I ask God to reward you and bless you in all ways as I hold you daily in my heart at prayer.

The shadow of the cross fell over my family again last May when my sister Catherine's oldest son, Paul, was discovered to have inoperable lung cancer. Since that time, it has spread to other areas. We ask the support of your prayers for Paul, for Catherine, whose own health is poor, and for all our family. We want to hold fast in faith surrendered to God's dear will in the certainty that light streams from that cross. He is all-wise, all- loving, and knows what is for our welfare, how to draw good out of everything, and chooses the best moment to draw His children Home into the brightness of eternity. May you experience His tender mercies and loving providence all you days. I so appreciate your goodness to me and my community.

We celebrated the Feast of the Epiphany yesterday and have just begun the final week of this cherished season. I pray your star of grace leads you to where the Lord wants you to serve Him in this New Year Virginia. I have read with admiration of the Cardinal's new order. Do let me know if you will enter and let me hear from you afterward if it is permitted you to write to me. I am sure those Gregorian Masses were much appreciated by your dear brother Karl who is also in my prayers. Thank you for remembering Ted. How wonderful Grandmother Burleigh could make the trip to the Holy Land. God Bless her. My love to her, your Mom, and Grandfather LaPointe. I will be having cataract surgery the end of the month. And yes, I know about dear Mrs. Keogh. You must miss her but what a blessed release for her saintly soul.

With grateful love, in Jesus, Our Redeemer,

Sister Mary Agnes Pozzouli

II A Trip to the Bronx

I was excited and I enjoyed getting my book bag, my navy suit together and The Liturgy of the Hours – the four volume set. Aunt Jane and Aunt Mary helped in getting me things. Then, in February, Uncle H.G. hired Bill Hogel to drive one of his vans to accommodate half of the family and my dear friend Christine on a road trip to the Bronx. They would accompany me on this day where I would be received as a postulant in The Sisters of Hope.

Everyone helped me unpack all my stuff in my room which was at the very end of the corridor. One other postulant, who was an older lady, had this huge statue of Saint Theresa, The Little Flower, which her entourage were helping her with. Oddly enough, she had a TV too which was brought into her room. Of course, that was not allowed and it would just be a holding place for the time being. My friend Christine also called "Chrissy", got a big kick out of this.

There were five entrants in my group, or the second group as the first group liked to remind us that they were the original foundresses.

They had entered a few months prior but they ran with the fact that they were the first.

Mom, Gramma and me
III. Entrance into The Sisters of Hope

Before the ceremony, three generations of women knelt side by side in the chapel at Saint Frances de Chantel – Gramma Farleigh, Mom and me. Then, we all made out way next door to the Poor Clare Monastery where Mass and our induction ceremony was held on this

Leap Year, February 29th, where I took a "leap". It was very beautiful. Indeed, thanks to one of the other postulant's father, I have a VHS tape of the ceremony.

Bill Hogel's van was waiting to make the return trip back to Ticonderoga – minus one passenger! After some emotional good-byes, I made my way through the new convent of Saint Frances de Paola.
There were several priests in the parlor, a couple from the rectory next door, and a priest from St. Peter's Church on Barclay Street– which incidentally, included my hometown parish of St. Mary's in Ticonderoga! This priest was our confessor and he was also selected by Saint Mother Theresa to be the Confessor to her Order of The Sisters of Charity.

"Confessor", I thought. That intrigued me. I had heard about them in books like The Lives of The Saints, but for one to actually have his own Confessor really struck me. I makde me feel a little ill-at-ease, and a little serious, and also , a feeling of what a privilege and honor. But could I really confess all my sins to that kindly – looking man. He seems so humble and he looks like he suffered a lot.

After the Mass, I returned to the convent of Saint Frances de Paola. Thirteen from my family had come and now it was time for me to bid farewell. As I was saying good-bye to each and everyone, so as to prolong it, I called fro Gramma Farleigh. "Gramma, come here! I want you to meet Monsignor Robertson." I had just ebraced him as it was the first time I had seen him since the retreat. I had enjoyed him so much on the retreat that brought me here this day. Gramma seemed delighted to meet the Monsignor. She was in her glory having met the Cardinal too. It also pleased her that her grandson Joseph, my cousin, served at the Mass where her pride extended to me as I was received this day – singing "Here I Am Lord". Could it be – they really care for me? Yes, or so the farewells would tell.
Now I must go. But first to my room, to be alone – only for a moment- as there are people waiting downstairs. I must not be rude on my first day. I washed my face – somewhat put together despite the whirling feeling in my head.

I returned downstairs. The living room seemed kind of barren in the way of furniture. I walked over to one sitting in a straight-back chair next to the couch. "Hello, how do you do? You are the Confessor, Father Halligan?" I shook his hands with both of mine. I liked him instantly and I felt that I was in the presence of a very holy man. I was in awe of him. Then I proceded to introduce myself to Monsignor Manselle whose first name is Henry. " Oh, I have a brother with that name!" Then I noticed one of the new postulants who entered with me sitting in the easy blue chair. It was Helene. " Ah, did you have tears?" She asked right in front of all these priests. I felt embarrassed. My family were gone, and "Here I was Lord".

We all went downstairs, basement level, to the refectory where a spaghetti dinner was served. Something happened to me that had never happened to me before in my life. But was it my life. I broke out in hives. I noticed them when I went up into my room. I think all the excitement and the fatigue brought them on. I was emotionally drained.

I talked to one of the new postulants who was in the room next to mine. We both loved everything Irish and we had exchanged stories about our respective travels to Ireland. Her name was Olive. She and I were closest in age. I really liked her and I felt that I could trust her. In addition to Olive, who was a Catholic school teacher on Staten Island, there was Margaret, Dorothy, Diane and Helene. Margaret was a nurse a couple of years my senior. She was from Staten Island. Diane came from Rhode Island – she was a widowed mother of eight who was very active in the church in Rhode Island especially where Pro Life work was concerned. Dorothy had been in The Sisters of St. Vincent where she taught in elementary school. She left that order as things changed dramatically post Vatican II. Helene was also a widow and a mother of eight. Helene was a nurse too. She had worked in the various hospitals in the city; well-acquainted with trauma.

Morning would come early and we were all given assigned tasks. There were two sisters who came up from Monroe, New York to help in the formation of the community. They had dark blue polyester modified habits. The first group were less than receptive in

14

having five new postulants join them. One in the first group was rushed to the hospital for appendicitus. One of the Sisters in the first group said that she had prayed to die. Thankfully, she did not die, but she did not return either which gave cause to consternation.

In the first group, there were seven. There was Sister Roberta from Minnesota. She was famous for writing lengthy missals to the Cardinal and then going on walks where she would mail them. There was Sister Josephat who was very scrupulous and she loved to have her picture taken. She seemed to analyze everything. There was Sister Christina whose family comes from Sicily. There was Sister Pio and she was very devout and obedient though I think she was misunderstood. Then there was Sister Agatha, who comes from an Irish family in Pennsylvania but because it is close to the New York border, she would rather you believe that she is from New York. She has a Master's Degree in Psychology from Columbia University. She is a little bit older than the others in her group and she has this air of superiority about her. She likens herself to Saint Theresa of Avila – one of the Doctors of the Church. She also compares her family to the Kennedys and she enjoys name dropping about the time that she saw Eunice Kennedy coming out of Saint Patrick's Cathedral. There is also an older Sister – Sister Gerard. Her son is a priest. She came from California. Then there was another one from the Mid-West but she took ill so I never got to meet her.

Dorothy is a beautiful letter writer. She so thoughtfully sent Grampa this letter upon my (our) Entrance:

February 29, 1992

Dear "Grampa",

Just a note to let you know that you are in my prayers. It was a hard day for you I am sure. You have given your Virginia to God. I am sure you are feeling a little sad and lonely. She will miss you terribly. She loves you very much. We will both be praying for you.

Please pray for us. She will write soon. God will take care of you and bless you for being so generous to Him,
Love and Peace,

Dorothy

IV. Helene of Troy

I got along with all the Sisters or so I thought I did. For some reason, Helene took a shining to me. Some deemed me too boisterous for the Convent and my friendship with Helene did not help matters. Helene had arthritis and she used to ask me to make her lemonade and take it up to her. I gladly did this as I would have gladly done for any of my sisters. However, they frowned upon this.
One day, coming from Sunday Mass, Helene and I met two ladies from Puerto Rico. They have a hair salon a couple of blocks from us. Helene decided that she wanted to get her hair done. She took her sidekick along with her. Long story short, (no pun intended), we both returned in time for Compline with new hairstyles. This did not bode well. The Sisters from Monroe, Sister Carol and Sister Rita were more tolerant of Helene. Helene admired Sister Rita. Helene adored the Cardinal. She was motherly towards him and she would think nothing of patting him on the shoulders. Helene was very human and she would let me know which priests she thought were "good-looking". Of course Helene herself was a real looker in her prime. She resembled the actress who is the daughter of Edward Bergen, the ventriloquist, Candice Bergen.

Helene has endured so much pain in her life. Her sense of humor matched this level of pain. Helene needed someone who would appreciate her humor. Enter me. It used to get us in trouble. Helene is a great impersonator and she was given to imitating any one of the sisters at any given time and then looking at me to get my reaction. I was a bundle of nerves and the schedule was exhausting which was a lethal combination for a place that adheres to silence and discipline.
In spite of all this, Helene had a great Faith. She loved her Saint Theresa, and Mother Mary. She loved to read and she was very well- read.

While I left my grandfather whom I was very close to, Helene left her grandson whom she had been raising. It was not easy.

Helene grew up at a time when smoking cigarettes was considered glamorous. Helene tried to give up smoking but it is a very hard habit to kick. She asked me to go and buy her cigarettes for her. I am more of a spirit of the law than letter of the law person. Once she got the cigarettes in her possession, she had me stand on the look -out as we both climbed the fire stairs to the roof of the convent. The Throggs Neck Bridge was in the distance. She would inhale and then do her lively imitations which would get me laughing hysterically. I nicknamed her "Helene of Troy".
Other times, on my way down the corridor, she would nab me as she would want to visit before turning in. It was so bad that we had to put a pillow on our faces to muffle our laughter. It was an outlet for all the petty things that went on throughout the day.

We had Confession every Friday thank goodness. Father Halligan would come from St. Peter's. It seems he was Sister Agatha's Confessor and she recommended him to the Cardinal. He had survived many heart surgeries having several pig valves replacing the original valves. He had this condition since he was 26 years old. Father would invoke The Holy Spirit before giving us these wonderful exegeses on different subjects pertinent to religious life. Mainly, he would emphasize abandoning ourselves to Divine Providence and pondering on The Crucified Lord. Humility was what he impressed upon us. I grew to appreciate and love this priest so much.

Father Halligan was hand chosen by the Cardinal with input from Sister Agatha as he had been her confessor. He was confessor to Mother Theresa's Sisters of Charity too.

I wrote to Grampa regularly and to many others back home. Here are some of my letters:

V. Letters from Home

17

This from my youngest sister Sarah:

3/2/92

Dear Virginia,

Howdy! How are you doing? Did you ever get your closet door
open? Did you get to sleep in and are you more rested? Is the food
good? How is the Card? How is Dorothy and anyone else I missed?
I just thought to open my letter that I would bombard you with
questions.

The bus ride home was just as entertaining as on the way down. I sat
between Georgie and Chrissy in the back seat. She was enjoying Sir
William's stories. Then we stopped in New Paltz at a diner. I had a
cheeseburger. Mom asked Bill if he would like to sit with us but he
said, "no thanks, they usually give busdrivers a free meal." So he sat
at the counter. Uncle Mike tried to pay for the dinner but Bill said it
was taken care of. I guess Chrissy took care of it though I think
Mom took care of Chrissy. On the rest of the way home, Joe sat
between Chrissy and Georgie. He was talking up a storm! After
Glens Falls, Chrissy sat up front, Joe and I fell asleep on the back
two seats but we heard Bill tell us how he doesn't bother to go to the
dentist. He just takes some old cow/horse teeth pliers, gets the rust
off, and then yanked out three teeth!! Chrissy said to tell you about
Bill's Bus/Dentistry Service!! When we got home, we were wide
awake. It was about 1:00 a.m. We told Dad all about the trip. Then
I went to bed and I slept in. When I got up, I got dressed and I put
on my new hat that you gave me. Then, we went to Ames to get
Mary some birthday gifts. Then we went up to see Grampa. Mom
told him all about the trip. Then she asked him, "Is there anything I
can get for you?" To which he replied, "If I hear that one more time,
I am going to bolt the door!" Apparently, Thomas stopped in, Jane
checked on him, Terry W. came by and someone named Fran ?
Asked if he needed anything.
Oh, Grampa told me that the hat looked good on me. Well, talk to
you later,

Loads of love,
Sarah

****

Tuesday 3 March, 1992
Saint Frances de Chantal Convent
Bronx,

My Dear Grandfather,

Hi Grampa! I feel bad as I meant to wash your feet before I left –
on Friday evening. How are you? You are wonderful! Very selfless
– and you are being strong for me – I know. You are making it
easier for me though I know your heart better.

It was a little unsettling to have one of the novices leave. I guess it
is something that she had been struggling with for some time. The
other one got the boot because she snuk and smoked. She wore
make-up, dyed, and, horror of horrors – curled her hair! She had
her family mail her cigarettes. She couldn't kick the habit so to
speak.

I miss going in stores.

Food is excellent – lots of fruit and vegetables. I like everyone in
my group. Some in the first group are hard to get used to. They are
still shook about that girl leaving.

I am playing my cassette recorder now. It really is a good little
machine.

Grampa, the Cardinal was asking for you. He said, "How is
Grampa?" And he called me "Heidi". He is a beautiful man.
Dorothy sends you her love. Some Sunday when you call, you must
ask for her first. It would make her feel good. She would really like
to meet you.

It was so good to hear your voice.

19

Did Aunt Karlene ever come down? I know how much you look forward to her visits.

Well, it is off to 9:30 a.m. class now It is so nice to have so many reminders of home around me. I have your photo on my bureau. I love you Grampa.

Tell Jane that I wear her apron.

Sorry so many people are bugging you.

Words can not describe the beauty of The Mass and the Ceremony on Saturday and then to have the support of the family.

How are the cats?

For now, and please stay well,

Lovingly yours,

Virginia

****
Letter from Mrs. Dechame:

Stephanie Pell Dechame
Fort Ticonderoga Road
Ticonderoga, New York 12883

Monday

My Dear Virginia,

No, you have not offended me, and never, never could, or will!! I thought of you every single second of the day you left to "enter" - I kept looking at the clock and thinking "now they are in Albany, now they are in the Bronx, now…., now,…. My prayers were and have been with you all the way. I have chuckled so often at things I have

heard or that you have written, and eaten up your precious letters. Your Uncle John (McDonald) repeated to me the incident of the locked closet door upon arrival! Good Virginia! That was really starting off on the right foot! Then, your Grandma Burleigh recounted each moment of the beautiful ceremony, and you can bet your life that I plied her with questions – she never lost patience and she obliged graciously. I loved the photo and your subsequent description of the Cardinal and the other women entering. I have a good idea of your room, your schedule, problems (the Sister Superior leaving); pleasures – walking across from Throggs Neck Bridge and, mmmm. I know from your Grandpa that after much searching, you found the right order for your talents. How happy he and I are that you did not find this at the North Pole or in Terra Fuega, Chile! He so looks forward to the weekly phone call (10:04) and knowing you are not too far away and "settled" means a lot to him. I sincerely hope this is really the case – remember there are no skies without clouds, and life is filled with small irritations that sometimes overwhelm us but in the long run don't amount to a row of beans in the larger picture. The picture is also filled with personalities that are pleasing to us individually, and others that "drive us up a tree"! Perhaps we are given a few of these to enable us to appreciate the others more! I will often say to Roger, that the world is certainly filled with idiots! (do they in turn say the same about me?)
 great satisfaction and entertainment.

I have been incredibly lax about writing for the very good reason that the last few months have been completely overwhelming. As you know, (or may not?), we are building a kitchen wing onto our house. The work has been going on since April, and will not be finished until October. Roger has long since lost his equanimity and I – almost, my sense of humor! I have had no stove to cook on for two months now, and a nephew visiting from France. I have just about run out of ideas for recipes that can be prepared on an electric 9 - inch frying pan, and a microwave which routinely blows every fuse in the house! Plunged into darkness, in the middle of an Olympic race, Roger's language then produces enough sparks by which to start a large scale inferno! Never mind, I keep telling him perhaps to reassure myself, it will be lovely!

Aside from the above, there has been a full scale ceremony of one sort or another at the Fort all summer long, in which of course, I have been (since my uncle's death five years ago) per force at center stage. I have truly felt that I have not "owned myself", since interrupting unexpected callers, constant entertaining has completely taken over. Most fortunately, Mrs. Stacy (Maureen), my dear friend of some 40 years, helps me with the house and every other way as well, and Cathy Burke pops in on Fridays. I am very lucky to have such good people for friends, and my appreciation knows no bounds.

(Thursday) Well, here I am! 3 Days later! Interruptions constantly – it is hopeless – I have so much to tell you – but am, (Oh dear! ?) going to mail this off, since I told your grndpa you would hear from me on or by Wednesday – This way, you will have this for the weekend.

Take good care of yourself dear little girl and I will write you following the Memorial St. Isaac Jogues Mass on Sunday -
Always lovingly -
"Mrs. Dechame"

And thanks for the little package fo goodies – I love the fleur-de-lys hand towel, which has the place of honor in the new guest "loo".

****

Dear Virginia,

Your mother dropped in last night and reported – seems everything good. She liked the whole set up and is happy for you as I am.

Things good here – everyone getting in on the act – (what can I get you, etc.) driving me up the wall. I just tell them that yo have made my day – and I do not need a thing.

This is just to let you know that I miss you and I pray my Rosary for you.

22

Keep me posted. Say hello to Dorothy for me.
Love,
Gramp

****

8 March 1992
Sunday 10 p.m.
Bronx

My Dear Grandfather,

How good it was to hear your voice today. Thank you so much for calling me. Your support is so encouraging. I know you are making a sacrifice. Thank you for offering your Rosary for me.

Well, I made the Catholic New York paper.

Dorothy reminds me so much of Margaret C. She laughs only when she wants to and then she is very bossy. No one wants to sit next to her. I feel kind of sorry for her. Helene is so loud and boisterous. She even spits when she talks. She has her daughter smuggle in book shelves, donuts, radio and she gets all kinds of phone calls. All she has to do is look at you, and you burst out laughing. She goes back for seconds or more often, she asks me to get them for he.

We are going to have a 'Ceili' on St. Patrick's Day. Another gal and myself are going to do the Irish jig.

Oh Grampa, Sundays at 10:15 a,m are a good time to call with the exception of the first Sunday of the month because we go to the Cathedral then for Mass. Our dinner is generally between 12 and one or 12:30 and 1:30 on Sundays. Vespers are at 4:45 followed by Holy Hour from 5 to 6 p.m. Supper is at 6:30 to seven-ish. So if you call around those times, you should be good. We have Holy Hour from 8 to 9 p.m. Monday through Saturday.

Sister Agatha is very nice. I like Olive and Margaret too. I feel like I am always in the way of the one from Rhode Island. I guess we are all as different as can be.

I am happy enough though.

All my love,

Your Heidi and
also, the Cardinal's Heidi!

****

Letter from my youngest sister Sarah:

8:18 p.m.
3/9/92

Bon Jour Virginia,

How are you? I just received your letter. I found it rather humorous. What was the $20 dollars for? The things you wanted? How is Dorothy and ToTo too (Helene)? So much has happened since I last wrote to you. The weather up here feels much more like Spring. The day after I mailed your letter, I was wearing your hat with my leather jacket in the Ti Market. I was looking at the meats so people could only see the back or side of me. A lady who was walking by said, "Oh, Hi Virginia. How's Grandpa?" I looked at her, and she said, "Oh my gosh, you are not Virginia!" I said, "I am her sister Sarah." She said, "I am sorry, but you look just like her!" She said it in a nice way but I was not sure how to phrase it correctly. I thought that was pretty funny. Then, March 4th, our Chorus went to the Empire State Plaza in Albany. We left school at 8:00 a.m. and performed at 12:30. Georgie and his buddy Chris came over to hear us. Thomas was at Mass or he would have come. Jim King gave us a citation but he could not stay because they were in Session. However, he came up to me and said, "Do you remember me?" I said yes. Then all the other kids wre running up to meet him saying, "Hi, nice to meet you – blah blah blah!!"

On Saturday, Jane came down in the morning and asked me to come to her house with Aunt Betty to entertain Alex. We went to McDonald's for lunch. There, I saw Chrissy. She told me that she wrote to you and about Bill Slater (aka 'B.S.'). She said that she probably should not have put that in, but she just could not resist.

Sunday I finished an earth quake project for Mr. Hall. Mom made a turkey for dinner – why is beyond moi. Tom came down to eat and stayed 'til 9:30 talking. The cat Grampa gave Jane got hit by a car. I don't think she told him though. Someone called the house and was wondering about putting on a shower for Lizzy.

Why did Sister Kate leave??

Monday, today, Allison and I walked up to the lake, past Clarke's house and back – about six miles. My body aches and I am tres tired. Oh well, I will look for socks and frames. Tell the "Card" I said Hey. Everyone sends their love. Oh, I called Georgie, jr. for his birthday. He had chocolate cake with chocolate frosting and cupcakes at school. Alex is registered at Saint Mary's Kindergarten. The biggest news is that Bridget is getting married one year from Memorial Day. Bye Bye,

Love,
Sarah
Will write soon. I know I am forgetting something.

Oh, I just remembered. Aunt Betty saw Teddy te Riele. She said, "Your daughter took my seat on the bus to NY." I guess Teddy laughed. Then Uncle H.G. explained to him that Gramma did not want her to go.

Grampa called us up a few times and Dad answered. But Gramp asked for Mom. He was excitd to hear from you. I hear your going to do an Irish jig on Saint Patty's Day. Oh, you can tell him I don't hug "big birds"!

Have fun, take care – write back if possible. Let me know what else you need and I will try to send it after Lent. I can smuggle you in some candy!! Love you, Bah

P.S. - did you know that little George asked his father why he was going to NY. Georgie told him you were going to be a nun. He said, "Oh, and I loved her so much!!"

****
*

March 9, 1992

Dear Virginia,

Hi! I really don't know where to begin! So many people have sent you good thoughts and prayers. Kay Wells, Claude Letson, Chrissy, Deacon and Mrs. Shaw and many others just to name a few.
I hope and pray all is well with you. I know you must be adjusting to your new schedule. Sarah filled me in on your trip! It sounded like you got off to a great start. I am not going to ask too many questions because I know how busy you are. Don't feel like you have to write back. I know how time consuming that can get. I just wanted you to know we miss you at school! The children ask for you. We have been praying for you during our morning prayers. I am sorry I did not get to say good-bye. Larry and I stopped by Grampa's on Friday but you were downtown.
If I can send you anything, please let me know. Take care of yourself and be happy. Please excuse my poor writing. It is getting late. I thought I would use up my old stationary.
Please know Virginia that we love you and miss you. You have touched many lives.
We're also proud of you! God Bless,
Love,
Karlene
Larry sends his love

***1

Tuesday
March 10th, 1992
Hi Gramp,

Trying to get my Irish jig ready for Saint Patrick's Day.

Maybe I will get your second letter tomorrow.

I usually take a walk towards the East River. The Throggs Neck and Whitestone Bridges are nearby.

We had some left over Italian food delivered tonight for our supper. It was from a Christening.

Am adjusting more daily though my heart looks for you.

Helene is a riot. I can not look at her in Chapel or I will bust out laughing.

Later, - oh, she just came in and plopped on my bed. She was doing her usual imitations – Dorothy et al. She says that if they serve brussel sprouts one more time, we will bust the convent windows out!
March 13th, 1992 (Friday the 13th)

I wish I had brought a dictionary to have in my room. It would be handy. There is one down in the basement office.

I do wear my knee socks occasionally and get away with it.

Olive gave $800 to the Sisters. This was from gifts that she received.

Well, time for Chapel now,
Love,
Virginia
Friday in March

My Dear Grandfather,

Hi Gramp! How are you? I hope this finds you well.

I am so happy – I could not wait to tell you, but guess who called me!! And guess who came?! Father Salmon – you got it! First, he called Wednesday night at 9:05. He left Brushton at 10:00 p.m. and arrived in Newburgh at 3:00 a.m. He came here Thursday at 11:15 a.m. Our chores were switched so I was still cleaning up. I expected him around 12:30 as I told him that was our dinner time. So I hurried and freshened up and went down to the parlor to greet him. He seemed genuinely happy to see me. The Cardinal was supposed to come on Thursday but instead is coming today. I am glad of that because he is giving a conference and it would be difficult to visit with Father. Of course Father and the Cardinal go way back to war time. Father Halligan comes at 2:30 on Thursdays for Confession. He hears right up 'til 6 p.m. or until everyone is finished which could even be later.

I showed Father Halligan your picture. I also asked him to pray for Karl. Father H. is a beautiful, humble priest. We are fortunate to have him.

Well Gramp, I had to ask permission for Father S. to come here and if he could say Mass. Fortunately, it worked out. He celebrated Mass for the success of our (The Sisters) endeavors. He was so powerful lending such presence. Everyone was so impressed. I felt honored and proud that my parish priest who watched me grow up was here.

Diane said, "Virginia, you beamed! The only thing that could have made it better for you was if your grandfather was here!"

Sister Rita, Sister Carol, Father and myself had dinner in the in the dining room – just ourselves. We used Ed and Dixie's new table cloth. We took pictures – so I will send you the disc when it is complete. That way, you can take it on a Tuesday to Arthur's for the two for one special – okay.

I felt that Father was proud of me. I remembered to look him straight in the eye too.

Helene's quote for the day which she wanted me to relay to you: "Everyone here has paper mache' asses!"

Can you believe that Sister Paula is serving the Cardinal fishsticks tonight!

Well Grampa, I miss you and love you,

Your Little Virginia
Bronx

P.S. - Happy St. Patrick's Day! P.P.S. - How are the cats?

My Dear Grandfather,

Hi! How are you Grampa? I was so happy to finally get your second letter yesterday.

Really, Dorothy is getting better. She always asks for you, "Have you written Grampa?" She looks out for you. I suppose that she was a little unsure of herself in the beginning, therefore a little bossy towards me. She has me changing her furniture around in her room. She has make-up, hot chocolate and a hot pot hidden in her trunk. Did I tell you that she uses a half can of hairspray on her hair! Hurricane Hugo couldn't touch her hair if it tried!

Helene has me in hysterics. When she is feeling a little unsure herself, she will come by and say, "Are you up?" Sometimes it drives me nuts but she is so funny. Olive came downstairs in her rather manly robe and slippers and Helene says to me, "My God, where is the pipe?!" I thought I would die!

I had letters from Annie, Nancy L., Nancy M. and Sarah. Sarah is faithful to me.

Glad you got the fifty okay. (I sent home to Grampa fifty that I received from Mrs. Dechame).

I really like Sister Agatha. She is striking. She seems very compassionate. She is always reading the autobiography of Edith Stein. Her sister died three years ago at age 32 of Cancer. I showed Sister Agatha your picture. She taught at Columbia University.

The Cardinal called Monday night and I just happened to answer the phone, "Is this my Heidi?" He said. I really like him.

Tomorrow we will get up very early and go to Mass at the Seminary in Dunwoodie. There is a 'Right to Life Institute there all day. The Cardinal will be there and people from all over the world will attend. Sister Lucille from Toronto might be there. If Father Salmon is back from his trip to South America, he may even be there.

Helene thinks that Olive has a crush on Sister Carol. Helene also told me something very hurtful. She said that she overheard one of the Sisters say, "Virginia is not as sweet as you think she is." I don't know how anyone could assault one's integrity and say something like that – especially in religious life.

Helene also thinks that I should take His Eminence's name because she says that he was hurt that none of the first group of novices took his name. What do you think? His middle name is Joseph just like you!

Yesterday I did the cooking. Sister Gerard helped me. She says some words like "Really" and "My Heavens" - it reminds me so much of Gramma LaPointe. Oh, I made chili.

Got my laundry done yesterday.

This Sunday is Family Visitation Day.

Well, I have to mop now, if I don't fall asleep first!

Dorothy sends you her love. Say hi to Tom B. for me.

30

Sunday – Aunt Karlene's Birthday
15 March 1992
10 p.m.

My Dear Grandfather,

Hi Grampa! It was so good to talk to you today. Thank you for calling me

I am so glad that the pictures made you feel proud.

I am sorry about Gramma Burleigh's shoulder. I must write to her.

Today was family visitation day. I acted as official greeter to everyone. The Cardinal came at 2:45 to 3:30 p.m. and then he returned at 6:35 to 7 p.m.He went to the airport with one of the novice's family. He gave up other plans to do that. He is very personable. He was very tired too. He has a lot on his mind with the Saint Patrick's Day parade and all. He asked me, "Where is your dirndl?" Of course he was making a reference to 'Heidi'. It is blue skirts and white blouses these days. Anyway, he was starting to tell me that one of my relatives wrote to him, but he changed the subject as I don't think he could come up with the name. So I have no idea who he was referring to.

Helene says right in front of him, "Oh Virginia is your favorite." I was embarrassed. It was awkward for him and for me. He is very perceptive and he is a natural diplomat.

I am playing my Irish music now – a guilty pleasure. I heard the bagpipes playing at the school the other night. I would have loved to have gone over there.

Dorothy came to my room in tears. Her sister is very sick. My heart ached for her.

Olive's family brought me three boxes of peppermint tea. They asked if I needed anything and they said they would get it for me.

They were affectionate saying good-bye to me. In fact, all the families were affectionate saying good-bye to me.

Helene was commenting on someone's feet in the bathroom stall next to where she was. All she could see were these big black shoes. "It is like going to the bathroom next to a man." She exclaimed.

Too bad about Molly C.

Probably forgetting something, but Happy St. Paddy's -
Lovingly,
Virginia
P.S. - Here is a rose applique for your lapel.

Your Little Virginia

****
******

Grampa writes:

Dear Virginia,

What an interesting letter.

I am so proud of you – so pleased to see that picture of you with the medal being bestowed on you.

You should know that some of the Irish in this country are unbearable. That is how Dorothy sounds. And Helene reminds me of loud mouth xxxxxxxxx. I just don't want you to be a scapegoat for them. I know you forgive and forget but the same goes for them to you know.

I will call you on Sundays at 10:05 except for the first Sunday. I do not want to overplay the privilege that is offered.

I am doing very nicely.

Jane is here every time I turn around. She means well.

I finally found out that cat I gave her got hit by a car – no more cats for them.

I am looking forward to a quiet St. Patrick's Day this year. I told Tom B. that I am not drinking. However, I do hae 1 and a half ounces of whatever there is on the sideboard in the dining room.

I do miss you, but the thought of you where you are makes me happy and that is all that is necessary.

Keep me posted.

Say hello to Dorothy if you want to – this is not an order.

Happy St. Patrick's Day. God be with you.

Love,
Gramp

17 March 1992 (I drew a shamrock)

My Dear Grandfather,

Hi! How do you like my new stationary? Well, I got a big care package from Sister Sharon. She is so generous. She sent three boxes of stationary, a pack of disc film – a five dollar value, a book of stamps plus ten more stamps. I am sending you the book of stamps. She sent me a book rack which I had been wanting, two packs of 'certs', a big album and a compact smaller one which holds lots of photos. She sent me a box of 100 envelopes and a folder filled with white paper. There was a memo pad and a letter from Karlene. Included was a letter from Sister Sharon and all the faculty including Diane O. Karlene's class made me a nice card. It was very nice. Mrs. Vilardo contributed in that she mailed the package out Priority Mail ($7.00). Sister said that she would call me on Sunday.

Well, I got a letter from you today with one enclosed from the Carrs. They thanked me for going to Liza's wake.

Today is St. Patrick's Day – my favorite holiday. I was in charge of the entertainment. Another Sister did the Irish jig and then I did too. I also did an improvisational dance to 'Song of Liberty' by Nana Mouskouri. Everyone was surprised – (stunned). We played Hal Roach, Irish songs and then my Wolfe Tones video. I guess I left the Clancy Brothers at home. Finnegan's Wake is the best Irish jig music. Well Grampa, it is going on 11 p.m. - so I will close for now,
With all my love,
Virginia
P.S. - Happy St. Joseph's Day!

There was a beautiful concert before Mass with Irish Tenors singing all these Irish classics: The Meeting of The Waters, Kathleen Mavoureen, Slievenamon, Come into the Garden Maud among others including O' Danny Boy. I thought I had died and went to Heaven!

Happy Feast Day of Saint Joseph!

19 March 1992

****

Letter from my dear friend Christine:

Dear Virginia,

Another week has gone by and I just have to touch base with you. Did you do anything special for St. Patrick's Day? I thought of you a lot yesterday, I know you always enjoyed St. Patty's Day. Dave and I had a quiet evening at home and didn't really celebrate as far as green beer goes.

Dave has been busy starting the seedlings in the greenhouse.
Brother Paul has been a big help to us. He comes every evening to
help out – transplanting, bring the wood in, etc. Spring is around the
cornere and I am anxious for warmer weather.

Dave's leg is doing great. Dr. Wilmot said he would be out from
work for at least another month. The x-ray showed evidence of
healing and she put a new cast on for him. Instead of groin to toe, he
has one that starts below the knee. The new one is much more
comfortable and not as bulky as the old one. Everyone's disposition
has improved. I hope the worst is over!

(3 – 19) Just received your letter and it was great hearing from you.
By the sound of things, you pack in a pretty busy day. How is the 6
a.m. wake-up going? Have you adjusted yet? You must hit the hay
pretty early at night. Are you sleeping well?? Virginia, I must tell
you that I savor your letters, word by word. By the way, your
stationary is very striking and beautiful and thanks for the "Roses for
Life". They have become my favorite flower! That is because they
now remind me of you and your ministry. Even in the shop, a red
rose will always remind me of you. Just think of how many times
you could be thought of in one business day at Dutchie's!! Wow!

Life at the convent sounds interesting. It is funny how you have
been there a short time and you already feel the "vibes" going on
about you. It truly must be difficult getting along with each other
and getting to knowone another when actually you are all pretty
much strangers. Feel free to fill me in more on Dorothy and Helene,
"Louise". It must be hard to suppress the humor. Is there another as
perceptive as you?? I can picture two women trying to be
"Christlike" and almost wishing that they didn't have to be across
from each other! God does work in mysterious ways (over – turn the
page "Louise"). Who knows? They could become kindred spirits!
You know Lucy and Ethel, Laverne and Shirley, Virginia and
Chris,. Anything is possible! Try to get some mileage and fun in
your exceptional sense of humor. I sensed both Helene and Dorothy
were the maternal type, and especially fond of you, in particular. I
knew you were in good hands. I sensed from Helene' daughter that

35

her mother was a riot – the nut doesn't fall far from the tree! Helene jr. sounds like a lifesaver – chocolate and all! I sensed that she was very generous and kind of "city smart". You know what I mean. Actually, she reminded me a bit of xxxxxxx. I really enjoyed meeting everyone and you were so right! I can truly envision "true" places and faces.

I am glad you enjoyed my last letter. I had to fill you in on the trip home. To answer your question, "No, I don't think Bill caught on the "prevailing laughter". It was more like suppressed snickering. He was too busy rambling on to notice. He's a swell guy all in all though – tooth plyers and all! "I can get you a reasonable dental plan if you need one!!"

You mentioned being "out of sorts" on the trip down. My gosh, Virginia, you don't have to apologize!! All the trepidation is natural! This is a very big and serious undertaking. I should apologize to you for being maybe too lighthearted. It truly was a very happy day for me, and I hope you know, that I know, how you must have felt. All I can think of, is "Maria' in The Sound of Music". Anyway, how do you feel now that you are there? Is it difficult? We talked about the detachment process. You are in my prayers. You know you are only a phone call away. I will even give you my 800# to the shop! Would it be okay to send you a goody box now and then? You will need chocolate to survive! If it is okay, I could send a box after Lent – then some of the burden could be taken off of Helene jr's. "smuggling"! I am going to close for now, please, please remember I am here for anything you need. I am not trying to take God's job, but Ti is closer than Heaven! Just kidding! You are the best!
Lots of Love,
Chris
P.S. - Dave and the girls send you lots of love, they talk of you all the time!

****

Dear Grampa,

Hi! I appreciate your letters. You are so sweet. I think of you all the time. I still must write to my parents. Mostly I have been corresponding with Sarah.

What about the little Tennian boy – is he going to be alright? I had the Sisters pray for him tonight at Vespers.

Woke up to snow falling. It is real pretty.
It is hard to fathom, but there is even back-biting in the Convent. I try to be oblivious to it, but there is no getting away from it. Human nature, I guess. There are a couple of "honeys" here.

Today we went to the Poor Clare Monastery which is a short walk from here. An elderly nun died last night. We went to show our respects.

We also celebrated St. Joseph's Day today. My stomach was a little queasy. I was able to have a little ginger ale on account of it being a feast day. I also made some peppermint tea. Some virus has been going through the community.

The water here is very dry. My skin seems extra dry. I even let my hair go an extra day before shampooing it to let the natural oils secrete.

We were going to visit "The Cloisters" today but we did not go there on account of the weather.

Helene said that Sister Christina has a "hatchet face". She makes me laugh when I shouldn't!

Am using more of the stationary that Sister Sharon sent me.

I am also working on my album.

Six a.m. comes early so I will close for now. Please tell me how you are feeling.

I love you,

Virginia

****

Note from the Parish Secretary:

Dear Virginia,

Just a quick note to say Hi!!!! I enjoyed your note. Write again when you have the chance.

Your grandmother says you are doing very well. Have you tried the "Folger's Switch" yet? What's this I hear about you and someone else giggling during prayers?

If you have to cook anytime, why not try some of the recipes in the bulletin. I know that you like the celery seed salad dressing. If you would like to have it, or any of the others, just let me know.

Tomorrow, Friday, Sister Sharon, Nancy L. and Linda D. are suppose to head up to Watertown for the Youth Rally. This does not sound like a relaxing trip.

Got to go now. Keep in touch.
Love,
Diane
On the outside of this envelope was a note from Father Alan -
"Please be assured of our prayers".

****

22 March 1992

My Dear Grampa,

Hi! Getting ready to hit the hay – how are you? I hope you are okay. Tomorrow is your Feast Day – St. Joseph's. You will be in the fore of my prayers. Weather permitting, we may visit "The Cloisters" in the Bronx. It is a museum.

I have to get up at 5 a.m. on Saturday as we are going to Brooklyn for a March for Life with Bishop Daly. We will have Fifteen Decades of The Rosary, Exposition of The Most Blessed Sacrament. We will participate in a peaceful, prayerful march where abortions take place.

On either Monday, or Tuesday (I forget which day), the postulants are invited tby the United Nations to go to a Gregroian Chant Concert. I can't wait. The novices are not included because they are to grow more spiritually at this time.

Helene and I went to Sister Gerard's room and tried on her veil. We took to fits of laughter.

Helene managed to get the Post (New York). Olive also loves this publication. Helene thought she would do a good deed and leave it in her room for her. "Let her think it fell from the Heavens!" She exclaimed.

The Cardinal plans to have his next retreat on the Fourth of July weekend. I heard that we may get our veils as early as in August.

These novices are too much. They all want to be Mother Superior. It sure makes one wonder.
Dorothy and Helene clash to the point where bouts of uncontrollable laughter occur. I have to work on overcoming this fault. Oh well - take good care, For now,
Your Loving Little Virginia

****

Letter from my sister Annie:

Dear Va.,

Thanks for the letter. You must be swamped with correspondence.

No matter how you slice it, people are all alike with their idiosynchocies. Nuns are no different – fuss budgets, takers, talkers, jealousy. You sound like you are in more of a college dorm. It would not surprise me if people are jealous of you. They envy you and they can't handle it; thus they become jealous.

Thanks for the nightgown, pillow cases, reading material and the box. I love the smell of the pillowcases – combination of fresh cloth plus the smell of the pipe. Appreciate the hair dryer too. Thank you for the twenty spot too.'

Gramma broke her shoulder and you are missed more than ever now. I went to relieve Jane at 8:30. I assisted with her bath. H.G. seemed very happy to see me. I tell you though, Gramma loves the attention. I waited on her hand and foot: lunch, tea, cookies snacks, change clothes, laundry, phone calls and 85 trips to the bathroom. I was totally exhausted!

Mom is a wreck over Gramma's fall. People don't realize that. Oh well, take care now,

Bye,
Love,
Annie

****

Monday 23 March 1992

My Dearest Grampa,

Hi Grampa! How are you? You are in my loving thoughts.

It was so good talking with you yesterday. You don't know how I look forward to your calls. I have your picture holding Karl as a baby on my desk.

40

I think that I will send a card to Carm Fosco in care of you for when the next time he visits. He has done a lot for you and for Lizzy too.

Well, I got a call from home yesterday around 1:30. Talked to Mom and Dad and Sarah. It was good to hear them. Mom said that H. G. told her not to leave her bag on Gramma's chair "winking" so that Joseph would get the message not to leave his bag there.

Sister Sharon called around 4 p.m. but I could not talk to her freely as it was Retreat day and we can not talk until after 6 p.m.

There is so much that I would like to tell you. The Cardinal came by yesterday and gave a conference on "Sister Poverty". That is the vow which will carry our charism.

Did I tell you that one of the novices was sneaking out and getting beer. She was reprimanded. I kind of feel sorry for her. She is 37. Her voice used to grate on me, but I can tolerate it better now. Sister Christina's voice is so drab and monotone and she is only 26. She is very bossy and a "know – it – all". Sister Pio has this loud, schrill voice given to hysterical laughter which puts everyone off. I think she has an eating disorder.

We were going to have Sister Luke come tomorrow for continued Scripture class but her Superior feels that she is overworked. It's a funny thing but I almost did not want her to come. I mean, she is good and all that – she comes from The Pontifical Institute in Rome and she has the face of an angel. I guess I just was not geared for it. Am still trying to finish an exam for credit on the Psalms.

Tomorrow it is my turn to cook. Chicken a la king is on the menu.

Got my laundry done today. Will have to send back bottom fitted flannel sheet as it does not fit my mattress.

Sister Sharon wants to get another care package out to me. She wants to call again so that Karlene can talk to me.

Boy, you should have seen the video we saw yesterday on Apparitions of Mother Mary. There is a priest in Washington who has the Stigmata and there are many religious statues of Our Blessed Mother that are weeping. Some emanate a sweet, rose scented oil and there is even one that weeps blood! It is incredible but the live footage reveals it all!

Our acting Superior, Sister Rita, goes to and from to Maryland to look after her aging parents. She takes them to their various appointments and all.

Sister Carol is from Ausable and she even knows Father O'Reilly. That will be great when he comes!

The Cardinal flew to Washington, D.C. for four days for the Bishops' Conference.

That was awful about that plane crash leaving 27 people dead.

An Iconist is coming on Wednesday evening. He is donating an Icon of Jesus – Unborn to the Sisters. In order for him to "write" this Icon, he must fast and pray. He is a Deacon in the church and he is married. He must also quit the bed chamber while he paints or more aptly "writes" an Icon.

You have an Icon above your chair Grampa. It is the one that I brought back from Belfast. It is Our Lady of Perpetual Help – except it is a print. Well, got to run for supper.

Take good care of yourself. Say hi to Jane. Am glad she is good to you. For now,

My love,
Virginia

P.S. - Diane from Rhode Island knows Father Salmon. She is very sick now. She sounds like she has pneumonia.

26 March 1992

My Dear Grandfather,

Just got a letter from you today with "stationary". That was very sweet of you. You are so thoughtful. I will use it to make labels for my current scrap book as it needs color. But really, I have access to the stationary now and Sister Sharon sent me some in the care package.

Anyway, that was nice of Father Salmon to visit Gramma. Did you see him too?

I hope I didn't look too gawky in the photos. I wish Aunt Jane would send me some copies for my scrap book.

I am sending you another Blessed Scapular so tht you will be sure to have one.

Well, I have not written you since Monday because I have been busy working on my first exam. You will be proud of me. I am enclosing a copy of it and you can show Mom too. The original questions I sent in with the exam. It was a relief to get it done.

No, Chrissy sent me her 800 number. On the Feast of The Anunciation, I took advantage and called her. I told her to get in touch with you.

I am glad that Jane is so good to you. She is constantly in my prayers. Hoping all my brothers and sisters go to church.

Really, I am fine. God gives me the grace. I hold my head up and I look people in the eye.

Thanks for sending on my mail.

I heard that we may get the veil as soon as August. Cardinal is givng his next retreat on the 4th of July weekend. Father Paul, an

Italian priest, wants to take the Sisters fo Life to Israel after the Novitiate. Keep it in your pipe as it is a long way off.

We had an Iconist come and explain all about Iconography – Wow! They are a w indow into Heaven – a genuine one is and they are worthy of veneration.

We saw a video of our Mass. Eventually we may get a copy.

I am so disappointed about my negatives – the original may be lost. They have been at this Indian store for over three weeks. I keep asking them about it, but I think they goofed. Will know better next time.

Time for supper – I will close for now,
All my love,
Virginia

29 March 1992
Sunday 9:30 p.m.

Hi Grampa,

Awful good talking to you.

Helene can be gross sometimes. She was picking her nose big time during a video tonight. Nonetheless, (nun the less!), she has my back. She was annoyed with Olive so she went to Sister Rita and asked her if there was supposed to be some kind of "Grand Silence" that was in effect. She said "Sleeping Beauty" is on TV and no one keeps silence. Olive was very noisey outide of her room she told Sister. She was jibber jabbering and worse yet, she was tough on Virginia. I suppose I was half of the blame because I was the one being "jabbered" at. Sister Rita said that we have not gotten into practicing 'Grand Silence' yet in this house. Some people are reading ahead in the booklets and they think they are already nuns. Helene, in effect, beat Olive to the punch by going to Sister Rita first. That way, nothing will be made of it. Helene is loud and feisty. If only she could hear herself!

I went to Confession today. Our Spiritual Director is a beautiful man who has suffered a great deal. God Bless Father Halligan. We also had Exposition of The Blessed Sacrament.

The Cardinal is coming tomorrow at 11 a.m. We have three or four different books (Biographies) on him. He will stay for dinner. Sister Sharon and Karlene called right after I got off the phone with you.

Night now, hope you feel better and sleep better,
I love you,
Virginia
P.S. - Here's a Blessed Scapular for you.

P.P.S. - Thanks for calling.

Tuesday 31 March 1992

Hi Gramp!

How are you?

Did you ever find out if Sister Juliana received that print of "The Madonna of The Streets"?

Did I tell you that the Cardinal, (Archdiocese of New York), pays $1,400 every three months for Health Insurance per person for those on the payroll as well as for the novices or postulants, like yours truly who does not have insurance.

We see lots of barges go by daily on the East River. We have a view of Manhattan and we are only 15 minutes from LaGuardia Airport (not far from where that plane crashed). Also, we are near the Maritime College where Babe Smith's son, "Smitty" went. Both the Throggs Neck Bridge and the Whitestone Bridge are in viewing range.

If Sarah has not sent that package yet, maybe you could have her put those cough drops in it. I feel fine but I do have a stuffy head. I try to catch a nap and I stay in bed as long as possible before rising.

The Cardinal came yesterday with a group of Sisters who broke away from another order which had gotten real liberal. They are the Religious Sisters of Mercy. They rise at 4:30 a.m.! They wear a real conservative habit. They are full of energy. One is from Russia – she is a doctor. Another one is a lawyer and another one a psychiatrist. They are well-educated and they also know how to run a tractor, chain saw, log chipper and you name it. They come from Alma, Michigan. They have houses in Rome, Germany, and in Bethelhem, Connecticut. We may go there for retreat in June. They put us to shame. They said when we go there, "Everybody works!"

Olive thought she would use her "teacher voice" to tell everyone at the table in the refectory to be quiet as Sister Rita was talking on the phone with the Cardinal. That did not go over well with Helene. She burst out, "Well, you are never quiet when I am on the phone!!" Helene said it right in front of Sister Carol.

Helene watches everyone like a hawk and then she gives me her assessment of the. She says that Olive is " big flop of sh--" and that she looks like a pinhead. She says that Margaret is on anti-depressants and that she has her up days and her down days. Helene will look at me and she will raise her hand up or down according to how she assesses Margaret's mood. Then, she looks in the sink to see if Sister Pio threw up her food.

It is interesting the things we are studying in class. They really reflect Olive's character. Being impatient and being a "know it all". Helene just grins at me. Olive acts so dopey in front of the Cardinal.

I was the last one in line for dinner and the Cardinal put his arm out and he said, "Heidi, please go ahead of me." I saw a picture of His Eminence in Africa where he was holding a starving Ehiopian child.

Grampa, how about calling me at 10:05 a.m. on Sunday because we are going to Mass here. It is my cooking day so I will get an early start in the kitchen. The seminarians are going to Mass at Saint Patrick's Cathedral. If we go too, coffee at the Cardinal's Residence will be too crowded. Instead, we are going on April 12th – Palm Sunday. So you can call me at 1:30 on that day. This Sunday afternoon, we are attending the Gregorian Chant concert at St. Pat's. We will probably leave around 1 o'clock.

Tentatively, the fourth Sunday of April will be family visitation day. They will have a buffet. Mom was wondering when so you can tell her April 26th. Is that when their Spring vacation is?

I am sending my absentee ballot to E'town. I figure I won't get a change of residence form until we get our motherhouse. I hate to give up "20 Carillon" as my residence!

Well, here comes Helene clicking down the corridor. I will sign off for now Grampa. I hope you are feeling better. Take care. I miss you and love you very much. You are in my prayers.

Lots of Love,
Virginia
P.S. - Looking forward to your phone call on Sunday at 10:05 a.m.

Thursday, April 2nd, 1992

Dear Grampa,

Hi! Was afraid that I wasn't going to hear from you. Just got your letter – thanks, and thanks for forwarding the other.

Well, I was flabberghasted! I sure did hear from the Knights of Columbus – to the tune of $500! $250 for me and $250 for the

Sisters of Life. Can you believe it?! I gave Sister Rita the one for here and I am sending you the other one. I have a favor to ask of you. I would like to send $100 to Bishop da Silva of Brazil in care of Father Salmon. This is for the destitute poor. Can you please write the
check for me Grampa. It is all set to go – see envelope enclosed. Just insert the check made out to Father Salmon. Thanks Grampa.

I am glad Jane is so good to you. She has always been generous. I can't believe that Sherrie did not invite Mom! What a lughead!

I will write to Annie. I had a letter from her on Monday.

You should let Jane know exactly what you could use as long as she is at your beck and call.

That is nice that Wanda called and Miss Harmon too.

No, I thought that you could show Mom the test so she could see how smart I have gotten!

Wish all my brothers were back in the Church.

Dorothy is just the same. She is more settled. She still sneaks off to the stores. Another Sister, an older one from the first group, Sister Gerard, broke her foot on a rock on the curb – while sneaking out to the store!

Helene's daughter keeps her in cigarettes. At the end of day, she goes up on the roof, and has a smoke while I keep watch. It is a hard habit to kick and she needs something to help her get through the days.

I miss you and I love you very much,

Your Little Virginia

Ash Wednesday 1992

My Dear Grandfather,

Hi Grampa! Received your nice letter today. Thank you for taking the time for me.

I am touched that you pray your Rosary for me. That means a lot. It is probably why I am surviving here.

Dorothy always asks for you. She tends to drive me up the wall though she did give me a nice, navy cardigan with white flecks on it – Shetland wool. Helene also drives me up a wall. They both bug me about being late for Chapel and I am generally there before they are! I wish they would just let me be. Helene will barge in my room and plop on the bed. Then she will procede to pick at her nails, face, ears, scalp - and there goes my chenille bedspread! She talks non-stop. She means well, but it gets tiresome. She also talks about other postulants and novices and I try to avoid that sort of thing.

No sense having any money. We are not suppose to have any possessions. If I get a box of chocolates, it merely slips through my hands. It is not passed out until the Superior deems it a good time.

I was thinking that you could see if Norm Thompson cataglogue has any of those delicacies. You could call toll free and maybe order something along the chocolate line. When I come home we can celebrate with champagne and chocolates! How does that sound?!

One Sunday a month is visiting day. Though if one's family were coming, it is possible that a couple could be put up for the night and maybe men at the rectory. Sundays we can receive phone calls.

Saturdays, we have classes all day in Monroe, New York at the Presentation Convent. We will have bread and soup for our penitential meal Saturday nights. Monday through Thursdays we have classes here. Then we have chores around rhe house. There is also time set aside for professors to come in and give lectures; other times for us to go out and visit the various Pro-Life agencies. This may include Hospice, Homes for Unwed Mothers, Covenant House, etc.

I am all set for everything. Dorothy and I snuk out yesterday to drop off the film to get developed. I need to get some scotch tape. Other than that, I won't be going to the store, that I know of and that which I will miss – especially the grocery store.

I wrote to Sister Sharon.

Grampa, what about your feet? Are you sleeping at night? You must keep your hands nimble (moving) and put them in warm water. This will help your arthritis.

Am probably forgetting something but must take advantage of this free time to write to you.

Dorothy sends her love – maybe you could drop her a line. It would mean a lot to her.

Well, as they say around here, "No Honey, No Money and a Boss!"

Take care,
Yours lovingly,
Virginia

****

Mar. '92

Dear Virginia,

Thank you for the fifty – it sure came in handy.

You must know that Dorothy and Helene are in the same boat as you. Do not let them run you. Stand up and be assertive. Look them in the eye and tell them so. Just because they are older does not give them the right to badger you. I am disappointed but then again – people act different in different situations.

The celebration sounds good, but that is a ways off – just go day by day. This is a chance to really do The Lord's work. I want you to succeed.

I am good and so are my feet. Don't worry about me.

Just put your mind to the best interest of the order and be happy doing it.

I miss you, but that goes with the territory.

My prayers are with you,

Love,
Gramp

****

Letter from Colonel Clarke:

Sunday April 5, 1992

Dear Virginia,

Loved the picture!

So glad to receive you letter and hear all about you again. It is a long time between letters and time passes so quickly these days.

So glad to hear of your work now. You will be so glad to hear of my work here. I was feeling very low and didn't know what to do. My new wife, Evelyn, suggested I do some volunteer work in a military hospital. With none around, I looked at the nearest Hospital and found "Holy Cross" - "Sisters of Mercy" and I volunteered. I requested work in the Emergency Room- being an old war Medic They immediately put me to work and I have been working ever since on Tuesdays and Fridays. It is very interesting work. We handle many patients from infants to very old patients. It sure improved my loneliness after Mildred and made a new outlook on my new life with a new wife. Thanks for your kind wishes of my new marriage. We are both so happy and now have a new life.

Did receive a nice long telephone call from Lynn today and that made my day. She is doing so good. That Bailey sure is cute and will start kindergarten this Fall. It does not seem possible We were just over to germany to see her when she was born.

Eveyln and I will go North the first of May. Will stop in Washington, D.C. for a short visit - Then on to see Lynn and her family; then on to see Judy and her family. We will be in Ti around the 15th. If and when you are in Ti, be sure and stop in and see us. We will be so happy to see you again and catch up on all your news. So good to hear from you – til then

Love,
Dad (Lynn's father looked on me as another daughter – something I have always cherished.

****

Monday 6 April, 1992

My Dear Grandfather,

Hi Gramp! I have the radio on. " Imus in The Morning" is on. And " Sam Adams is the best beer – two years running and made with the freshest, most pure water."

Went to the Gregorian Concert at Saint Patrick's yesterdayl The Friars were from Verona, Italy. The Cardinal was in attendance.

Thank you Grampa for calling me. I hope and pray that you are alright. I love you so much.

I will have to write to Sarah and ask her to include or perhaps if I ccould tell Annie before she comes down, to bring me a small tube of Vicks Vapor Action, a toothbrush and a pack of gum. Sometimes,

I get the urge to "chew". Well, visiting day is definitely on Sunday, April 26th from 1 p.m. to 6 p.m. It is okay if Annie is a little early.

We will go to Saint Patrick's on Palm Sunday.

That Helene has me in stitches imitating everyone. She was a tough nurse. She pulls no punches. I am the only one she trusts. Her daughter gives her a hard time. Well, after she told Olive off the other day, on Friday, she went to her room, slammed the door, and yelled, "You Jerk Ass!" I thought I would die. The Superiors are in Monroe, so they did not hear. Also, we are on the second floor.

Sister Rita and Sister Carol are supposed to go to the Cardinal's Residence later this afternoon to have a meeting with His Eminence.

Olive is becoming more tolerable. It seems that once she gets put in her place, she reflects on the day's lessons which would seem to pertain to her.

Well Grampa, that is about it for now. Oh, Sister Rita called a special class with the postulants because I think some hae spoken to her about Helene. I keep my mouth shut!

Take care, Supposed to get in the 60's today!

All my love,
Virginia
P.S. - Am enclosing article on the Weeping Statues in a Virginia Parish; and I cut some coupons out of Sundays Papers for you too.

****

Dear Virginia,

Good to hear you Sunday.

Sarah has been avoiding me like the plague. Just can't understand you LaPointes, or should I say Burleighs.

Still getting 900 calls on my phone bill – this month there were two calls for $42.00 I called and they were surprised, because you put the block on in December – so they gave me credit.

I had to get a new stack control for the furnace – something all the time.

Ordered a pair of striped overalls from Sears.

The check came today – have sent to Father Salmon.

Well, Sarah came tonight to pick up the rest of the things. I told her to mail it UPS for youto get it quicker. I will pay for it.

Now the pump on the oil burner went Bennie is coming to work on it.

Cats are good. Nothing new – suppose to rain today but warmer.

I miss you and happy for you. God Bless you.

Love,
Gramp

7 April (Avril as I used to like to use my French!) 1992

Dear Gramp,

 Hi! Just wanted to add a couple of items to the ever-growing list. I think that there is a pair of sunglasses in the second left-hand drawer (in a case) of yor desk. If I can't find part of my frame on my "AARP" sunglasses (the kind that are given to patients after eye surgery), I amy have to ask you to order mea pair either in lavender or dark green. You can get them for $7.95 through AARP. There might be additional for tax and shipping. I can probably hold off on the other bedspread unless of course Annie comes up to Ti before she comes down here. I love that chenille style – old New England!

There are little holes in it that I have been mending. Those towels are great! They remind me so much of Gramma Audette.
Next Day – 8 Avril – in the 60's today

Grampa, you don't have to worry about the sunglasses. Today, I found the other part of my frame.

However, a bottle of Witch Hazel, Ti Market carries this, and a small jar of carbolated (sp) vaseline would be useful – that is, if Annie were to stop by.

Those darn planes overhead are so noisey! Plus, one always hears car alarms sounding.

Also, Sister Roberta, who used to like to take a nip, plays the kazoo in Chapel. It is supposed to help us get on pitch. This is something new and it sends Helene and me into hysteria!

For now, and with love,
Your Heidi
P.S. - I hope you are okay. Here is a prayer card to Blessed Solanus Casey. Oh, and here is a copy of the letter that Helene wrote to me on Retreat Day. She has named me "Sister John Joseph" after the Cardinal himself! She was on dish duty on my cooking day:

"Dear Sister John Joseph, SV,

I must thank you for your delicious dinner. It was the best one I have had since moving to Throggs Neck. I must also thank you for using every pot and pan, bowl, silverware, and anything else you could get your hands on! I also noticed that you did this undertaking on the day that I was to do the

dish washing along with the pots and pans and everything else! This was also a day of "SILENCE So a scream was out of the question. I hope that you are planning on pop corn and tea for supper!
I will write again after supper.
Yours truly,
Sister Mary Magdgalene, SS"

Helene loved Saint Mary Magdalene and she always referred to herself as "Sister Mary Magdalene" - the "S.S." is for Suori Spes – Sisters of Hope

****

Had a letter from Miss Hall:

Apr. 8

Dear Virginia,

What a nice surprise! I was so pleased to hear from you, - to know more of your surroundings and your daily routine. Your description of the view made the Bronx less terrifying to me, But I can't forget that Hilda Muntzes and husband had to leave their family home there because of vandalism, etc. Hilda and Bernie are deaf - that was a further complication.

The day I received your mini-letter, your grandfather sent me the mimeographed copy which your mother had made. Presumably, you recall its contents. And in the same mail I had a whole page from the Catholic New York. That was sent to me by the Carmelites in Saranac Lake. I have a little love affair going with them from way back when. When they came to Saranac, Kate Hopkins was their benefactor in the days when life was so rigid – couldn't see anyone, talked behind the grille. couldn't even see the Sacrifice of the Mass! I am glad, and so are they, that Vatican II changed so much of that. Kate delighted in loading the car with edibles (no meat) and her joy was complete when she pushed them through the turnstile.

I have told the Sisters about you; hence the paper which described the reception of the first group of novices, and a good bit about the habit, rules, etc. They pray for you as do we all. We want you to be able to discern if this is your calling . The days ahead will tell.

Your friend Ruby Noel is in better health and Lee has bronchitis, asthma and is in much discomfort, loss of sleep, etc. They have three ladies helping through the course of the day. Ruby has to have her first check with the cardiotonic "Black Box" - a monthly check-up on the pacemaker. Kathryn has a pacemaker, so I am accustomed to seeing her get her "Black Box", clock, 'don' the apparatus, and sit by the phone waiting for the N.Y.C. office to call, Previously, they notify you of date, hour. There really is nothing to it – all over in six minutes. Ruby was nervous about it, so the county nurse was going to be there with her to reassure her.

The Lambertons are having it hard. Jimmy falls often. "Riddy" is in the hospital with an aneurysm in her groin.

We pray for the hospital every Sunday, but I think we will have to pray harder if Moses Ludington is to be saved. I can not think the voters would approve an added tax. That is so sad. We need the hospital so much. But I can understand why many just can't see where they can come up with an extra $185 a year. For one, Joyce C. couldn't. Only this month, with her Social Security is she able to come up with the Town and County tax due in January. Then, in June, there is the large Village tax. How could she, and so many others, pay more as great as the need is.?

Don't chide yourself for not overcoming your spirit of detachment for family and friends. I am sure there is a place for that in religious life and I am convinced of that when I read letters from Sister Agnes Pozzouli, Sr. Mary Ellen, S.A., - she e ven took time off to visit her sister, Sr. Maria, S.A., who was ill at Graymoor.

I'd like to be remembered in your prayers. Arthritis has a real grip on me and walking becomes more and more of a problem. I have a driver, and Joyce lends an arm when we go to Mass. In the store, a grocery cart is a "must". I'd use a cane but I lack security. It is not easy to accept this inadequacy and thank God I can see. And I hope to see even better as there is a cataract operation planned for later this month. My left eye was "done" in September. God has been so good to restore my sight there. Now, I am praying for equal success with the right .
  We think of you with love,
  Irene Hall

****

Dear Virginia,

 Sorry to hear that Harry is coming – just about ruined my day and this until August 3rd! God help me! His eyes are worse. Edna walks him over. He fell on the porch going out – did not hurt himself – thank God. Don't trust his walking.

Nothing new here. Just miss you.

Saw the Cardinal's picture in the paper.

Your mother and father enjoyed the trip to Bellows Falls. Your mother had a three hour meeting. Your father enjoyed driving around.

I will take care of the film and get the pictures to you as soon as I can.

The Clancy Brothers were in Saratoga – the boys went down. Tom McDonald and Linda really enjoyed them. Tom B. met Ron down there. Thomas went but I have not seen him.

Do you need any stamps or anything? Just let me know.

No obits today.

Sarah is enjoying the bike. She is careful – wears the helmet.

Well my best girl, take good care. God be with you.

Love,
Gramp
****

9 April 1992

My Dear Gramp,

Hi Grampa! Just had a letter from you – thank you for 'stipend'. You are so good. Thank you for sending the other to Father Salmon.

The Postulants seem to be in a slump. Some of the novices are under the impression that they are better or above us because they have the veil. Most of them are so into themselves. One of them who is in charge of cooking, cooks one third of what should be cooked. I miss my spaghetti and red wine with you!

My stuffy head is getting better,

Had a letter from Sister Julian. Grampa, did she ever get that print I had for her – the one that Miss Sullivan sent me?

Had a nice letter from Colonel Walter Clarke. I enjoy corresponding with him.

Could you see if there is a full slip in my top drawer – that too could be sent down with Annie.

Helene is so funny ! You should hear the names that she calls the different ones here. She refers to one as Sister Olive Oil as she says her feet look like Olive Oils on the Popeye cartoon. She calls Margaret "the original frump" and she calls Sister Christina "Ole Hatchett Face".

I guess we are going to Monroe for Easter with the Parish Visitor Sisters.

I am preparing the Psader Meal for Holy Thursday – to be continued -

There is a lot of back biting here. I have to say that the postulants are a better group than the novices.

Can't believe that you are getting 900 calls on your phone bill.

That is too bad about the stack control and then the pump on the oil burner. It sure rains when it pours.

I am glad that you are getting some new striped overalls but the fabric is apt to be like your other ones.

Thank you for seeing that I get all my stuff. Truly, I am spoiled.

Yes, by all means, you can tell Tom how pleased I was with the gesture of the K of C.

What about the shoe catalogues? Some of the Sisters are anxious to order those sandals like mine. Annie could bring them down. Gramma B. has some of those catalogues.

Did Jane say she got my letter?

Oh, I have plenty of paper to write on now. You need not send me anymore of that green paper.

Hope someone brings you a palm.
All my love,
Virginia
P.S. - I bet the kitties are cute

****
Dear Virginia,

Good to hear you yesterday.

Miss Harmon called and asked about you. She wanted to know if I had any news that she could relay to you - she is writing to you.

Your mother did not go to Sherry's. She was not invited. We had a nice talk.

Wanda called from St. Thomas. She and Wolfgang are fine. She did receive the box you sent her in Florida.

60

Nice letter from the Bishop.

Henry brought me a nice dinner with roast pork – great!

Annie called – drop her a note. She wants to go down next visiting day.

Jane wanted a scapular so I found one for her.

Father Salmon stopped to see Gramma B. - she showed him the pictures taken at the convent.

Virginia, there will always be back biting no matter what. People are different.
 Just ignore it.
Snow is all gone. Suppose to warm up. Cats are fine.

Francine came to see me.

I miss you.

Love,
Gramp

****

Letter from my sister Jane:

April 10, 1992

Dear Virginia,

Hello! How are things going for you? It seems like yesterday you left. I can't believe you have been away for seven weeks now.

I saw the pictures of you and the Pope (she meant Cardinal) at your brunch with everyone. They turned out good. I like the one with you giving him the cake.. The one with everyone together was nice too. I talked ot Chrissy a few days after you left and she said she

61

had a nice time. Dave said you called one Sunday – they enjoyed hearing from you.

Grampa seems fine. I know he misses you a lot, Mother cat had three kittens. They are so cute. Baby looks like she is ready to have some as well. Sometime soon I will take Grampa on a catfood run.

His legs ache so, but it is nice for him to get out of the house now and again. I have been going there to fill my water jugs. The water is so nice and cold. Our water tastes like the pipes here and it is always warm.

Gramma B. is feeling better since her episode. She loved all the attention she was getting! It was funny to hear her tell different people how the accident happened. I have been helping her out these first couple of weeks. Lizzy has been a big help getting her in the shower and Annie has been coming up helping her too. Poor Gramma – to think this is her first broken bone in 85 years!

Thank you for recommending me to that job with that elderly couple. They are very nice, but their niece sure is odd – enough to drive anyone crazy. No wonder they can't get help.

Alexandra has her screening with Saint Mary's. I am so excited. She can not wait. She told me to tell you that she drinks water and she washes her hands.

Well, everyone asks for you. I hope this letter finds you well. Doug says hi. Take care.

Love,
Jane and Alexandra

****

Notes Helene and I passed:

Dear Sister Mary Magdalene,

Have you confronted your feelings of jealousy over me talking with "Woolsey" If you think those peds are going to cut it, think again.

Is it true I overheard the bishop from Africa say to you, "Meet me in Malawi." The monsignor is not a bishop, but he does have a good tan. By the end of summer, he might even rival your friend from Malawi.

Au Revoir,
Sister MJJ
Dear Sr. J.J.,

I am taking a shower. If you would like a report, see me afterward.

Sr. M. M.
("Reports" were the re-hashings of the day's events. Helene liked to discuss everything and give me her take on the situation which always resulted in fits of laughter. Often we would take to the roof because our laughter was so loud. There Helene would do her impersonations of all the Sisters).

Dear Sr. M. J.J.,

Helene replies intentionally writing with a very shakey hand:

Dear Sr. MJJ,

Don't worry. I am not nervous at all about you and 'Woolsey'.

Sr. M. M.

Sr. M. J. J.,

What are you doing? Please answer. You are not suppose to be doing anything between 11- 12:30 except for studies.
Sr. M.M.
Then, I find this note in my room,

Sister,
What does this mean? Come in and explain!
Sr. M. M.

****

Dear Virginia,

Great to hear you Sunday-

Have not seen a soul all weekend – Jane of course – she is doing my laundry today.

I think school is out for twelve days over Easter.

Tisdale sent me tobacco – everyone there is good. Tisdale is back to work.

Bucky Lynch drops in every other day to see if I need anything.

The Kings have gone to Florida over Easter.

Benny S. finally got the furnace working okay.

Heard your family called Sunday night – that was great.

I just do not have much to say, except Happy Easter and all-

Love,
Gramp

****

Easter 1992

Hi Grampa,

Just got off the phone with you – it was so good hearing your voice.

The Easter Vigil at Saint Patrick's was out of this world! Just to go to the bathroom was quite a performance. I went down the gold elevator, and walked through the Sacristy, and then past these meeting rooms. Two ushers had to let me pass these velvet ropes. The choir is unbelievable!

Thank you for the gum – you are so thoughtful. Also, for the money – you did not have to send so much. I wish that I had something for you. You have my loving prayers.

So the Kings are getting a house in Florida? Which part? Some parts are nice..

Glad the furnace is running okay.

Next Sunday is visiting Sunday. You can call meat 10:15 so that I don't have to call you – okay.

That is good that Jane is back to work.

Sounds like a good vacation what with twelve days off.

That was nice of Tizz to send you tobacco. Will probably get my parcel this week.

The Cardinal may not ask anyone anything, but he never forgets to ask about you.

Also, I had a letter from Sister Damien and a small card from Margaret Corsiglia which I am enclosing.

Well, I am off to Easter Mass now. Take care of yourself,
All my love,
Virginia

****

65

Letter from my baby sister Sarah:

4/25/92

Dear Virginia,

I really am sorry that I haven't written to you in such a long time, but the truth is, I didn't forget you, but I had hoped to see you on visiting day. I am working on your 2nd package. I just want to get it a little bigger so it will be less expensive to mail!!

How are you doing? Say hi to Helene for me. I just vacuumed my room and thought I would write to you. I also baked cookies today. Aunt Mary went to Middlebury today to find a dress for someone's wedding. Yesterday, I was cleaning upstairs and I found an old letter that you wrote to Lizzy when she was in college. It is funny to see how similar we are or were. We received your letter yesterday. Also, is Margaret mean to you? I was not sure after reading your letter. I don't think Annie is going to visiting day because she has been kind of sick. I guess I really don't know though. Lizzy is due the second of May. She is rather large. I must say I am kind of excited.

I'll tell you about vacation. Easter, we ate at the Big H. Monday, I went to see a movie, "Fern Gully" with Julie and family. Also, Mary spent the night. Tuesday, Mary spent the night again. Temperature was 80 degrees! It was nice and hot! Tues – cont'd. Mom and Dad went to Gutchells to see Marc. Wed., Mary left. Thurs., I babysat for Julie; Fri. cleaned, Sat. - wrote you and got to church. Sunday – might go to movie to see "Rockadoodle" with Julie but not sure. The 'Chieftans' tape was from Grampa – Tom B. or Julie gave it to him. K.J. swallowed a marble. Julie took him to the emergency room. He just has to pass it now. Tommy B. broke up with his girlfriend and has new interests now. Mom is kind of tired today so that is why we can't go to see you but maybe next month.

Jane, Joe and Thomas went to Cooperstown Thurs. & Fri. When do you get your break? Mom was wondering. We made Gramp and Easter Basket. I saw him Sun. Can't think of much else. So I'm

going to close for now. Take care and if they treat you bad, tell 'em
I'll kick their a---es off to Halifax – Ha Ha Ha Oh well, bye
Love your #1 sister,
Sarah
4/25/92

Dear Virg,

Later today, after I mailed your letter, I went to church. Forgot to
tell you that Father Jerry had a kidney stone and didn't pass it!!
Also, if you want that navy blazer from Sears, let Mom know.
Baaa,
Love,
Sarah
****
****

Throggs Necks
Easter Monday
27 Avril 1992

My Dear Grandfather,

Hi Grampa! Awful good hearing your voice yesterday. Thanks so
much for calling.
Talked to my mother and father last night too, and Sarah. They
called at 8 p.m. thinking that I had Recreation on account of visiting
day. However, we had our Holy Hour from 8 to 9 p.m. instead of 5
to 6 p.m. which would be on any given Sunday. So Grampa, I will
plan on you calling me at 10:05 a.m. this Sunday, May 2nd, unless I
hear differently.

I apologize but Mom's call went on the answering machine. When I
returned her call, I used your calling card. I hope it won't be too
much.

Thank you for the five dollars. You don't have to send me any more plain green paper as Sister Sharon sent me this white paper.

I guess that Annie has been run-down with anemia. She had to work night before last, so she could not come down.

Karlene and Larry had to take the Garden State Parkway so they could not have been very far from here. It would have been ideal if they could have come yesterday. She did send an Easter card.

The "supposed" dietician in the kitchen did not want to put out the two big Sara Lee boxes of chocolate brownies which Sister Rita had planned on using. Sister Roberta kept them in the freezer. I was in charge of desserts. There were some muffins and scones that Sister Roberta would only permit me to put out. I mentioned this to Sister Carol. Everyone is getting disgusted with Sister Roberta's frugality!

I told Sarah about the sheets and the dictionary in the corner hutch. She sent me one but it is too basic – for junior high level.

Mom was saying that she wished that we would move to Suffern and then she could more readily visit. That sure would be nice, but then there is talk that we might even move in the monastery – assuming that the order grows - next door. They only have seventeen sisters there.

Margaret's father said that he would make a copy of the video from our Entrance day for me. It shows me giving the Cardinal the Irish sipping cake. You can see it then!

Oh Grampa, can you send me the obituaries and the one on the Barber baby. I went to school with a lot of these people. I could drop them a note. Thanks.

Well Grampa, we are supposed to be getting out more this week to visit the various Pro Life centers.

I love you and miss you. You have my loving prayers,
Your Little Virginia

P.S. - Helene really liked talking to you.

P.P.S. - Oh, Sister Catherine Kenny told a lady entering next September that our group is getting along better than the first group.

****

Sister Sharon has been wonderful sending me care packages and honing up on me. Here is a note that was in one. She would also call to see how I was doing.

Dear Virginia,

Hope this finds you well and well-fed. Your Mom told me that you can get calls on Sunday. So I will probably call then. I am not much of a writer.

We just dismissed Crown Point at 10 a.m. because of flooding – What weather we are having!

We all miss you! It hit me on Monday that you wouldn't be coming. Mrs. Bush is here today. Well, Mrs. Vilardo is going to mail this for me, so I'll close. Take care, keep the faith,

Sr. Sharon

****

Card from Nancy:

Dear Virginia,

"Hooray for Spring!" Although it still feels like winter up here. I promise to write a letter soon but I just had to get a card in the mail for Easter.

We miss you so much – you really became a part of our family and there is a very empty spot without you.

I hope you are well and happy. Keep in touch with your Chilson cousins,

Love,
Nancy

****

14 April 1992 – 2:50 p.m.

My Dear Grandfather,

Hi Grampa! So good to talk with you. You are very encouraging and comforting.

Well, I did my laundry, ironed blouses, shampooed my hair; I took my shower earlier. Today we are going to the Chrism Mass at St. Patrick's Cathedral. There are supposed to be about 700 to 800 priest renewing their vows. They also get the fresh oils for Christenings and Anointings. I guess our priests back home go to Ogdensburgh as that is the Diocese there.
That Sunrise Service at the Fort on Easter Sunday sounds real nice.

I see they quoted the Cardinal in Saint Mary's Church bulletin.

Well, Sarah, my mother and father called me around 6:35 p.m. on Sunday. It was very nice to talk to them.

Forgot to tell you that I met Mary Alice Williams at the Cardinal's Residence after the High Mass on Palm Sunday. She is the New York newscaster for NBC. She probably knows Tom Brokaw. She is very pretty. Her husband is a famous producer. I met him too. They have a two-year old daughter.

Well Grampa, you will be happy to know that I went out and got a box of tea cookies which I have now hidden in my room. I make a cup of tea which I bring to my room. I also got an Italian Perugina chocolate bar. Got Helene some Fig Newtons.

Boy Helene has some gross habits – always picking and then I don't think she washes her hands.

Well, I want to get this in the mailbox by three – so you will know that I am thinking of you. My Easter Mass and Holy Communion at St. Patrick's will be for you – my "Alm Uncle".

God Bless you Grampa and thank you for being there for me,

Your Heidi (Virginia)

Can't find the first page of my letter which has a postmark of April 21st, 1992 on the envelope.

I told Grampa that I photo-copied the letter that I had sent to my mother and father so as not to be repetitive.

Then I continue saying how the Sisters were hanging around after the Chrism Mass waiting for an invitation to go to the Cardinal's Residence. They, particularly the Novices, do this after all the Masses that we go to at the Cathedral. It is awful!

Some of the Sisters here are finding it hard to adjust when they were big organizers in the outside world. One Sister made the comment that "Virginia isn't as nice or innocent as you think. That girl has been in Bulgaria. She has been around." I had trouble warming up to her in the beginning then I was giving her a chance. One would not think that this sort of talk would go on in a convent. I keep hearing stories through Helene.

Then this one who knows that Olive looks up to her will use her to get through to the superiors. This other one, Margaret has a heart tremor. She is on anti-depressants according to Helene. Sometimes, she has the countenance of a mad woman. It would seem that she, Olive and Diane are attempting to take over.

Dorothy tried to climb on the Novices' bandwagon in the beginning, but it did not work. She is disgusted with them.

71

Helene, although tiresome at times, is the most real person here. She is a lot of fun. We both carry on with our Irish brogues. We also both pick up on the same things. Sister Agatha of the novices seems alright. Sister Gerard goes with whatever way the wind blows. Sister Roberta is introverted but I can take her. The rest are for the birds. The present acting superior and her assistant are real nice though. Of course they are from a different order. They have come here at the Cardinal's request to help get this new order underway.

We had a Penance Service and there was one part where we had to extend our hands to whomever was next to us. Helene had to hold Margaret and Dorothy's hand which was comical as she can not stand either of them. Thank goodness I was at the end.

Helene and I have ordered veils from a catalgue in Philadelphia. So when I go home on break, I will be able to wear one! Mum's the word!

We ended up staying here in the Bronx for Easter. We had ham and party favors. Then we hunted for Easter eggs. Oh, and I did an improvisational dance for everyone. It was with the music "Prepare Ye the Way of the Lord (Godspell). Sister Rita liked it. She even asked if I had professional training! Am enclosing Herb's letter. You will recall he was part of the Lester Lanin Trio that played at Basin Harbor. He is very witty. Then he sent me Dick the drummer's rebuttal which is equally clever.

Well, no classes this week until Saturday when we have our three-hour class up in Monroe. We will watch Pro Life videos and hopefully get to the Botanical Gardens and we have yet to get to The Cloisters.

Helene refers to this one sister as a "big lump of sh--!"

The reason we are not having classes this week in Monroe is because Sister Rita has to go to Maryland to take her parents to their doctor appointments. She goes one week a month there.

I received nice cards from Mom, Gramma F., Father Wright, Father Lamica, Nancy M., Nancy L., Jeannie teRiele and a few others.

I do have a supply of cookies in my room!

I wonder if Annie is coming this Sunday. Maybe Karlene will stop. I gave Sister Carol a head count of approximately five people – just in case.

The Easter Vigil Mass at St. Patrick's was magnificent!

Thank Mom and Dad for calling me; and for the dictionary, thesaurus, the other book, the angel. It was a wonderful care package!

Well, take care now,
  Your Loving granddaughter,

Virginia

P.S.- I hope you are okay Grampa. Dorothy always asks for you. We have a few barracudas here! Oh well, I am fine - lots of love, Virginia

****

Note from Helene:
Dear Sister M. J. J.,

Did you notice the large lily arrangement on the altar that Father Keehan sent? He sent them to me!! But of course his card was in code.

See you later,

Sister M. M.

The flowers were sent for the May Crowning but Helene ran with it!

****

Throggs Neck 4 May 1992
Monday 2 p.m.

Hi Grampa,

Didn't want to waste this paper – I copied the very nice letter from Lynn on the back.

I am sorry about you having to get a new oil burner. If I get any money, I will send it to you. Uncle Tommy and Aunt Arhturlyn sent me a check for $20. I sent it to Mom for Mother's Day (that was before I knew about the oil burner).

Thanks for sending me the obituaries.

I finally got to the Post Office today. I sent home a package to you. I have my album in it and cookies for Dad. There is stuff for Mom and Sarah; a bag for Mrs. Dechame, something for Nancy M. and something for Diane O. (St. Mary's Library). You could give Sarah that one to have Karlene give to Diane. I appreciate your taking care of all this.

Yesterday, Sister Sharon called. Her father has Congestive Heart Failure. He has lost fifty pounds.

Margie Ann and Marty Fay also called. It came through on the Fax machine. She said that she just had to hear my voice. She said Georgie was doing some work for them.

I asked the Cardinal, by way of letter, if he could call my father for his birthday on Sunday. I don't know if he will be able to, so don't say anything. I think Dad would like that – he would get a kick out of that!

I had to laugh as Jane said that she liked my picture with the "Pope" when it was indeed His Eminence.

Any ideas on what name I should take? St. Mary's is having its Centennial – we have St. Isaac Jogues. There is John James Cardinal O'Malley. There is your dear grandmother Mariah which is Scottish/Gaelic for 'Mary'. Joseph is your middle name. Then there is dear Father James Halligan. He has helped me so much.

I love you and am praying for you,
Your Little Virginia

****
***********8

Dear Virginia - letter postmarked May 12, 1992

Great to talk with you Saturday night.

Your Sunday seems to have made your day.

The Cardinal calling your father – that was great! Your father called me right away. He was excited as Hell! That made his day. It was great of the Cardinal because he is so busy.

No obits this week.

Stephanie's package delivered – also one to Nancy.

Jane, Doug and Alex took off to Florida. She says "hello". They should be back sometime next week – Tuesday.

Well the bright spot of my life, keep me posted.

Love,
Gramp

****

Letter from Tisdale:

Dear Sister Virginia,

Well, long time coming, how is everything going with you?!

Rick received a beautiful birthday card from you. I received your rather humorous letter on "Gardening"! I will have to make a few copies of that one!

I heard you had a visit from "The Duke" - (reference to Father Salmon who resembles John Wayne).

You seem pretty happy. Don't worry about Grampa's pipe tobacco. You can count on me.

I think Mootse is coming in August. I want to get up to Ti for Mom's birthday. We'll see....

Very, very good – check with you later (Uncle H. G. jargon)

Your loving sister,

Tisdale

****

7:58 a.m.
Thursday
May 7, 1992

Dear Virginia,

I am sitting at your desk looking at your picture. Guess where I am?

This package and letter were long in coming. The usual craziness kept me from sending it sooner,
In this package, you will find 1). grapevine basket with linen liner. The flowers on the linen are wild flowers. 2.) In the basket you will find a. a brioche bread, b. a chocolate brioche bread and c. assorted cookies. 3.) a plaster of Paris paper weight with the imprint of the rose & small cones from the cedar tree in the shape of a cross. 4,) Three bars of soap from Newberry's.
Mrs. Kenney sent along this calendar with pictures of our loving children. Sister sends along a new picture book (I picked it up at Ames -Newberry's didn't have any more of the other). Let me know if it is okay, plus a roll of film.
On Monday of this week, your sister Karlene brought in a batch of choco-carmel brownie just for you, but she took them home again! She says they were "too crumbly" - but I think she and Larry had a party with them! (Ho-Hum!!)
Yes, I miss you. There, now I have said it. What's worse is that now it is even in writing! Whenever I think of you, I feel happy. I know you are happy.
We are all good. The kids are doing great in school.
The Library is good though the kids miss you. Emily E. said in Litany fashion, "But why, why did she leave?!" I tried to explain to her, but she kept repeating "But why". It was somewhat amusing but her sentiment was genuine. Please write to her if you can.
I'll write again sooner next time. Let me know if you need anything. Have to get to work. I love you Virginia, Say a prayer for me,

Diane
(Diane came from the Bronx ironically - a beautiful Neopolitan – Naples – lady who helped out at St. Mary's School)

****

12 May 1992
Tuesday morning 8:45 a.m. Throggs Neck - Saint Frances de Chantal Convent

My Dear Grandfather,

Hello! I am late writing to you this week. Our schedule has been very busy and yet very wonderful.

Hope you don't think this is impersonal because it is type written.

Anyway, it was so good talking with you Saturday night. If you want, you can call me this Sunday at 10:05 a.m. This Sunday is our visiting day. Have been occupied writing my term paper on Mariology. Am also typing up Helene's for her. I really like her though she can be overbearing and demanding at times.

I guess you heard that the Cardinal did call Dad. That really made his day – and mine too. The nice thing about it was that we were having coffee at his residence, when, right in front of everybody – including Assemblyman John Deerey, and an African bishop, His Eminence says, "Heidi, come here..." Well, you should have seen how everybody was looking. I would not tell them why either but some of them were buddying up to me to find out why. I only told Helene. He had indeed called Dad to wish him a Happy Birthday. The funny thing is, that my father was so incredulous that when he heard the Cardinal say who he was on the other end, Daddy said, "No sh---!" The Cardinal was a long time Navy Chaplain so he must have gotten a kick out of it. He likes it when people are themselves.

About this Assemblyman Deerey – he knows our neighbor General Jim King pretty well. It is funny how all these po liticians carry themselves in a similar manner. Oh, and I was throwing around a little French with the Bishop. His Eminence caught wind of this – seemingly impressed. It was my accent to be sure.

Those who have seen Gramma Audette's picture here say that we share an uncanny resemblance.

I appreciated your last letter and all the forwarded letters. Hope you are feeling okay Grampa. Sorry about yellow cat.

Another reason that I am typing this is because if I were in my room writing it by hand, Helene would be in there gabbing up a storm!

I look forward to talking with you on Sunday.

All my love,

Your Little Virginia

****

Easter card from Gramma Burleigh:

Dear Virginia,

Your lovely card and beautiful calendar with the picture are greatly appreciated.

I am sorry that I am not able to write myself for a while but I want you to know that I am most grateful for all that you have done – especially, the prayers.

I hope you are happy with the way I took care of the money you sent for the altar.

Hope to be able to write soon.

Love and Best Wishes for a Happy Easter,
Grandmother

P.S. - Kindess of your mother. (Gramma had hurt her shoulder)

****

15 May 1992
Friday 9:06 a.m.

Hi Grampa,

You shouldn't be sending me money. Really, I don't need it but thank you. I bought a new notebook yesterday. The day before, I went to the Bakery. The lady there stuffs a little bag full of cookies and she only charges me a quarter. Helene was annoyed with me about this. "Is that all you paid her?" She said. Meanwhile, she thinks nothing of taking a five dollar discount from the lady who gave her a pedicure!

I can't wait to see Father Halligan this week.

Yesterday Father Keehan came for dinner. It was his 38th Anniversary of being a priest. There were two pieces of cheesecake left. Helene wanted me to get her one of the pieces. And, as Murphy's Law would have it, someone took the other piece – and then there were 'Nun"!! It's okay, I get my sweets. Sister Sharon sent me another box. It was filled with homemade cookies from Diane Olsen. She also put soap in it, and, a pretty table cloth. She sent me an album and film. She is awful good to me. Plus, Sister Sharon called me.

I keep meaning to tell you – remember that episode of the Burt Reynolds show where three men are stranded on an island with no clothes – so they wear branches. Well, Sister Rita was trying to get The Shroud of Turin on the VCR and that particular segment kept coming up. It was hysterical. She was pressing the remote control furiously to no avail.

The Cardinal wants to have private talks with each of us within the next two weeks. He comes on June 1st to celebrate the anniversary that he founded the Order. Then we will go on retreat with the Religious Sisters of Mercy in Bethlehem, Connecticut. We will return here June 9th, so please understand if I don't get a letter out. That is why I got the new notebook because we will have speakers.

Joan Andrews and her husband Chris Bell are coming here on Monday to speak. She is amazing. She has been arrested for silently praying for the unborn in front of these abortion places. She has even gone to jail.

Finished my paper on Mariology and got Helene's typed too.

Have to do my chores now. I will make banana bread for visiting day.

Well, take care, again, I am so happy the Cardinal called Dad,

I love you,

Your Little Virginia

19 May 1992
Tuesday Noon

My Dear Grandfather,

Thought that I would recycle the program cover from the First Holy Communion Mass.

How are you? It was so good talking with you on Sunday. I love the pictures of Mary Evelyn you sent me. Thank you.

Grampa, don't send me any more money. I promise if I need anything, I will let you know. God only knows you are so good.

I pray that you will call one of the priests and that one will bring you the Sacraments.

Anyway, I can't wait to see you – probably in late August.

Yesterday Joan Andrews Bell came with her husband Chris. She has been in jail for months on end for her rescue work in the cause for the Right to Life. She even accompanied Father Salmon on one of his trips to Brazil to give witness to the people. She spoke at the church in Brushton and she stayed with

Miss Sullivan same as I did. Joan is very frail and holy-looking. She is expecting her first child. She is 43 years of age. Please God, everything will be alright for her and baby.
Had a nice letter from our neighbor Jane King.

Helene realizes now how far she can push me. I had to ask her not to repeat everything I share with her at the table in the refectory.

Tomorrow I cook. It will be macaroni and cheese. There is no meat on Wednesdays and Fridays. Helene is cooking now. I will go and help her put things out.

We are having speakers all week. It looks like we are going to Washington, D.C. on Saturday. If we get back before ten p.m., I will phone you that night.

Take care,

I love you,

Virginia

****

Around this time I suffered a humiliation. The Cardinal came by for an impromptu visit. Everyone ran down to the community room to see him. It was a hot day in the Bronx and I had my usual blouse and skirt on. It never occurred to me to put on my blazer. In fact, I find them rather "man-ish" and it seems more feminine without them. One of the novices says in front of everybody, "Where is your blazer? You should have it on. You know the Cardinal is here." I was taken aback – actually stunned. I meant no disrespect. We were going out doors, perhaps for a picture, and the Cardinal asked me discreetly if I would get my jacket. He did it in a nice way. He is a military man. It reminded me of parochial school. Of course I went to get it. I would have put it on in the beginning had I known it was some sort of requirement.

****

21 May 1992
Thursday 6 p.m.

My Dear Grandfather,

I just had a letter returned from Ireland, It says "Service Temporarily Suspended". So I don't know.

That is too bad that the nurse you worked with has Cancer.

What did you mean about being careful what I write to people? I can not think of anything untoward that I have written.

How is Lizzy's new baby?

The latest is that we are getting our veils on August 15th – the Feast of The Assumption. It is also the Feast of St. Mary's Centennial! How about that?! Should get home around August 1st.

Sister Gerard discovered quite by accident that Dorothy has been in another religious order. What is even more bizarre, is that she actually taught one of Helene's children.

They are installing air-conditioning in the convent. Only two people want it – Helene and Sister Gerard.

It is pretty awful what goes on behind the scenes at Planned Parenthood. You would die if you knew – that which the public never hears about.

Today, I walked to the mailbox. I bumped into Monsignor Devlin, "Hello Virginia….. it is killing the others that I know your name." He is one sharp cookie. He is old school. He says the same kind of stuff that you would say. He is 81. He had been serving in "Hell's Kitchen".

Went to the beauty shop. The lady from Puerto Rico who I invited on visiting day trimmed my hair. She did it gratis. I tried to give her the five bucks you sent me. My hair looks neater – that which could cost me in other ways because people can not mind their own beeswax!!

Trip to Washington canceled.

Lots of Love,

Your little Virginia

Had a beautiful letter from Ed and Dixie. Ed writes on March 1st, 1992

Virginia,

We were happy to receive your letter and thank you for the Valentines. Also, I am happy that you are getting into something that you have wanted for a long time. Sounds as if you are getting in on the ground floor of that Order and I'm sure before very long you will make them very proud to have you. We wish you the best.

With all due respect to you and the bishop, the nearest I intend to come to the Bronx or any part of NYC is the Garden State Parkway. We don't know yet if we are coming North. We saw Penny the other day and she wants to make some changes and will write us when she gets home. We are not sure we will like what she has in mind.

Dixie is at work. This is a long day for her from 9:15 a.m. to about 10:30 p.m.

It has been quite cool here the last few days. Plenty of sun. We have tomatoes, beans, and flowers growing on the back porch in pots. The tomatoes are good, but the beans are several weeks away.

Yes, it was Cardinal Spellman that I met. He was a fishing guest of Mr. W. A. Fisher in Michigan. Mr. Fisher was a very wealthy Catholic. Also with them was Mr. K.T. Keller, the head of Chrysler Corporation. Mr. Fisher introduced me and I did not know exactly what I was supposed to do. The Cardinal put out his hand in a handshake position, So I shook it. He had a lot of experience with dumb country boys because he spent a lot of time overseas during the war. I am sure I told you but I hd another interesting handshake there. I was standing in the bar one afternoon when four people came in with a dog. I knew two of the people and I heard one of them say, " Go over and shake hands with Eddie." This big dog came over, sat down in front of me, and stuck out his paw. I shook that too. Probably was afraid not to. It was "Rin Tin Tin". Many of those people there had a lot of money and liked to bring celebrities there to show off to their fellow members. It was a fun place to work.

That's enough of my life story for now.

I am sure the Sisters will keep you busy, but do arrange time to keep in touch. Also, I am reasonably sure your prayers mean more, but mine, unworthy as they may be, are for you and your happiness and all the good you will do in this world.

Love,
Ed & Dixie

Also had a post card from Father Salmon. It was dated March 14th, 1992. It was from Brazil where he was at a Pro Life Project in Viana with Bishop da Silva.

Father Salmon had written to Grampa to thank him for his generous gift to Bishop da Silva. The people in his country are very poor.

Had a letter from Mr. Clarke. He sent me the newspaper clipping announcing his second wedding to a life long friend and widow which was to take place on Valentine's Day.

Margie Ann from Albany wrote me. She was my brother's landlady:

April 10, 1992

Dear Virginia,

We received your letter Monday, April 6th. And I can't tell you how happy we were to hear from you. I didn't think you would forget us in memory, but with your brother and his wife and my babies gone, I didn't know if I would hear from you being so far away. When I saw the outside of the envelope, I noticed the return address, first I thought it was for George and that somebody didn't know that they moved away. Then I saw our name! I came running in and told Marty that "M. (Mildred) Virginia LaPointe had written us!

Well, well, when I opened it, (no first), I said to Marty, this envelope is thick. It is either a wedding invitation, or, an invitation to Virginia's joining the Convent. I really did suspect that! You can not imagine how happy we were and are for you! I tell you, you just made my day! No, my life! This will go in the LaPointe album. Oh yes, I have a whole album of pictures of George and Loretta and thekids from every occasion since they moved here. And the pictures of you before you went to Medjugorie and the picture of you lighting the candle for me in the Grotto. Plus, I have all your letters, cards and notes; and all the drawings from the kids.

I will never forget your kindness for bringing me the Holy Water. Believe me Virginia, the Water, your candles, and prayers answered my request. It was a miracle. I will tell you sometime.

Yet, I know in my heart that your prayers, like you, are special. I swear they go right to Our Blessed Mother and Her Son. This was before you entered the Convent, just think what we can expect now!

To me, Virginia, you were like a nun before February. There is something special about you. Maybe it is the way you pray. You will have to tell me or teach me sometime.

I am glad Grandpa is content. And I am glad your fmily was able to go down and see you enter. I called Loretta. I am going to call her and tell her that I was going to kill her for not letting us know – just kidding, but she said you didn't tell anybody 'til just a short time before you decided to join. So all is forgiven, ha ha. We had a nice long chat and I talked to George also. And you know me, I was worried about the location of the Convent. George said it seemed like a nice, "safe" neighborhood. Thank God. Well, Virginia, please keep us posted.

I will write again soon, more slowly and carefully. As you can see, this was written in a hurry. I was out shopping and I have to go out again.

We love and miss you, but we will think of you often and remember you in our prayes – that you are happy and stay well. Think of us in your prayers.

All Our Love,
Marty and Margie Ann

Actually, I never got to Medjugorie. I was in Northern Yugoslavia, but the war was going on there. I got Margie Ann the Holy Water from Epesus in Turkey. It was there in the Grotto where I lit a candle for her and her intentions. That is where Our Blessed Mother spent her last days on earth.

****

Dear Virginia,

As usual, great to hear your voice.

Lizzy brought me a ham dinner – very good – just the right amount of everything. Of course she is as big as a hot air balloon.

I heard that Burleigh Pharmacy is closing.

Jane takes good care of me. She gets me so much to eat. I don't know what to do with it all. I try to stop her – but forget it!

Barbara and Mrs. Crammond had a garage sale – junk. Mrs. C. asks for you as does Mrs. King.

The kittens are raising Hell.

Dorothy sounds like a basket case. It seems to me that the purpose of the order is compassion for all – but those novices have a clique all their own. I think they are a little jealous of you.

Georgie stopped in – he is something else – such a good kid.

"So and So" is about as useless as "ti-s on a bull".

Say hi to Helene for me.

Love,
Gramp

P.S. - Bucky fixed my wind chimes. He said he missed hearing them when he would walk by.

****

6 May 1992
Wednesday 12:30

Dear Grampa,
 Well, I hope this finds you well. I meant to tell you about the Monsignor who lives next door. He is your age. His name is Monsignor Devlin. He is Irish. He is a real, no-nonsense, tough priest. He reminds Helene of Humphrey Bogart the way he talks.
 Well, I had to laugh. We were coming from the May Crowning Procession which was held outdoors. Monsignor says, "Hello, Sister Virginia…." The novices were taken aback. They don't think that

we should be called "Sister" yet. On top of that, he did not know any of their names. Sister Christina says, "How come you know her name?" He replied, "Because she works." Well, you should have seen their faces! I was enjoying this moment where I seem to confound them.

I hope you pour the Listerine into a cup before you gargle and not take it directly from the bottle. I did that with Scope and some bacteria was growing in it! Also, be sure to change the paper cups!

Ed and Dixie sent me a beautiful table cloth. It says "Religious" on it. That was very sweet and kind of funny. I turned it in to the Superior.

Grampa, The Cardinal led us to believe that we would have traditional habits. Instead, they are wearing these tan tops and skirts that look like something a European maid would wear. The novices do not want our input at all! Helene did voice her opinion and Sister Agatha was practically in tears. She puts on this poker face. She is stubborn and she thinks that she is running the show. I am wondering if I have a right to express my opinion on this. Afterall, I hope to be wearing one and I am not crazy about this one.

Also, we had our third meeting regarding a newsletter. I presented some good ideas. Of course they all got shot down. But then all the ideas got shot down. Sister Agatha had it all pre-determined. Then she tried to use her psychology to infer that we were all contributing.

Well Grampa, you would have been proud of me. I looked everyone in the eye, and spoke eloquently defending one of my proposed titles. You should have seen Sister Agatha's face. I thought she was going to cry. She must be going through her change. But these people are like concrete – narrow and set in their ways. There is so much pride. I ask, is it worth it. Do I be humble and let them do what they want. Or, do I voice my opinion.

Afterall, God gave me a brain to use. I feel like I could contribute. I could write for this newsletter.

So Carmel,(a girl I met on retreat), called you. I just got off the phone with her. I am not surprised what happened to her. That's too bad. I bet you were surprised to hear from her. Carmel met up with this fellow from Central America. He wants to marry her in order to get his Green Card. Her parents tried to talk sense to her. I did too. But youth will have its way.

Got to run to lunch and then we have a speaker. God Bless you,

89

All my love,
Virginia

P.S. - How do you like my homemade stationary. I photocopied the poem and the sweet picture of the cat.

On May Day, I sent Grampa a post card of Country Life. It shows a blacksmith putting "shoes" on a horse. I write, "Dear Grampa, Time to get out the boots! Hi! I got your letter yesterday – Thank you!
Also, finally, got Janes – postmarked April 21st. Received one from Mary too.
Well, today Helene and I scrubbed the statue of Our Blessed Mother in the convent. We had a blast doing it. We are going to have a procession now.
Got all my chores done today.
Wrote down Hilda G. and Harry K. in our prayer intention book.
That is too bad about Hilda – so young. Thanks for all the news. I find myslef getting more adjusted - though I do miss you. Take care. Oh, Helene says hi. I love you, Virginia

Ascension Thursday
10:00 p.m.

My Dear Grampa,
Hello my special person! How are you? Received a letter from you today, and insert – you naughty one – shouldn't be sending me anything, but, thank you.

Well, the Cardinal came today. I was waiting to write to you after he came. He talked to us as a group. He is always using parables.
So, I can't quite figure out, but he did talk to the novices as a group for an hour in the parlor. Then, after Benediction, he asked the postulants to stay – in the Chapel. He asked if we had any problems; and, were the novices helpful ot us. Well, it was hard to answer in the Presence of The Blessed Sacrament. Olive, who is the biggest brown noser is two -faced. She said, "Oh yes, they are nice."
Meanwhile, I hear her talk disparaging behind their backs. I kept still because I do not trust any of the postulants – only Helene, and

90

then, up to a point. But I met the Cardinal at the door and he did say that he received my letter. "Oh, you did?" I replied. And that was that. He will talk with us individually after our retreat. He brought us pizza and cookies for supper. I do believe that my letter made an impact on him.

Enclosed, a program from the Recital of Classical music that was held at the Church. I slipped out, and it was beautiful!

Also, had a couple of post cards from Father Salmon. He was at a wedding in Kansas City.

Oh, I will give you my number for where we will be at on retreat in Bethlehem, Connecticut. It is for emergency only. I won't be able to write to you that week. But I will call you as soon as I can afterward.
Love,
Virginia
P.S. - Had a nice letter fro Ed and Dixie. They will be back at BHC.

P.P.S. - Received sheets and scatter rug from mother and father.

9:40 p.m.
Memorial Day

Tuesday, May 19th (Letter from Ed and Dixie)

Virginia,

We were glad that you were able to put the table cloth to such instant use but we were surprised it received such an exalted beginning. We thought from the picture on TV that it might be appropriate but really did not know if you were permitted to own personal things. Anyway, we are happy for you.

Things have changed for us. Aurie called to find out when we would be there so she could have our room ready. We explained we would not be there unless we heard from Rhonda. The next day Rhonda called; they expected us so wear are going back.

We enjoyed the Keys but the fishing was terrible and the last day we were there, the wind blew so much, you had to sit down or keep your feet apart to keep from falling over. We leave here the 26th and will be in Atlantic City; then go up to Vermont to drop some stuff off at the Harbor and then go to Maine for a few days.

It was a good picture of you with the Cardinal.

I am sure you deserved the highest grade on the Psalms exam. There is an amount of personal satisfaction in such a thing. I had an experience like that once. In Infantry School at Camp Lejeune they posted the grades on the bulletin board every week. There were captains and lietenants in the crowd. One day, I was passing the board and I heard one officer ask another, "Who is this Corporal Watts who always has high grades?" I did not say a word, but it was a good feeling. Field stripping a light machine gun in the dark was not my best subject.

Say hello to Grampa when you talk to him. If we ever get to Ticonderoga, we will stop by I wish you were going to be with us this summer, but that is selfish. You are much better off where you are and the world and the world will be better because you have been there. God Bless you and Much love,
 Ed & Dixie
P.S. - Our cat was named Rachel. We took her back to the Rescue League

****

Letter from my sister Lizzy:

6/2/92

Dear Virginia,

Sorry I am not good at writing. But I think of you often. We are all doing well.

Thank you for always remembering the kids – Michael on his First Holy Communion. They all miss you. Thank you for your note on Mary C.'s death. I spent as much time as I could with her before she died.

Robert is beautiful and perfect – a good baby. I love him right to pieces. I am so thankful I had such a perfect child. They all are though.

Well, take care now and God Bless you – We miss you!!

Love,

Lizzy

****

****

My Dear Grandfather,

Hello! I was glad to get you Saturday night but you concerned me as you sounded very tired. I am sorry that your legs ache so much. Your suffering will be meritorious for you!

I had a letter from Sister Mary Agnes Pozzouli.

Well, I did it. I decided to write to the Cardinal. By the time that you get this, he too will have his letter. He is

on Thursday. I have enclosed a copy (confidential) of my letter.

I was annoyed with Margaret last night because I discussd the possibiliy of a more traditional habit and she thought I was way out of line. Such audacity! The more I thought about it, the madder I got. That was when I penned the letter to His Eminence.

Today we went to the Parish Visitor Sisters in the Bronx. It is not in the best section. We are spoiled here. We had a barbeque. There were three Korean Sisters there. It was very nice. Then, a Sister returned from West Virginia, Her little five-year old niece died. She had been severely sick since June. She only had Holy Communion for Sustenance in the last two weeks of her life. She kept calling out

93

for Jesus. We saw a video of her First Holy Communion and Confirmation which she got to receive simultaneously on account of her terminal lung disease. The poor thing. Her father has a beard too.

Sarah called last night. I got to talk to her and Mom.

Tomorrow we are celebrating Sister Rita's Feast Day as she as away on the

22nd. Feast Days are a big thing in the Convent. We are doing a satire on 'Hello Dolly'. We made up a biography of a saint – Saint Rita of Marycrest. We have been busy rehearshing all day.

Well, they had a fabulous Baroque Concert, 18th Century, at the church yesterday. It was our retreat day. Helene said that I shouldn't go which was all the more reason for me to attend. It was magnificent. I sat quietly – albeit reflectively.

Sorry about your losing those kittens. It must have been very upsetting.

Please take care of yourself Grampa. I will be able to tell you more after meeting with the Cardinal.

God Bless and keep you.

I love you,

Little Virginia

Letter to the Cardinal

24 May 1992

Your Eminence,

Am glad you are back home and getting rested up from your arduous schedule.

It is with much consternation that I write to you regarding what has become a highly sensitive subject. While chanting this morning's Office, The Canticle of Sirach 36:1-5, 10 – 13 confirmed my decision; thus, "Give new signs and work new wonders; show forth the splendor of your right hand and arm."

94

Some minds are like cement all mixed up and set like concrete. Others agree out of fear because they desperately want to belong. I suppose I am a "mindset" of a dissenting opinion risking all because I believe His Eminence deserves the best. This brings to matter, the subject of the habit.

Your Eminence, when you extended your invitation to enter the postulancy, you wrote, "You will be part of establishing the foundation and creating the history for the Sisters of Hope. There is no precedent, no model to follow – only Jesus – who is the Way, the Truth, and the Life. You also stated on the retreat that the Sisters would wear a traditional habit and, you implied it again in the Rationale for the Sisters of Hope.

When this has been broached to the novices, the reaction is, "We have taken a vow not to discuss it for eight months." or "We already have our habits." I have heard that it was already written up in the Constitution that it was not to be changed. I do not know for sure because the postulants are not privy to their meetings though we are most welcome in the domestic area of the kitchen.

I know there are five of the postulants who would welcome a more traditonal garb. I believe there are also a couple of the novices who would like to change their "outfit". The reason I use the word "outfit" is because that is exactly what a lady referred to it as on Saturday coming out of church. The same lady is a Religious and she did not even recognise it as a habit.

A lovely habit was sent by the Daughters of Saint Paul, and I wonder if it was shown to you. I propose something with the scapular, or the effect of it, and a straight cut lending a dignified appearance. More importantly, Kind Father, is that your Sisters of Hope would be making a powerful statement. There would be no need for a seamstress as the Fitzpatrick catalogue has them made to order. Please understand that this is not my personal desire as such, because if that was the case, I would say lets get a pretty light blue one like the sister, if you will forgive me, on the bottle of "Blue Nun" Lieframilch.

Where I come from we eat oat meal and pitch tents. I propose we "pitch" these tents or modified habits and represent the Cardinal with aplomb!

I have the honour to remain
His Eminence's most humble servant,

M. Virginia LaPointe

P. S. - I don't even mind if we eat like Eule Gibbons! (This was a reference to one of the novices in charge of the kitchen who was a bit of a health nut!)

On 31 May 1992

His Eminence, John Cardinal O'Malley
Archbishop of New York

Dear Eminent One,

Firstly, you are to be commended on this first anniversary of the founding, Your founding, of The Sisters of Hope. I tender my warmest felicitations Your Eminence.

Secondly, I wish to express my contentment with our spiritual director, one Reverend Father Halligan. I am very much at ease when conferring with him. He has taught not only me, but all of us some lofty things in which to aspire. He is offering his Mass on June 1st for all the Sisters and their intentions …..a magnanimous gesture which touches me deeply.

Thirdly, I am still repining having not gone to your Mass at The Shrine in Washington. You should not have had to change your homily. The Sisters of Hope should have been there and I apologize that it was not carried through.

Next, I want to express that I have a great devotion to Our Lady of Perpetual Help. So badly did I want to tell you this when you asked us if we had thought of any titles, but the previous night, I was told not to mention it as you would pick one. Just want you personally to know that I took heed of what you said earlier in the month Good Father. It is no wonder that the Child Jesus's Strap of His Sandal was astrew!

Let it not go remiss without thanking you and Father Whelan for going out of your way to treat us to the delicious pizza and the gourmet bakery cookies. Mmmmmmmm, Thank you!

As a matter of conscience, there is one other small matter that I must beg your pardon for Gracious Emininence. That is, when you arrived I had every intention of paying you homage, but awkwardness won out. So, I beseech you Dear Cardinal to allow me to make up for this disparagement in asking you to extend your hand so that I may revere it not once, but twice.

Am looking forward to the retreat, and hoping that its effects will foster such growth that we may live up to your ideals. Thank you for permitting this time for us.

So it is that your loving daughter of Christ closes asking to

Remain His Eminence's most
humble servant,
M. Virginia LaPointe (Sometimes called "Heidi")

P.S. - Grampa says that Daddy is still taking about that singular call on his birthday. All of Ticonderoga is talking about it; it may even make the Times of Ti!

My 31st, 1992

Hi Gramp,

Good talking with you. Here is a copy of my next test which I have yet to do. On it, you will see notes that Helene wrote to me during class.

I am sorry you lost another cat. Also sorry your legs bother you so much. Everyone is busy getting packed. I have yet to pack. I am exhausted and I feel my hayfever kicking in.

Well, I wrote the Cardinal another letter which I will give him tomorrow – except, I used two sheets of paper for the original.

I feel like I forgot to tell you something, but am just too tired to think what it could be. Will finish this letter in the morning.

I told Father Halligan you said Hi. Sister Mary Paul says to say hi too. She is really nice.

Well Grampa, take care, I love you very much.

Your Little Virginia's

Helene's "notes":
"You better watch out for 'Rosie', she is watching to see if you are going to pass a note."
"Here is your test !!! Better watch out for Rosie, you are making noise! Stop!" (My stomach was growling.)

"What's wrong with his (the instructor) shoulder?"

And I reply on the paper, "I don't know, but he has a good head on his shoulders."

"S.J.J.S.S.. - Notice, no fig newtons or cookies! @ lunch none either! He's very funny, isn't he? Please answer correctly and use medical terminology, S.M.M.S.VS" (Helene is a nurse so she is accustomed to those abbreviations. The initials stood for Sister Mary Magdalene and the Latin S S for Sisters of Hope. My initials she used were for Sister James John and Sisters for Hope. This was before we would receive our veils and names.

I reply to this "test question", " I appreciate his Peter Sellers style. Can you picture him singing?"

Helene responds, "Father H----- used to be an opera singer. Sister Carmen told me."

To which I add, "Yes, and he sang 'Carmen'.

Helene continues on her note or as she puts it, question number 5., "I am trying to watch him so we can have a good meeting tonight – watch when he puts his hand and arm behind his back."
My response: I think he has a Werther's butterscotch in his back pocket.
Whenever Father H. looks away, 'Rosie' looks at me to see if I am going to pass you a note.
That's a good position for you to put your elbow in for me to pass you this.

"Please, don't tell me about Rosie (Helene's nickname for one of the postulants who has rosie cheeks) again. Her friends Sister Christina and Dorothy always pass notes. PLEASE USE MEDICAL TERMINOLOGY!

6. Could it be a lazy mouth? Are you trying to make me lose it?! Hilarious!
Rosie thinks she has a monopoly on C.S. Lewis. What does Diane use that broom for?

Helene replies, "She sweeps off the dandruff of Father H------

"Charlie Brown" wanted to know how Father Tony knew where I was from.
"Don't tell her. She is jealous." Helene responds. Then she says, "You must tell "Hally" that I am being good!!" Then she goes on to

99

say that "that Peace Corps girl is going to do the reading." and she finishes, "by the way, I had a little nip today."

Gramp, had a letter from Nancy today; also one from Ed and Dixie.

VI. The Retreat from Haedes

The retreat proved to be more than a time of reflection. I remember the Sisters there saying how they worked with tractors to clear the land and build their convent. They said there were a lot of snakes. It seems the "snakes" are still there. They are so big into their academic degrees and psychology. They video taped our times together that we had open discussions. They had a purpose. It was not a time for reflection and drawing closer to Our Lord. It was more like the "Living Stations of the Cross." It was each man (nun) for himself.

The Cardinal was visiting on one of these days and during one of these taped "discussions". I was made a mockery of. Margaret was quick to point out my disobedience for having a chocolate Freihofer cake in my room. Then, Olive chimed in, "I saw you with it." She also pointed out that someone yells in the night – implying that someone is crazy here. Well, I have been given to nightmares – especially when I hold everything in. These two, along with Dorothy, resented me for doing kind deeds for Helene. Helene sat there and she let me take the blame when I had gotten the cake for her. She wanted me to keep it in my room. Everyone was playing it safe in front of the Cardinal. The novices sat there in a self-righteous manner. Real issues were not discussed. It was, gang up on the "fall guy" Virginia. Make her look ridiculous. It was all so ridiculous. I admitted, at the "trial", "Yes, it is true, I did buy a chocolate cake and I gladly would have shared it with any of my perpetrators." Then I noticed Monsignor Walsh slap his knee laughing. He could not believe that a mountain was being made out of a mole hill and then, at my expense. I felt humiliated and all alone. I could not eat. I learned that day not to trust anybody – not even Helene. Dorothy was quiet. I sensed that in her own quiet way, she did not think this was right. Later, that evening, I was sitting next to Dorothy at dinner. Her hand reached over and clasped mine. I kept to myself the rest of the time there. I also went out in the night for a long walk alone -

****
**

Wednesday 10 June 1992
St. Barnabas
10::06 a.m.

My Dear Grandfather,

 Hi Grampa l I am back in the Bronx – Throggs Neck. It is good to be back.

 Was glad to get a hold of you over the weekend. Sorry if I sounded down. The retreat was more of a workshop and it left me completely drained. I disagree with their methods. They use too much psychology and anthropology. The Sisters there kiss on the for the Sign of Peace gently on the lips and they bow to each other before and afterwards. They are into imagery and their degrees. They wear their Birkenstock and sandals and long polyester habits, but the way I see it, they are very self-serving.

I believe their modus operandi was to give the Cardinal a more in-depth report than he was getting from Sister Rita. I had heard that he wanted them or The Parish Visitors to get us started. I am so glad that it is the Parish Visitors. Remember last year I visited a convent in Meriden, Connecticut on my way back from Darien – well this outfit is just like them – WEIRD! I did get a little satisfaction in erasing the part where the sister told me not to bring something up after the other sister told me to bring it up. They call each other "Mother". They have about twelve Mothers! It must be because they are "well-educated" women that the Cardinal goes for them; that, plus the fact that they are self-supporting. Well, I will not hesitate to tell him what I think of them! They don't even pray the Rosary. They taped and videoed most of our retreat. The food was good and plentiful; the setting was nice (bucolic), and the dogs were

101

friendly – but, that was about the extent of it. My hayfever was in full force. So you can see why I had to talk to you.

VII. Dorothy

Helene hated it and so did Dorothy. Dorothy has been kinder to me as of late. Even the novices have been a little nicer to me than usual. I think Sister Agatha was not keen on this outfit too. Perhaps they are too much alike.

Helene can be miserable at times, but at other times she is all heart. She is protective of me in her own way. She tries to keep me under her wing.

Got a whole slew of mail when I got back. Today I have a letter from Mrs. Crammond. Lizzy wrote. Mr. and Mrs. Shaw wrote also and I had a letter from Georgie.

Will be anxious to discuss the "retreat" with my spiritual director Father Halligan.

Saturday, we are going on a Prayer Vigil with the Cardinal.

Can you call me Sunday morning at 10:05 -
I love you Grampa,

Your Little Virginia

Sunday Night June 14, 1992

Dear Grampa,

Recognise my stationary? Look, only about six more weeks and I can see you! I can hardly wait! Mom called tonight. She snuk in a call!

I guess Grant had food poisoning though he was rushed to St.Peter's and they had him in the Cancer Unit.

Thank Goodness for a restful day today.

Father Halligan is going to Daytona with his sister this Wednesday – so we won't see him 'il the 25th. He is a beautiful priest. I marched with him yesterday. He is only 57 years old, but he seems older on account of his frail health.

Well, thank you for your letter.

Sister Gerard threatening to leave – but then she always does. Maybe she will make good on it this time.

I guess I don't have too much to say. I am a little behind in my writing. Have an exam to work on, plus two articles for the newsletter. Plus ti do the filing for the archives. Now we, the postulants will be included in the meetings with the novices. I just hope the Cardinal does not decide to have those Alma Sisters do the formation. I do not like their methods!

Sister Carole is leaving because she was elected superior for the Parish Visitors.

I will write again this week, For now,

Your Loving Little Virginia

for June 21, 1992

My Dear Grandfather,

Hi Grampa! Happy Father's Day. You could call me at 5:10 p.m. - but if you have company (Harry), you can call me at 7:00 p.m., or at 8:35 p.m. We go to the Cathedral on Sunday. We will probably be back around 1 p.m. - depending on if and how long the Cardinal wants to meet with us. He met with Dan Quayle yesterday.

Boy, I sure met some loonies on that March. There were a lot of "marginal" people. One woman told me that she had a rather unique job. She works in a morgue! Then she went on to describe an autopsy! I thought I would die!

Well, now we have to have a meeting about whether or not to use the dishwasher. Can you believe it?!

I am learning an African dance for Sister Carol – for the farewell dinner. She spent time in Africa.

Well Grampa, God Bless you. I love you,

Virginia
P.S. - I cut a bunch of coupons out of the Sunday papers for you. Maybe you can use them.

Monday
22 June 1992
11:40 a.m.

My Dear Grandfather,

Hi Grampa! It was so good talking with you on Saturday and then again on Sunday. So what did you think of me finding that song by Richard Harris. I couldn't believe it! Then, I heard our other favorite - 'Ballad pour Adeline'.

This is a picture of Jesus Laughing. Helene gave me this prayer card.

Helene can be a lot of fun, but she also can be very bossy. Then she tries to pry into my affairs. Even when I called you yesterday, she is telling me not to play all of the song. She takes right over! She gets on my nerves. Today she is puzzled because I have been aloof towards her. She will cut down Sister Agatha one minute and then she kisses up to her the next. "Well, she is on the Council, so she deserves my respect." She will say. She and Sister Gerard are so fickle. Gerard is leaving. She told the Cardinal. He asked her to stay an extra month, but he goes to Italy in July so she will be leaving right after the next retreat. It will be a good riddance because she is miserable.

I am going to Chapel to pray. I will finish this after lunch.

Later, 1:35 p.m. - Father Paul stopped in. He had lunch (dinner) with us. He is a short Italian priest who looks like a little boy. He thinks that the devil is trying to cause dissension in the community and I believe he is right. I can't stand anyone here. It is awful to say, but true. I am trying to pray to overcome this. The minute a priest walks in, they all get giddy.

I can't wait to get the photos.

Talked to the folks last night at 10:30. It seems they were visiting you at 7:00 when I anticipated their call.

I hear they are selling centennial tiles for six bucks from the church. It would be nice to get a couple. I could give one to the Cardinal.

Oh well, I love you and I can only try my best with God's Grace. Human nature is not likely to change.

Say hi to Harry and Edna.

Lots of Love,
Little Virginia

We are having a meeting now!!

VII. Spring Exam Paper

Grampa, here is a copy of my Spring Exam on Jesus Christ – Spring of 1992

The human impression Jesus would have made to pepole who encounterd Him would be firstly that He is a man, a truly human man. He would want us to know that He is like us in all things except sin. His mind, body, and will are all human. He has a human nature - a mysterious blending of body and soul. In His mind, like in our minds there is an intelligence - a capacity to learn and a will to choose; decisions to make. Jesus could get tired. He could enjoy a good meal, feel hunger, and be happy hearing a nice song. Jesus was a man, but not just a man, rather a just man with a difference.

Jesus Christ is also a divne Person who intrinsically has that right to speak of a new law. He has Divine authority because of a special relationship to God. In Matthew 5: 17, "Think not that I have come to abolish the law and the prophets; I have come not to abolish them, but to fulfil them." Also, in verses 21-27, Matthew continues to convey Jesus as Lord telling His people not to kill, or to judge; to forgive, and to make peace with your brother; not to commit adultery. Jesus claimed authority to forgive sins; in Matthew 11:25, Jesus declared, "I thank Thee, Father, Lord of heaven and earth, that Thous hast hidden these things from the wise and understanding and revealed them to babes."

We must not downplay Jesus's humanity, we must revere Him. In Luke 10:21, the same theme is paralleled as Matthew 11:25.

In Act II: 21, Peter describes our Lord, "Being therefore a prophet, and knowing that God had sworn an oath to him that he would set one of his descendants upon his throne." God raised up this Jesus, a true descendant of David.

Hebrews 4:5 refers to Jesus not as a high priest who is unable to sympathize with our weaknesses, but one who in every respect has been tempted as we are, yet without sinning. Just as this Jesus could

106

be tempted, so could his apostles, and He would tell them to pray for strength to overcome temptation (Luke 22:39).

Jesus could be terce and unsentimental – speaking in direct plainness, Matt. 16:21, and reproaching in pointed terms. Luke 9:55. Jesus was confrontational to the Pharisees, Matt. 23. This is evident again in John 3:4 when He puts Nicodemus in his place. Just as Jesus could be angry, He was also compassionate and affectionate; happy, yet He wept. This is the reality of Jesus.

However, in every way, Jesus reveals Himself as being "ad Patrem" - glorifying and revealing the Father in all his actions. Only the Son knows the Father, and the Father knows the Son.

Jesus reveals that He existd before His Birth, "Before Abraham was, I am." In St. John's Gospel, "I am Who am." Jesus took the Divine Name, The Unspeakable Word. At that point, the Apostles wanted to stone Him for saying He was The Lord God of Israel. Later, in the Garden of Gethsemane, Jesus was asked, "Are you Jesus of Nazareth?" He replied, "I Am Who Am", the apostles reacted by involunarily falling at their feet.
Christ also has a Divine nature. He performed miracles: healings, raising from the dead, exorcisms, walking on water, multiplication fo loaves, control over nature. These supernatural acts were caused by God for a moral or religious purpose.

Jesus was humble and obedient to the Father. Phil. 2: 6-11, He did not deem equality with God , something to be grasped at. He had a great love for His Father (Jn. 10-28). He claimed that intimacy with the Father (Matt. 11:27).

Jesus also had/has an unspeakable love and devotion for His Mother. Theirs was an inexpressable love. Mary is Co-Redeemer. She went to Calvary with Jesus. Finally, in this act, we His people must know how much Jesus loves us to subject Himself to that cruel, bitter suffering for us and for our salvation.

The second question of the final exam was: What was the significance of the Council of Chalcedon's teaching that Jesus Christ

107

was one divine person with two real natures, that of God and that of man?

The significance of The Council of Chalcedon's teaching that Jesus Christ was one Divine Person with two real natures, that being one of God and one of man was that in 451 A.D., the Concil of Chalcedon met in order to lay down in solemn dogmatic decisions the doctrine of the two natures of Christ united in the Second Divine Person. This Eternal, Only Begotten of the Eternal Father was born of The Holy Spirit and The Virgin Mary. This temporal birth took nothing from that Divine and Eternal birth, and added nothing to it. Its whole purpose was the redemption of deluded man, to conquer death and to destroy the devil, who had dominion over death. For we could not have overcome the author of sin and death unless he, whom sin could not stain nor death hold fast, had taken our nature and made it his own.

He was conceivwd by The Holy Spirit in the Womb of the Virgin who bore Him without loss of virginity as she conceived Him in a like manner.

The Holy Spirit indeed made the Virgin fruitful, but the true body was taken from the body (of the Virgin) - 'Wisdom hath built herself a house' - Rev. 9:1 'And the Word was made flesh, and dwelt among us' John 1:14. - that is, in the flesh which He took from mand and animated with a rational soul.

With the character of both natures unimpaired, therefore, coming together in one person, humility was assumed by majesty, weakness by strength, mortality by eternity, and in order to wipe out our guilt, the inviolable nature was joined to the nature subject to suffering so that, as our salvation demanded, one and the same 'mediator of God and man, the man Christ Jesus, (1 Tim. 2:5) could from one element be able to die and from the other not.

The true God, therefore, was born in the complete and perfect nature of man, complete in his (nature) and complete in ours .....

So the Son of God enters this lowly world, descending from His heavenly throne yet not leaving the glory of his Father.

Jesus comes in a new order, born in a new birth, invisible in His own, He became visible in ours. Existing before all time, He began in time. The impassible God did not disdain to become a man subject to suffering, and the Immortal to subject Himself to the laws of death. In this birth, was also born a body for inviolate Virginity, knowing no concupsiscence. The Lord took His mother's nature. However, His nature is like ours even though His birth was miraculous. For He who is truly God is also truly man. In this unity, there is no lie, for the divine majesty and the human humility penetrate each other. As God is not changed by His mercy, so man is not consumed by this dignity. For each of the natures accords with each other, the Word doing what pertains to the Word, and the flesh doing what pertains to the flesh. One of them shines forth with miracles, and the other one is subjected to insults. As the Word does not leave the equality of glory with the Father, so also the flesh does not abandon the nature of our race....

The Council of Chalcedon met in order to lay down in solemn dogmatic decisions the doctrine of the tow natures of Christ united in the Second Divine Person. This was to counter the theandric view which Dioscoros took. Around the same time, the monk Eutyches, in Constantinople, adhered to the view of monophysitism. This view holds that divinity and humanity were separate before the union, but on union they fused and there remained only one new nature, hence, "monophysitism". The theandric view envisages Christ's unity of divnity and humanity as unity of person but also to recognise one divine – human nature in Christ. This brought about the successful Latrocinium Council of Ephesus in 449 A.D.

In his famous Tome addressed to Flavian, Leo the Great declared against the new heresy. Up to that time, the Tome contains the clearest expression of the Doctrine of Incarnation. Thus the General Council of Chalcedon against monophysitism ensued.

"Following therefore the Holy Fathers we unanimously teach that the Son, our Lord Jesus Christ, is one and the same perfect in

Divinity, the same perfect in humanity, 'in all things like as we are, without sin: (Heb. 4:15), born in recent times for us and for our salvation from the Virgin Mary, Mother of God, as to His humanity. We confess one and the same Christ, the Son, the Lord, the Only Begotten, in two natures, unconfused, unchangeable, undivided and unseparable. The difference of natures will never be abolished by their being united, but rather the properties of each remain unimpaired, both coming together in one person and substance, not parted or divided between two person, but in one and the same only-begotten Son, The Divine Word, The Lord Jesus Christ. Jesus Christ Himself has taught us this previously with the prophets and the Creed of the Fathers has been handed down to us (Sanction). The above having been considered with all and every care and diligence, this Holy Ecumenical Council has defined that no one may advance any other belief or inscribe, compose, hold or teach it in any other way....."

Christ is really one of the Holy Trinity, that is, one holy Person from the three Persons of The Holy Trinity.... God did truly suffer in the flesh..... the glorious and holy Mary, ever a virgin, is in a real and true sense, Mother of God....

Due to the Monophysite schism continuing in spite of Chalcedon, yet another Council called the Fifth General Council with Pope Vigiius presiding, allowed for the healing the breach concerning "The Threee Chapters".

Four Centuries of trying to come to grips with who Jesus is, and, the classic and permanently vlid standard on which to judge morality giving definitive precision to what the church thought about Christ sums the importance of Chalcedon. It also gave a definitive stamp on previous councils; Nicea, Ephesus, and Constantinople I and II.

Bibliography and Footnotes:

1. The Teaching of the Catholic Church edited by Karl Rahner, S.J. 1966 c., pp. 151 – 155, 247, 291, of Dogmatic Letter of Pope Leo I Against Eutyches (449 A.D.), or 'Tome'.

2. Article 293 of same source

3. Articles 250, 294 and 251 – paraphrased from same source

4. From the General Council of Chalcedon (451 A.D.) against Monophysitism

5. The Holy Bible, Catholic Edition RSV Nelson, 1965 c.

Then, I selected question number 4, which was: "Why is it so crucial that we realize the nature of sin? What does it mean that Jesus is a Savior? What were some of the sins Jesus was particularly concerned to sway us away from?"

It is crucial that we realize the nature of sin because we can freely consent to it, and in doing so, we forsake all. An absence of unity, oneness, and an absence of love prevails. The propensity to sin is so strong as C.C. Lewis puts it, "You can leave hell anytime you want, but we don't want to – we are attached to our sins and selfishness." As a result, four kinds of relationships are disrupted: Man against Nature, Man against himself, Man aginst Man and Man against God.

In the letter to Titus, Chapter 3, verse 3, "For we ourselves were once foolish, disobedient, led astray, slaves to various passions and pleasures, passing our days in malice and envy, hated by men and hating one another;"

God gives us the freedom, but we must ask ourselves, "Are we getting away from God's way?" Our sins punish us in themselves. In Romans, Chapter 3:9 - "both Jews and Greeksare unde the power of sin, as it is written: 'None is righteous, no, not one' no one understands, no one seeks for God. All have turned aside, together they have gone wrong; no one does good, not even one." Then, it goes on to say in verse 20, "For no human being w ill be justified in his sight by works of the law, since through the law comes knowledge of sin." Chapter 3, berses 21 – 27 go on to say about answering to the righteousness of God. All are ustified by the grace of God since all have sinned – as a gift, through

111

the redemption which is in Christ Jesus, whom God put forward as an expiation by His Blood, to be received by faith. This was to prove Jesus' mercy and righteousness.

We must be ever aware that the force to do evil is very strong. If only one person sinned, Jesus still would have suffered and died on the Cross for that one person. Jesus repairs the damage done to us, and He restores and renews us. In John I, chapter 3:1, "We are God's children." Therefore, what father would not do that for his children. Jesus is an offering for our sins and for the whole world (I Jn. 1-7). We have become by adoption what Christ is by nature.

St. Athanasius says, " the Son of God was made the Son of man that the children of man might be made the children of God."

Ephesians 2 – 10, "For we are his workmanship, created in Christ Jesus for good works, which God prepared beforehand, that we should walk in them." It further goes on to say that we should put away our old self and put on a fresh new spiritual way of thinking. That is why we put on the white garment at Baptism, and why we exult at the Easter Vigil – Christ comes to rescue us.

There is objective and subjective redemption. Objective redemption is what Jesus actually did to save us, and subjective, or applied redemption is suffice for everyone's salvation. Jesus Christ came as Mediator with the Father for the salvation of man. He achieved the redemption by his Sacrifice of the Cross by which He made atonement to God and merited all grace for man. All the faithful are united in the community of his Mystical Body.

The greatest sin is pride. Jesus is also concerned with us succumbing to sins of the flesh – anything against the Ten Commandments. He does not want us to judge or slander or be unjust to our fellow man – e.g. - giving unfair wages to a worker. Pride leads to all other sins. We lose the beatic vision, and forsake all when we sin. We are lucky to get to Purgatory. We have to be guarded that we might give glory to God and feast with Him forever and ever. Otherwise, we could end up in "Haedes" and there is no turning back. The main thing is to not want to sin for love of our

Lord – not just out of fear. We are like nothing, and anything we have, we owe to God. Thank God for the Church and the Sacraments which sustain us, our souls, along the way. If we are in the state of mortal sin, we can not receive sanctifying grace. It is vital that we avail ourselves to the sacraments and make amends so that Jesus our Savior, our Redeemer, can rescue us. Amen!

The fourth question and final one out of a possible five I selected was: Describe the Paschal Mystery, and why it is of such towering importance to us.

The Paschal Mystery is the mystery of the death and resurrection of Our Lord and the Ascension of Our Lord. It must be regarded harmoniously with the salvific meaning of the Incarnation of the Word of God and that of the saving power of His resurrection. The word incarnate is through His deeds and words the fulness of God's revelation to the world. This has been expressed in the Second Vatican Council with great clarity – moreso than in past documents. It also emphasizes the significance of Christ for the Christian understanding of the mystery of man.

It is of such towering importance to us because as stated above, Christ contains the fulness of God's revelation, and, He is the mediator between God and men. He has saved all mean through the sacrifice of His Cross. Christ saves and liberates. He has satisfied and merited for all. By His resurrection He has become for all the source of a new life. Thus, He has universal Lordship and Kingship. Christ is the goal of history. He is the new and perfect man who manifests man's true vocation. The truth about Jesus Christ may not be distorted!

We as Christians, and moreso as Catholics, celebrate the Paschal Mystery sacramentally at Mass. A renewal is produced as we reflect what shapes our way of being, thinking, and acting.......having special connotations.

By gift of nature, we are endowed with freedom, the faculty to make our own choices. However, our nature is tainted, and often we err. Alas, we are spared of death, the inevitable consequence of sin due

113

to the new freedom procured by Christ the Redeemer (cf. Rom. 8:2). The reason we falter in the first place is on account of original sin, the sin of Adam.

We were subject to separation from God, moral sickness, and death – as slaves in a very sad fate. Throught Baptism, Christ freed us from the effects of original sin, and, by our participation in the Mystery of His death and resurrection – The Paschal Mystery. He gave us the grace to free ourselves from personal and present sin, and to raise ourselves up from it. Through our own resurrection, He promised us that we too would overcome death – a rpofound and incomprehensble truth.

In the Old Testament, the first liberation of the elect People from Pharaonic slavery and the law of Sinai promulgated with it – Christ was fulfilled and the religious economy was set up. However, good law that it was, it was insufficient. The law of grace was necessary, the law of the Spirit. Christ conferred this on us by dying for us, and rising from the dead. This is the liberation that came to us from the Paschal Mystery.

Therefore, we must live in charity and in faithfulness carrying out the supreme duties of love of God and love of neighbor (Matt. 22-37). We must imitate Christ who is the model of ascetic and perfect life, and in the living of Christ – Gal. 2:20, the principle fo mysticallife, the initial consummation of our eternal endowment ith the divine life, the supreme liberation.

While we are free, our freedom must be born of the Holy Spirit. The Christian is bound more than ever to God's will, to respect for natural and civil laws, obedient to the hierarchical and pastoral functions of the Church. This blessed freedom is among the most beautiful and original experiences of our Christian election, never to be renounced.

Phil. 2: 6-11, refers to Christ's Sacrifice on Calvary as a "Kenosis" - that is, and emptying of Himself. We too must grasp at his form of God. St.Paul says we are bought and paid for; Christ is our ransom. Jesus had to go so that the Holy Spirit would come. Gal. 5:22

114

speaks of the Fruits of the Holy Spirit which come forth as a rsult of the Paschal Mystery: knows as "Objective Redemption".

Christ has did, Christ is Risen, Christ will come again!

****

June 9, 1992

Dear Virginia,

What happened on that retreat?! You seemed kind of down last night. Do the best you can. Now you know who your friends are. You made your speech. I am surprised at the attitude of the others. You all took the same oaths. It seems the others are not honoring them – the compassion, honesty, etc. Know that I am proud of you. Keep your chin up. If they want to isolate you, so be it. Just ignore them. You made your point to the Cardinal. I think he knows what is going on. I only hope things improve. I do worry you know.

Miss Hall had her 90th Birthday Sunday.

Sarah went to Montreal with the French club.

Your mother and the Burleighs went to Isle La Motte on Sunday – to the Shrine there.

No obits

God Bless and keep you,
Love,
Gramp

****

One thing about being in the Cardinal's Order was that we were accorded some of the best classes with renown theologians.

However, Helene would get bored in the classes. Then she would look for me – to try to get a rise out of me. She would slip notes usually with a reference of one of the instructors's features. One resembled Mister Rogers. Helene ran with that from his lips to his cardigan. The awful thing is, I know the priest picked up on it. I was right in the middle.

22 June 1992

Hi Gramp,

Guess what?! I just got my first fax from Chile It was great to hear from Herr Oehr – just had to share it with you!

Maybe you could slip me two dollars in your next letter. I have to get out and get some chocolate – in need of a chocolate fix!

Hope you are alright.

I love you. I am off to prayer now.

P.S. - You will be billed for $8.00 for a veil I ordered. Hopefully, it won't be more than that. Oh, call me on Sunday at 10:05. It's Thomas's birthday; if he is around, tell him to call me so that I can wish him a Happy Birthday.

Copy of the fax that I received:

Santiago de Chile

Virginia LaPointe
Sisters of Hope
New York

Hi My Dear Virginia,

How could I dare to forget my Little Ginia....

116

Many thanks for your lovely letter which I got today.

Family is fine, business is horrible. We might change house, so please let us know where we can always reach you.

We are thinking a lot of you. Last Thursday, we got card for Frederick's birthday.

We all love you and I give you a special big kiss,

Winfried

29 June 1992

My Dear Gramp,

Hi Gramp! Finally, Helene has left my room. She thinks she wants to leave, but she says that she will wait for the veil first.

Well, we got our veils we ordered originally from Philadelphia. Then the other one I ordered just came today with UPS. Sister Gerard and Helene brought the box up and they said, "Okay, what's in it?" Like they knew. Nothing is sacred around here! But Gerard is leaving soon. She is miserable anyways. She does, however, have a son who is a priest, and he is lovely.

Sister Carole just left. Yesterday I asked Margaret if I could have half of a brownie and she said no. Then I asked Sister Carole and she said no also. I was feeling kind of faint like I just needed something to tie myself over. Was kind of upset about it. Helene told Sister Carole. She said that if I ask, I can

ave something sweet, but she also said that I don't like to be told "No" which I suppose is true. So I was happy to receive your note with "sweet possibilities". Thank you Grampa.

I love you, Little Virginia

P.S. - Enclosed is a copy of the letter I slipped under Helene's door:

Dear Sister Helene,

His Eminence is coming this Thrusday June 24th to celebrate Mass. Monsignor O'Reilly and Father Arcuri will be concelebrating. I would like you to read the first reading. Virginia will do the responsorial pslm and Sister Carole will sing the verse in the back of your office book.

Thank you and God Bless,

Sister Rita

P.S. - For some reason, I always find this particular reding a mouthful to get through. Good Luck.

Then, I included a copy of the First Reading which was from the book of Genesis:

Abram's wife Sarai had borne him no children. She had, however, an Egyptian maid-servant named Hagar. Sarai said to abram: "The Lord has kept me from bearing children. Have intercourse, then, with my maid; perhaps I shall have sons through her." Abram heeded Sarai's requst. Thus, after Abram had lived ten years in the land of of Canaan, his wife Sarai tookher maid, Hagar the Egyptian, and gave her to her husband Abram to be his concubine. He had intercourse with her, and she became pregnant. When she became aware of her pregnancy, she has been looking on me with disdain. May the Lord decide between you and me!" Abram told Sarai: "Your maid is in your power. Do to her whatever you please." Sarai then abusd her so much that Hagar ran away from her.

The Lord's messenger found her by a spring in the wilderness, the spring on the road to Shur, and he asked, "Hagar, maid of Sarai, where have you come from and where are you going?" She answered, "I am running away from my mistress, Sarai." But the Lord's messenger told her: 'Go back to your mistress and submit to her abusive treatment. I will make your descendants so numerous.," added the Lord's messenger, "that they will be too many to count. Besides," the Lord's messenger said to her:

"You are now pregnant and shall bear a son; you shall name him Ishmael, For the Lord has heard you, God has answered you. He shall be a wild ass of a man, his hand against everyone, and everyone's hand against him;"

Hence that is how we survived in the Sisters for Hope!

In another missive I gave Grampa instructions to have film developed at Arthur's drugstore on a Tuesday as we could get two for one then. I needed a photo for the Centennial directory for the Church back home.

Tuesday 9:30 A.M.
30 June 1992

Dear Grampa,

Hi Gramp!

Guess what?! I just got my other veil! Maybe I told you.

I photocopied some of my journal, and my latest letter to the Cardinal. Retreat should be good. I like it at St. John Neuman.

Olive's mother and father brought me a beautiful African violet plant on visiting day. Her mother also gave me a pretty handkerchief with violets on it. It was Olive's grandmother. They also brought me Earl Grey and peppermint tea. I think this was to make up for the "Ollie North" trials in that unholy town of Bethlehem, Connecticut. I surmise Olive felt a little guilty afterward.

119

Say hi to Jane. I will call you from Riverdale this weekend.

Loads of Love,

Virginia

From my journal:

Just got off the phone with Mr. Williams. He is a riot! I just asked the Sisters to pray for him during Holy Hour. I prefaced my plea saying that God is a jealous lover because I planned on a back-up visitor if my sister Annie could not make it. And now, and I laughed, my friend Mr. Williams has fallen down a flight of stairs in his new slip-on Foursheim shoes. It hurt him to even laugh as he told me about it on the phone. He was funny though. Then he told me about the time he fell off a ladder attached to the roof and how an axe landed on his head! Still can't figure that one out! He is a card! He is as comical as Jack Lemmon or Jonathan Winters. He is in severe pain, but God love him, he is going to attempt to make it tomorrow for visiting day. I told him not to feel obligated. He asked if I would like a statue of Saint Germain Cousins - " though it could be any saint, that is the name posted on the bottom of it." he said.

Today, the postulants went to the Blue Army Shrine in Washington, New Jersey. Talk about funny things happening!

First there is "Hop along Cassidy" with a patch on his eye and glasses on. He walks with a limp. He has sort of a poor boy's version of Ernest Hemmingway look to him – real eccentric! He is parading back and forth with all his camera paraphernalia taking pictures of Bishop Vaughn. He is also photographing mothers with their babies and the scenery around the Shrine. I recall seeing him at The Right To Life Institute.

Then, there is this woman with a 1960's bouffant hairstyle with a poker face. She wears a lot of pan cake make-up and it is caked on. Her arms are outstretched as she sings in this ultra-high falsetto voice. She is dramatic with her rendition of Ave Maria. She is from Staten Island same as the photographer is. They both attend all the Pro Life functions. I had all I could do not to look over at Helene during her rendition of Ave Maria. It seems Olive knows them but she was being rather aloof. She did not want to own up to the fact that she actually knew them. There are all kinds!

Some woman from Pennsylvania talked endlessly to me about the messages of Our Lady of Guadalupe. A fellow from South America was receiving the messages and Our Lady of Guadalupe spared a lot of babies from being aborted. These messages were approved by the Bishops. Then, another woman buds in and says, "It was a fellow from Nicaragua." The people from Pennsylvania sound like hicks. That must be why Agatha likes to tell people she is from New York as her Pennsylvania family home is in Pennsylvania but evidently not too far from the New York border.

I met some lady on the Indian Trail the other day and she said, "You are not from around here, are you?" I said, "No," and then she asked if I was from Pennsylvania! Now I was insulted!

Then there is Elizabeth Laplinski from Elmhurst, Pennsylvania. She worked with the Cardinal when he was stationed in Scranton. The funny thing was when the spokeswoman for the American Life League Lobby got up to speak, she went up and sat right next to her. Then, Miss Laplinski procedes to fall asleep and she begins to snore! Loudly! I thought I would die! And Helene beside me – a lost cause. Dorothy was getting perturbed with me. I find myself having to apologize more and more for my laughing at the wrong, albeit funny, times! The worst was, we were sitting less than a foot in front of the speaker as the setting was to be more personable. I did apologize for my nerves after she rattled off the 62 pages of her well-reseached report. Mr. and Mrs. Sadict were very cool and Mr. Sadict said that he saw me laughing and he actually enjoyed it. Of course that was during the part about "intercourse" which was doubly funny because Helene and I were in mass hysteria over a reading from Genesis, Year 1, 12th week – Thursday which of course this reminded us of. It was awful. No control for the wicked! To make matters worse, there was this large, approximately 275 pound woman, with huge ankles and as big as the all outdoors – which is sort of where we were – outdoors – an outdoor amphitheater setting. God help every pound of that woman, but the sight of her was more than I could handle at this point. On top of that, there was this guy with slick, black hair greased back – perhaps in his 40's. He draws his inspiration from Elvis Presley. He was wearing light blue pressed trousers and a matching vest. He was placing the statue of Our Lady of Fatima down in a meticulous manner. His stance – almost like he was posing for us as he arranged the roses. His expression, and his exacting manner, the hairdo, and Helene – starting to lose it. It was more than I could bear!!

There was also this woman wearing a long gold veil, a red tunic blouse and slacks. She was raising her arms to the high heavens. It was quite a show though I don't doubt her sincerity. It is part of her Hispanic culture.

To top it off, Bishop Vaughn missed a step coming down the altar at the recession. His angels were with him, as he caught himself, miter intact. That is always good for cracking a smile. I met him afterward, and kissed his ring.

People watching – that is what it is all about. I get a lot of mileage out of that.

I am hoping Annie comes down on Sunday for Visiting day.

Then, on June 25, 1992 in a letter to His Eminence

Your Esteemed Eminence,

Welcome home! I guess everywhere is your home though. Herr Oehr, who is the head of the Franco-German household where I used to mind his children sent me my first fax! I was so excited. He came to mind because today is his birthday. He always said, "June 25th is the greatest day!" Thus I write to you Holy One.

I wanted to be sure and thank you for the lovely wall hanging of The Madonna of The Streets. It was a very personal gift and it ensures all who enter, a warm welcome. What a beautiful way to commemorate the Sisters of Hope's First Anniversary. With that, warm thoughts of her founder are evoked.

Have been trying to get caught up on the filing. Baked cookies this week, completed Reverend Father Hubbard's exam and am working on possible newsletter submissions.

It was very nice to see Sister Catherine and my friend, Monsignor Harrington. While fully aware that they take the role as liason, I did want to reiterate a stance I took at our meeting. That is, I feel that the incoming group should not be postphoned, or at least not for any length of time. Once the decision is made, it is agonizing to prolong the waiting period. Saint Catherine said, "The thing is to cut, not to untie." The other contention is that the issue we are fighting is one of urgency and immediacy. Life is too short. The Little Flower comes to mind as she made herself appear older upon her appointment with the Bishop so as to be accepted more readily.

Cognizant of good wine and cheese needing ample time to mature, I adhere to spiritual growth developing in doing what has to be done in the present tense; even if it means being challenged by disquietude. Give me the "pioneer spirit!"

I apologize as it is now June 29th....

Your homily last Sunday was very moving – about the Christening in Alice's family.

Am relieved you are back in the states safe and sound though I admit my inspirations at 2 a.m. come from sipping Earl Grey tea in the evening! Can't wait for the retreat at St. John Neumann. I really liked it there.

Yesterday was visiting day and I have come to the conclusion that God is indeed a jealous lover because my sister was unable to make it. I called up this man whose daughter is from Ticonderoga, and as fate would have it, he fell down a flight of stairs in his new Floursheims! But all was not naught. We prayed for him during Holy Hour and he put in an appearance.

Your Eminence, I am anxiously awaiting the dates of our break. You see, I have been asked to lector at the Centennial Mass of Saint Mary's in Ticonderoga on August 23rd. Don't know what the possibilities are, but thought I would bring it to your attention.

The postulants went to the Blue Army Shrine on Saturday. It was not as crowded as one would expect. His Excellency, Bishop Vaughn celebrated the Mass.

The altar boy washed the van so there is a chance that I may get to bake more cookies as a token thank you.

Forgive me, I get carried away with the keys (type writer). I shall close now. Oh, I am sorry you will be losing your right hand man – Reverend Father Sullivan.

With devoted affection,
I have the honour to remain
His Eminence's most humble servant,

M. Virginia LaPointe, ss
7 July 1992
11:17 a.m.

Hi Grampa,

I can't remember if I sent you this – please read the other side – all of it. I wrote the note on it and gave it to Helene.

Well, maybe we won't go to Monroe after all. The Cardinal said the Dominicans of Hawthorne made an offer to take us for canonical novitiate. Then, I guess he met with the novices and he saw their true colors. One said that she did not want to touch people with Cancer. Most of them did not want the direction from these nuns. I heard he got annoyed with them. Let him see them for what they are. I am wondering if he heard the tapes from Connecticut. He seems to know everything and those crazy sisters recorded what one would have thought would have been a peaceful retreat.

Grampa, it was so good talking with you this past weekend. I know it was awful hard for you and I thought a lot about you and Gramma. I hope you are okay.

I also heard that Sister Agatha told the Cardinal that we were not ready for our veils and he said that as far as he is concerned, we were getting them!

Sister Gerard, big pain in arse, getting ready to go (leave).

NYS (HESC) sent me my note – bill. They will probably send it here now. Well, my grandfather, take care of yourself,
Love,
Your devoted granddaughter,
Virginia
On the back of this letter was the reading from Genesis that I told Helene
Sister Rita wanted her to read.
IX. White Smoke Over the Convent

Also, was enclosed a note from Helene who was hoping for a smoke up on the roof.

"Virginia Dear!

Where in Hell do I get a match?

Get me one fast!
H."

After I procured matches for Helene, I found this note on my bed:

"Thank you virginia,
I was going to buy you a bottle and not give you an opener!
H"

Monday
9:14 a.m.
13 July 1992

My Dear Grandfather,

Hi Grampa! You are so lucky to be having cool weather. It is wicked hot and humid here.

I had a nice birthday and thank you for remembering me.

It was good talking to you though you sounded down. You know you are in my loving prayers.

Well, the Cardinal came yesterday. He stayed for nearly three hours. He seemed disgusted and impatient with the sisters – moreso, the novices stemming from their last meeting with him. We did not press him on the issue of going home – and he did not say. Hopefully, we will find out this week Please God.

It seems that there are two priests who are in big trouble in the archdiocese. The Cardinal fears scandal. I don't know, but more and more, I see the politics of the hierarchy.

Looking forward to getting the photos. Thank you for getting them developed.

I just don't know where I stand – which is good in that I rely on God, but which is disconcerting in respect to myself regarding the Cardinal. The Cross, (The Chalice) which I am to embrace/partake.

Father Halligan has had three heart surgeries. He has had three heart attacks. He was only in his 30's when he had his first one. He appears older than what he is (57) on account of his sufferings. He is a beautiful confessor.

Take care Grampa,
I love you,
Little Virginia

P.S. - Helene said to me, "You know, I am mad at you." I said,
"Yeah, I know" Then she said, "I don't want to talk about it either."
Then, I replied, " Well, I didn't mean to walk away, but that subject
tired me – re: formation in future."

The Sisters all signed a homemade card for me with a cute cartoon
of a bunch of children and two nuns at a hamburger/ ice cream stand.
They captioned it: The Sisters celebrate Virginia's birthday with
the town of Ti!!

Here are some of the messages:

Dear Virginia,

Ti's loss is our gain! Thank you for the joy you bring the
community and your graciousnes to everyone. Love, Diane

Another one writes,

"Who needs 'The Greatest Fourth in the North' when you can spend
your birthday with us?

Happy Birthday!"

The novices mostly quoted a verse from the Bible – which was nice,
- and safe.

Sister Gerard wrote a motherly message which was sincere though
she kind of made fun of me in the beginning.

Margaret was offering a Rosary for me which was very thoughtful
(even though she would not let me have a brownie!)

Sister Agatha wrote - "May God Bless you richly during this year of
formation." There is something peculiar with her. She plays it close
to the grindstone. I get the feeling that she does not like it that I
have a good rapport with our Confessor. I think she views him as

her personal Confessor and that we might all benefit by him, but he is such a wonderful one that everyone feels he is exclusively theirs.

Included in this letter are two pictures from the May Crowning: one with everyone around the statue of Our Blessed Mother with the Cardinal, and another one with the Cardinal and me.

2:24 p.m. 20th July 1992

My Dear Grandfather,

Hi Grampa!

Delighted with the coffee cans – keep saving them. The Sisters love them. I appreciate the trouble you went to – to get the Saint Josesph's oil.

Everyone is happy with the Crucifix too.

Thank you. You are a doll. You sounded good this past weekend. Sorry about the fridge – here is little something to help you out with it. Mom said my father would buy you one.

It was so good to see Mom and Sarah, Joseph and Gordon. Trust they got home okay. We had a nice time though I hardly had two minutes alone with her.

I heard that Betty has a twelve pound tumor and that she does not want Dr. Wilburta to operate on her as she blames her for not saving Karl. Aunt Betty has always been fierecely loyal.

I feel confident that I will get to come home for the Centennial celebration. I mentioned it to Sister Rita and she said that it would be nice if I could get home for it.

Wicked hot here.

Yes, I do read your letters Grampa. I love you – stay well,

Your Little Virginia

****

Dear Virginia,

Great to hear from you as it always is.

Did you enjoy your company on Sunday? They got home about 12:30 a.m. The weather was good.

On IMPIOUS – the dictionary says \im-pe-as adj. (L – impius or Whatever!)

Well, I broke down and bought a new refrigerator and stove – don't know how I am going to pay for them, but I will worry about that tomorrow.

The cats are good. Mother tiger is expecting – that's all I need.

Are you getting Times of Ti?
If you get the notice on your loan, let me know.

Well, Heidi, keep up the good work and God Bless you -

Love,
Gramp

P.S. - Enjoy your chocolate – my pleasure!

****

27 July 1992

Hi Grampa,

Here is $40 towards the shoes. They can be sent directly here.

I cooked Swiss steaks yesteday for the Cardinal He is coming today and again tomorrow. He will celebrate Mass here. Father Salmon is supposed to call and come by this week with the little Bishop.

Sorry about all your expenses. That is good of mother and father to get you the new refrigerator.

We have the Crucifix up in our refectory. I took pictures of it with the Cardinal so I will be able to. show Chrissy.

Don't send me any money. I am fine.

Chrissy is going to look into getting me 'The Times of Ti'. She is such a good and loyal friend.

Thanks for the pronunciation on 'impious'.

Can't wait to see you. I love you
 Your Heidi,

 Little Virginia

Sunday 8:50 p.m.
2 August 1992

My Dear Grandfather,

Hi Grampa! You sounded a little better this week.

I hope you are enjoying your peace and quiet after crazy Harry!

Thank you for ordering the shoes for me Grampa.

I trust you called the rectory and I thank you.

Well, it looks like it is going to be an exciting week. Guess who I just talked to – Father Salmon! He is planning on coming Thursday with Bishop da Silva. They will concelebrate Mass and then Father will give a talk. Then they will stay for lunch. I can't wait!

Then, on Tuesday we are going to the big Knights of Columbus Mass at the Cathedral. And – we will meet Mother Teresa! There will be sixty-two bishops there from all over the world. I would not be surprised if Father Salmon and the "Little Bishop" would be there. We are invited to go to the Cardinal's Residence afterward.

It is a busy, exciting week. We are also going to find out the outcome regarding our next step in formation.

Helene called this evening. She sounds like a different person – a hundred times better. She is going on the bus with her grandson Liam to to Fort Lauderdale where her son Joseph is. Her daughter is in some sort of dilema. I doubt Helene will ever come back now. I will have to do some heavy duty packing for her; and then ship all her stuff. I do miss her even though she could be a pain in the arse.

Grampa, don't you be going up in the attic now! You wait for me or for one of the kids to come in. I am surpised that Tom B. isn't going to this K of C affair down here.

I can't get over this being the coldest summer since 1795 – it sure is hot here!

Thanks for checking on the tiles.

Not much longer 'til I see you again. Hang in there! God Bless you!

Your Loving Little Virginia
P.S. - Went for a bike ride today

Enclosed is 'My Daily Prayer for Miracles':

O, Lord, as I begin each day, help me to speak the truth in the face of the strong. Help me never to lie to gain the applause of the weak.

If you give me power; Please don't take my happiness, insights; wits, success; humility; dignity.

O God, help me always to see both sides of any problem, and do not allow me to accuse any opponent of treachery just because he may have a different point of view, especially with members of my family.

Lord, help me to love people more than I love myself and to keep myself in check as I do others.

Do not let me become boastful if I am successful, and do not let me despair if I should fail. Keep reminding me that any failure I may experience is just an experiment before your true success arrives.

Dearest Lord, letme be gentle with others; teach me Lord that forgiveness is the highest standard of power, and that revenge is the greatest indication of weakness.

If you take my health, leave my Faith; if you take my serenity, leave me hope; and if you should take everything I have, then leave me your love.

Lord,if I have wronged others, give me the opportunity and desire to apologize; and if others have wronged me, then give me the power to forgive.

God, I know you will never forget me, may I never forget you.

Amen

Friday 10:10 a.m.
7 August 1992

I did get to go home for a week after my Postulancy. It flew by. I was home for the Church Centennial and yes, I wore one of the veils that Helene and I ordered. It was wonderful to see Grampa, and all the family and all of the good folks of Ticonderoga!

****

My Dear Grandfather,

Hi Grampa!

What a week! I met Mother Teresa of Calcutta! What a woman! I sat three feet away from her in Saint Patrick's Cathedral. I rubbed her back with some Holy cards and with Mary Evelyn's picture. I also held both of her hands. I spent at least five minutes one on one with her. There were sixty-two bishops and three cardinals in the same room – not to mention a nice food reception.

Then, Father Salmon and Bishop da Silva came yesterday at 9:45 a.m. They stayed 'til 2:30 p.m. Father was a riot throwing around his Portuguese. He really seemed to enjoy himself. The Little Bishop had a good time too. I danced a Kate Smith song for them - 'Climb Every Mountain'. They seemed to like it. Father took a lot of pictures. It was so nice to see them. They celebrated Mass for The Feast of The Transfiguration.

Helene is gone for good. I do miss her.

Father Halligan is coming today for Confessions and Exposition of The Blessed Sacrament.

Still waiting on dates and the outcome.

Have to clean now as it is Friday.

Got your letter, thanks. Still, no letter from Mrs. Dechame – maybe today it will come.

My Higher Education Loan came again today. Can you chew them out again. Gotta go,

Love you,
Virginia

VII. A New Acting Superior – Mother Regina

2 September 1992
11:40 a.m.

My Dear Grandfather,

Just a quick note before lunch - how are you? It was reassuring to hear your voice Sunday night. I could not sleep well that night. I felt sapped. It was much harder leaving than I expected. The worst is not knowing when I can see you again.

I like Mother Regina. She is fair. She also runs a tight ship. We will have to be getting up around 5 a.m. next week! We are in the process of cleaning and moving into new rooms. I am very pleased with my new room. It has two windows. There is a huge beehive on one of the windows. It is noiser on this side of the convent. The planes seem to fly directly overhead. Plus the road is outside my window and I hear the traffic go by. At least I don't have that air conditioner! I have a pretty pink bathroom. And, guess what Grampa – I even have a bath tub! The toilet needs to be fixed; it is bone dry.

You weren't kidding about having only the crucifix in the room. There is that along with only one other devotional picture. We have to clean every nook and cranny from top to bottom. I had to wash and clean a complete bed in the basement and a desk.

I miss you. Talk to you soon.

My love,
Virginia
P.S. - Mother Regina has got everyone's number! She met with us all individually. She told me to try and get my rest as we do all this work.

P.P.S. - Should get veil by end of month!

Horarium

Monday, Tueday, Thursday*, Friday**

5:00 a.m. Rise
5:30 Angelus, Meditation
6:00 Lauds (Morning Prayer)
6:30 Holy Sacrifice of The Massachusetts
8:00 Breakfast
 House Duties
9:00 Class

10:00 Break

10:15 Class
11:15 Prayer, Study, etc.
12:00 p.m. Angelus, Petitions, Divine Mercy Chaplet
12:20 Dinner

1:30 Recreation – Free Time
2:30 Prayer, Study, etc.
3:00 Class
4:00 Prayer, Study, etc.
5:00 Vespers, Evening Prayer

 Rosary, Angelus
5:30 Supper
6:30 Formal Recreation
7:30 Holy Hour
 Spiritual Reading, Silent Prayer

Compline
10:00 Profound Silence
11:00 Lights Out

Thursday*

6:30 p.m. Compline
7:00 p.m. Class

Friday**

1:30 p.m. Confessions
Spiritual Direction
Benediction
6:30 p.m. Compline
7:00 p.m. Recreation (optional)
8:00 p.m. Silence Bell

Wednesdays

6:00 Rise
6:30 Angelus, Meditation
7:00 Lauds
7:30 Holy Sacrifice of the Mass
Breakfast
9:00 House Duties

9:30 Class
10:30 Break
10:45 Class
11:45 Break

rest of schedule follows Monday, Tuesday, Thursdays

Saturday

6:30 Rise

7:00 Angelus, Meditation
7:30 Breakfast

8:15 Lauds
9:00 Holy Sacrifice of the Mass
9:30 House Duties
12:00 p.m. Angelus, etc.
1:30 - Recreation – Free Time
3:00 – 5:00 Prayer, Study, etc.
5:00 Vespers, etc.
5:30 Supper
6:30 Formal Recreation
7:30 Holy Hour, etc. - follow Mon, Tues., Thurs.

Individual Conferences will be held each day immediately after
Dinner and Supper
Names will be posted.

****
**

Received two post cards from Father Salmon. One was written on
September 1, 1992 from Saint Louis, Missouri:

Sorry I missed you in Ti. Preached at St. Simon Stock last
weekend. Preaching at SS Peter and Paul and O.L. of Mercy in
November (Call Bronx 8 and 15); St. John Evangelist (NYC) on
Sept. 20.
God Bless to all,
Fr. Salmon

And the other from Indianapolis, Indianna

16 VIII 92

Pro-Life meeting here (with Cardinal), then VFW Conference.

So good to see you again.

In Christ,
Fr. Salmon

****

Monday
Labor Day
September 7, 1992

Dear Grampa,

Can't believe my last letter has taken so long to get to you.

So how are you? It was very good talking to you on Sunday.

I talked to the Cardinal on the phone tonight.

Father Halligan got us an ice cream cake to celebrate Mother
Mary's Birthday.
Everyone here can't get over how I call Mother Mary "Mother
Mary". They all say "Blessed Mother".
I guess I never thought about it.

How do you like my stationary? I make a beautiful fleur de lis to
honor the French in you.

Hope the cat situation isn't wearing you out too much.

How is your arthritis? I have to laught when I think of when you
would be mad at me and I would look at you and say, "How is your
arthritis?" Do you remember that?

Sad about Paula Gauchet– she was a year ahead of me in school.

Father Halligan was asking for you.

The Cardinal thanked me for coming back.

My friend Sister Marie Ange is dying. She is 81 and she is a living saint.

Someone just broke a street lamp outdoors. Also, there was blood on the church steps last weekend as a result of a wild fight.

Toilet working like a charm – only it runs. Have to get the ball and chain, (Hmmm- interesting analogy), working now.

Up early, early!! I cook tomorrow. I helped Diane cook today. Made French-Swiss cinnamon cookies from a recipe Mrs. Dechame had given me. Everyone loved them.

Father Salmon will be in NYC September 2oth, and November 8th and 15th. He may stop by on any or all of those dates. That will be nice.

Feel awful you spent so much on sending packages – they should arrive tomorrow.

Thanks for all you have done for me.
Love you and miss you,

Virginia

Sunday
September 13, 1992
9:05
My Dear Grandfather,

Thank you so much for calling. It was so good to hear your voice. You sounded pretty good.

Thanks for your letter which I received on Friday. I am glad you are using the white paper.

You make me feel good that you believe in me and that you are proud of me.

I have felt pretty confident this week as I have been doing a lot of cooking and baking receiving rave reviews! Plus, I speak more eloquently with Mother Regina being here as everyone is forced to listen. She is real nice. She meets with each of us for a half hour every week. She is good.

I told Father Halligan that you fixed my toilet over the telephone.

Tell Jane I said Hi. I must write her a thank you note for all she has done for you and for me.

I appreciate your keeping me posted on everything.

Here is a roll of film to be brought in to Arthur's on Tuesday for their two for one special. When you send it to me, just remove the big envelope and put the photo envelope in a business size envelope with a couple of stamps.

Did you see my schedule!!!

I wrote down some ideas for a Christmas care package – if someone were coming down this way. They would fit in one of your empty tobacco envelopes; except hold off, and have someone bring the bell – the crystal one in the dining room. Dixie and Ed got it for me. It has The Lord's Prayer on it. That and the maple syrup can be sent with someone. Those Swee- Touche- Nee tea bags could be put in with the photos perhaps.

Thanks Grampa, I love you,

Your Handkerchief Girl,
Virginia
St. Matthew
September 21, 1992

Dearest Grampa,

It was so nice to hear your voice yesterday. Thank you for calling me.

I suppose you have heard that I have had visitors. Annie surprised me with Kenny and her new baby; and her daughter Francine along with a friend of Francine's. It was so nice to see them. Everyone loved the baby. Dorothy immediately put the baby on the Altar like the very Abraham offering up his son Isaac! Sister Christina took right over with the baby. She loved her. Annie enjoyed herself and the nice lunch we set out for our visitors. I think she will come again.

My friend Mr. Williams cake. He really enjoyed Annie. He said that she reminds him of his daughter.

Solie and Myrna came. They brought a huge spice cake.

Helene called on Friday. She was asking for you. I think she has had her fill of Florida for now.

I am enclosing a copy of the letter from Saint Joseph Cupertino that I read Friday during breakfast. It sent me in hysteria and everyone else too!

"It is said that the life of St. Joseph Cupertino was marked by ecstasies and levitations. The mere mention of God or a spiritual matter was enough to take him out of his senses; at Mass, he frequently floated in the air in rapture. Once, as Christmas carols were being sung, he soared to the high altar, rapt in prayer. On another occasion, he ferried a cross thirty-six feet high through the air to the top of a Calvary group as easily as one might carry a straw."

It just struck me funny because if you tell anyone something like that – that person would say you are crazy. But this is true and these events were witnessed.

Well, on that note -

Stay well,

Love,
Little Virginia

****
My Dear Grandfather,

Hi! I am on cooking again today. I enjoy it and I must say that I do a pretty good job with it and the people here never cease to be amazed by it.

Am enclosing a copy of Father Halligan's letter. Can you see why I would want to pick his name? He is so holy and humble. That with your dear grandmother's name – Irish for Mary – will complete it. I had to get special permission for Father to come to the reception of habit ceremony. Canon Law forbids it, but since Father is our Confessor, he can come.

Forgot to send you this article. Looks who is in front on the pre-dieu! We had more reporters here this afternoon.

Have you ever heard of "Goo Goo Clusters"? They are the official snack of The Grand Ole Opry. A friend of Mother Regina's sent a huge box of them. They are chocolate covered marshmallow and carmel and peanuts – like a round candy bar. And boy, are they good!!!

I slipped out to the hairdresser's while on my walk – to get a trim – a sin I may have to pay for, but my hair will look nice for Investiture day.

Grampa, thank you for all the things you sent me. I put the new laces in my shoes, I have enjoyed the Cadbury's, and I am enjoying the tape (cassette). The flashlight sure comes in handy too.

I slept through my alarm twice this week!

Have to clean out another room for a new postulant. Have to bring in storm windows and, I have a lot of reading to do. Busy!

Your loving
Little Virginia

29 September 1992
Feast of Guardian Angels

My Dear Grandfather,

It was so nice talking with you on Sunday. I really enjoyed our conversation. It was good to laugh.

I am a bundle of nerves as I prepare for Investiture day. Please pray for me to have grace and be peace-filled.

I expect that my college transcripts and the photos will come in today's mail.

Mother Regina and a couple of the novices, Sister Agatha and Sr. Joseph, wen to a Conference for Catholic Scholars in Pittsburgh. Father Salmon was there. He told them that he would be coming here in November. That will be nice – still have to talk with Mother Regina about her meeting him.

We just had an etiquette class – about no elbows on the table and sitting "ladylike". Mother Regina and I are the only ones here who do that quite naturally already.

Well Grampa, we start our retreat today for preparation for next Saturday – so I shall close for now.

All my love,

Virginia
soon to be: Sister James Mariah,s.s.

P.S. - Karl loved that song - 'They Call the Wind Mariah'

143

P.P.S – I know this sounds crazy Grampa, but I dream of all our family being together in Heaven!!

CANONICAL YEAR

October 12th, 1992

My Dear Grandfather,

Letters are few and far between now.

Today, we had a barbeque in the garden. The food situation has improved vastly since Sister N---------- has been d ispensed from the kitchen detail.

There is just hardly any time for one's self. There are so many studies – but you know me, I love to learn.

Did you see anyone on Columbus Day?

I thought I had that "Mull of Kintyre" tape. Maybe Sarah could make a copy of the one I gave her. Also, did I send you the order form for the Deanna Durbin cassette?

Thanks for sending me the absentee ballot.

Am enclosing a copy of 'The Rite of Initiation Into Religious Life'.

Received a beautiful card and letter from Gramma B. Also had a long letter from Irene Hall. She sent $5.00 – God love her.

Dorothy has has really gotten nice to me. I think she found out who the real villains are.

Visiting Day comes early in November – the 15th. You can call at ten of one.

Father Halligan was real intrigued by that musket.

Had a post card from Father Salmon – he is supposed to come on November 8th.

I will try to get you a Catholic prayer book.

We had a retreat day today with Exposition of The Blessed Sacrament – very beautiful. I want to share a poem, that which was my meditation, with you from my favorite poet, Reverend Father Abram Ryan:

A Child's Wish

Before An Altar

I wish I were the little key
That locks Love's Captive in,
And lets Him out to go and free
A sinful heart from sin.

I wish I were the little bell
That tinkles for the Host,
When God comes down each day to dwell
With hearts He loves the most.

I wish I were the chalice fair
That holds the Blood of Love,
When every flash lights holy prayerful
Upon its way above.

I wish I were the little flower
So near the Host's sweet face,
or like the light that half an hour
Burns on the shrine of grace.

I wish I were the altar where,
as on His mother's breast,
Christ nestles, like a child, fore'er
In Eucharistic rest.

But, oh! My God, I wish the most
That my poor heart may be
A home all holy for each Host
That comes in love to me.
Rev. Abram Ryan

****

Your loving granddaughter,

Virginia – Sister James Mariah

****

Sunday
October 25th, 1992

My Dear Grandfather,

Thank you for all you have done and are doing for me. Appreciate
your getting the film developed.

Oh how I wish that you could meet Father Halligan! He is also the
Confessor for Mother Teresa's Order – The Sisters of Charity.

Heard from Father O'Reilly. He is very witty. He is also one of the
finest, if not, the finest philosophical mind I have ever encountered
in my life. He sees a much greater picture when he sees things,
people, etc. He also has an easy, light hearted laugh. I am so glad
that he came down to see you.

Wow! I am shocked about my neighbor Smitty. He went to the
Maritime College right down here beside me. His poor mother.

146

Was he Cyrus's age? Didn't he used to come to the house with Jackie G. too?

I hope Aunt Peg is alright. Will keep her in prayer.

Glad your electric bill went down – hmmm – wonder if I could have had something to do with that!

Had a nice visit with my father on the phone.

Father Halligan and his sister Betty came on visiting day. Poor Betty – she has a lot of health issues. She bruised her head on the brick wall, but Annie, being the good nurse that she is, reassured her. Thank God she was alright.

Have you got Tisdale's new address? It is funny, because there is one postulant here and she reminds me so much of Tisdale. Her name is Maura. There are two other ones who entered along with her at the same time we were invested.

Sister Sharon sent me a print, poster size, of "The Laughing Jesus" - appropriately enough! I will send it with the folks when they come down. I want Hank Hossack to have it.

If Sarah can pick me up a pair of cream colored tights that would be great. They would be warmer than regular stockings.

The clamp has been put down on our letter writing. We can only write three letters on the first Sunday of the month and one to our family. Mother Assumpta has, however, given me permission to write to you every Sunday. It really jolted me as I was hoping to write to you at least twice a week because phone calls have been cut back. I am trying to get caught up and I will abide starting this Sunday. I should be grateful that this privilege has been extended to me – and only me.

One of the new novices in my group had a muscle spasm last night. She was taken to the hospital as she was in dire pain.

Have been writing a little poetry lately – perhaps you would like me to share it with you.

Am still waiting on the official transcript from NCCC.

The Cardinal came for lunch on Monday. He is still pretty weak. He has to take it easy. Quite often his attorney brings him. Her name is Alice. She is very beautiful with dark eyes and hair. She is also very smart. Her father and the Cardinal go way back. However, Alice lost her father young – to Huntington's disease or something like that. The Cardinal is like a father to Alice – well, to everyone. He has that way about him.

Had a letter from Ireland – Mrs. Grimes. She is not well. Her daughter Frances is getting married. She sent me an invitation.

I am in the schola – soon I will be a cantor.

I am sure Henry or Doug will see that you get some venison.

Tell Harry, (the pest), I said Hi.

I try to get a dance in for recreation but I think Mother Superior is trying ot discourage it. Yes, we are being asked to give up a lot, but all for the glory of God.

Hope you are okay – it means a lot knowing you are there for me.

Lovingly,
Sr. James Mariah
Litle Virginia

****

All Souls Day
2 November 1992

My Dear Grandfather,

Can't wait to show Father Halligan the clipping you found. Thanks for coming up with it. If you ever get lonely, you can call him. Here is his number: (212) 233-8355. He hopes to visit the Fort someday. He is very interested in history. Plus, he is a skilled sharp shooter.

Had a letter from Mrs. Dechame today. It came by way of Watertown. She had sent it to Sister James Marie by accident. Sister James Marie forwarded it to me along with two pictures, one of Mom and me at the Centennial and the other of Sister James Marie and me.

Also had nice letters from Miss Hall, Joyce c. and Miss Harmon.

Dorothy has been so nice to me lately. We dressed up as two jailbirds for Halloween. Mother Regina wore one of those grotesque "Freddy Krueger" masks. It was so scary that no one could even look at her. When Maura bumped into her in the cloister hall, she exclaimed, "Holy Sh !" upon seeing her in it! It was so funny. Maura is always getting in trouble for whistling or talking. Maura and I went up on the roof tonight to look at the bridges. Dorothy came up later to join us.

Helene sent me this cup that has a profile of a witch. She said it reminds her of Sister Agatha. I am supposed to turn these things in too! The features are exaggerated, but................

_We are fasting today for the elections.

We had carmel apples, hot cider and pop corn for Halloween.

Last week, we had a group photo taken of the Sisters.

Thank goodness my stuffy head has improved.

Oh, we went to a Byzantine Catholic Mass yesterday. It was so beautiful.

149

Had a beautiful letter from Babe Smith – God rest Smitty. Also had a nice letter from Martha McC.

Take good care,

Your loving granddaughter,
Virginia – Sr. J.M.S.S.

P.S. - Got a flu shot. I felt like Houdini trying to get my arm out of my habit for the kindly Black man to administer the shot. He was embarrassed and looked away. God love him.

****
Sunday
November 8, 1992

My Dear Grandfather,

Hi Grampa!

You are not going to believe who I saw today – The Wolfe Tones! I saw in The Catholic New York that they were going to be at Mount St. Vincent College in the Bronx. After Mass, I proposed it to Mother Regina – telling her that if I went after intermission, it would not cost anything. Otherwise, the tickets were $20. She said that I could pick one person to accompany me. Since Sister Olive and Sister Peter discouraged me and said there is no way that I would be going, I ruled them out. I wish I had asked Maura but Sister Agatha overheard me asking Mother Assumpta, and she does have Irish ancestry, so I asked her. She seemed excited. But boy, what mistake that was. Remember how they would play the music and ask me to dance – well, they did. Sister Agatha assumed the role of "Mother

Superior" and said, "You better not dance." The Wolfe Tones remembered me from Ireland and from attending numerous shows of theirs. They said, "Aww, come on Mother Superior, be a sport." But no, she was the killjoy of the century. The Wolfe Tones were so nice to us – offering us sandwiches and soda. Sister Agatha was

150

right over my shoulder. I did, however, get some good pictures. They gave me a great big poster and signed it in Gaelic for me. They are so cool. I told them that you enjoyed them too. I knew, some how that I would get to see them. I prayed in chapel the night before and I asked Karl to pull a few strings for me. Be sure to tell Tom Blanchard. Oh, and the two sisters who were "naysayers" were green with envy.

27 November 1992

Bob Hope's wife Dolores just sent a huge donation to the Sisters. Dorothy can not wait to write her a thank you note as that is one of her jobs. Incidentally, Dorothy has a pack of Ritz cracker in her brief case – she sits in front of me in class at Monroe and munches on them. She thinks that no one notices.

I am cook today. The other day, I was the reader in the refectory for breakfast. Well, I did not "proof-read" it. Then came the part about "the repulsive self covered with sores!" This was too much - I just lost it. Mother Regina rang the bell for me to stop.
Speaking of bells, Sister Francis Mary (Dorothy) is giving me the "Rising Bell". This means, that I have to get up at 4:55 a.m. and ring the bell through the cloister. Plus, I have to set the security alarm at night to make sure all units are secure. So I have to be up 'til ten in order to complete this ritual.

I miss having my Advent wreath. Tomorrow, the first Sunday of Advent, is Retreat Sunday.

We got to watch 'Miracle on 34th Street' last night. Naturally, Santa Claus made me think of you. And, as you know, "Kris Kringle" sleeps with his beard outside of the covers!

Everyone seems kind of burnt out lately. I suppose the Holidays and all. They say that the months of November and Frebruary are the hardest in the novitiate.

We did have a very nice Thanksgiving Dinner. I was on for cooking, but I did not have to do much cooking because Mr.

151

Gallagher donated the entire Thanksgiving meal complete with the trimmings. I kept busy with the serving and clean up though.

We watched a rather bizarre movie on St. Therese of Lisieux. It was a movie made by the French. It portrayed St. Therese as being a bit neurotic. The funny thing was that the actress portraying her resembled me – that is what Sister Immaculata was saying. On top of that, in the film, it said how Theresa was craving custard filled eclairs and how she wanted to hang on to her father's handkerchief for a keepsake (I have a drawer full!). She also embraced the elderly dying nun as though she were her grandmother. Yeah, I can relate.

Had another letter from Dixie and Ed.

We drew names for Advent and Christmas. I got Rosario who is one of the new postulants. She is a doctor from the Phillippines. In my room back home, there is a little picture I have of Mother Mary. Perhaps you could send that down. I think Rosario would like that. We are suppose to do nice things secretly for this person throughout the season – but most especially pray for that person.

Grampa, I was very touched, the Sisters made sure that I had a Mass for Karl on his anniversary. Father Paul came over and celebrated it. I brought the 'Gifts' up.

Let me know when Annie has to have that operation – even if it means calling here and leaving a message. I may even be on phone duty.

Maybe you could send me some "Ticonderoga" pencils – I could hand them out at Christmas.

I had no idea that Karlene called or Helene. I was never told.

This sweet 13-year old gal came up to me and hugged me and told me that she had missed me. I met her once last June! Then, upon coming out of Confession, this kind man gave me a warm embrace – for no reason.

Mother Regina wants us to use the Four Volume set of The Liturgy Hours. She will have us turn in our Christian Prayer books. I was kind of hoping that I could give it to Mom, but she has promised them to Father Paul's prayer group. Here I had it blessed by Sister Gerard's son – Father Lee. Oh well, Blessed Detachment.

I wish I had something I could send to Frances(for her wedding) in Ireland.

Well Grampa, I hope you are okay. Oh, next visiting day is on your birthday!!

God Bless,

All my love,

Virginia (Sr. J.M.)

P.S. - Guess what?! We are going to Mid-night Mass at St. Patrick's Cathedral for Christmas.
Then, the Cardinal is having us for breakfast after the Mass.

****

St. Margaret of Scotland

Hi Grampa!

Thet tights will probably arrive tomorrow. Please thank Mom for the slip she sent me. I also received the English book which will come in handy. The dictionary is a big help too. Now I am all set.

Mother Regina said that she would love to meet you.

You are so sweet sending all the candies and goodies. Tell Sarah that I was thrilled with the cinnamon Mentos.

I will go to bed and finish this in the morning.

Next morning, before class – have my house cleaning duties to do in addition to laundry.

This week, I am the cantor. That means, that I intone and sing the psalms. They tell me that I do alright. I read during the meals.

Yesterday morning at 5:30, I managed to knock over the music stand with all the books on it! Call me the Convent Klutz!

Grampa, can you find out if Mom ever got the soap I sent her. It is called "Virginia's Soap". It was in the bag with her cardigan. I am so glad that she finally got to meet Father Halligan. He made a sacrifice in coming as he had a head cold and he had to walk twenty minutes from his car each way to and from the subway.

Annie said she hasn't been up to Ti since I was home in August. She came with Mary Margaret who is a doll.

I kind of felt sorry for His Eminence today. He seemed a little forlorn. He came with his niece today. She is very attractive and smart – a lawyer. Her father was the Cardinal's best friend. He died nine years ago. I am sure the Cardinal would just like some quiet time with his family.

Things are very strict here (repressive). If I thought it was going to be lke this, I doubt that I would have come. I don't agree with everything.

We did a special dinner for Mother Regina on her community's feast day of Saint Cecilia. We prepared a Southern meal complete with bread pudding and a boubon sauce! Then we put on a Grand Ole' Opry-style show for her.

I don't trust Sister Agatha. She is not very nice to me for some reason.

At least you are rid of Harry now.

Take good care now,
I love you,

Virginia – Sister James Mariah

****

Saturday December 5th, 1992 was the Baptism of Sister
Immaculata's fifteenth grandchild, Robert Joseph Manning. His
Eminence officiated with Father Keehan and Father Greg assisting.

That evening, there was a concert at Dunwoodie in their most
beautiful chapel. Father Sorgei directed the orchestra. We listened
to Advent and Christmas music – indeed a foretaste of Heaven.

Sunday, December 6 – Father Groeschel came and celebrated Mass.
He also gave a very good talk.

On Tuesday, December 8th, Helene's good friend Father Jacob came
and gave us a retreat using fifteen Icons he celebrated Mass for us
for the Feast of The Immaculate Conception. On that same day, we
went to the Sister Servants of Mary to witness a final profession of
vows for three sisters: Sister Margarita, Sister Beatrix, and Sister
Helena. Bishp Garamendi celebrated the Mass in Spanish. We did
not stay for the reception as we had to get back to celebrate Sister
Immaculata's feast day with the steaks that Mr. Honerkamp brought
us. (I met Mr. Honerkamp at the Basin Harbor Club where I used to
work). That night, we continued our Advent retreat with Father
Jacob. Father Jacob had a sister who died from Cancer nine years
ago. She had several children. We had another class with a Sister
Janet on Wednesday. One loses track of time being so occupied.

Thursday, December 10th, (Anniversary of Emily Dickinson),
concluded our retreat with Father Jacob. His delivery has been
captivating. He uses as few words as are necessary.

In the evening of that Thursday, we joined the Sacramentine nuns for
Holy Hour. It was damp, cold and rainy. We had supper there with
several other religious communities. We had chicken a la king. I sat

155

with Sister Mary of Mercy. She had been cured of TB in her younger years. Now, she is 82 years of age. With her, is Sister Genevieve, who had a very comforting way about her. She is in her 70's. They are both Sisters of Christian Doctrine from Mount Vernon. We all stayed for an Advent ceremony. The Sacramentines sing beautifully, but boy, those benches sure were getting hard after a while! I returned back to the convent where a humongous parcel from Mrs. Dechame awaited me. In the midst of hundreds of styrofoam chips was a gayly wrapped package from Williams & Sonoma. The green wrapping paper had pineapples on it (which takes on added significance since "Pineapple" was my childhod nickname growing up, and a beautiful cream colored grosgrain ribbon adorned this gift. I noticed there was no tape on it – that is the way they do it in Europe. I think that is neat. There is a little wooden spoon on the ribbon. I will not know what it is until Christmas as it sits in the Superior's office.

That night, an eerie wind made it difficult to sleep. The next day there was a huge rain and wind storm. It took down a large pine tree in front of the convent – completely uprooted it. There was flooding everywhere with people being evacuated. Tiles were flying off the roofs of people's homes and aluminum siding was coming off of people's houses.

Friday night, Mother Regina let me put on "The Little Princess". I was supposed to give the news report for the week, but we watched it on TV on account of the storm. The situation in Somalia is very sad. Also, how unfortunate that Lady Diana and Prince Charles are breaking up. Lady Diana looks up to Mother Teresa. I think she would find great solace in the Catholic Church.

Sister Carol called to cancel our Saturday class in Monroe due to heavy snowfall. Instead, we went to the Church of The Immaculate Conception in the South Bronx for Mass and a Pro Life prayer vigil. We saw Bishop Garimendi again. The priests in that parish are very edifying. God Bless them. It was very rainy, slushy and cold but all seemed oblivious to the elements as a force stronger led us in prayer.

Also, on this day, the Feast of Our Lady of Guadalupe, we had a Mexican dinner. Sister Paul's sister flew in for a medical conference in the city. Later, she joined us for dinner which was nice.

That night, Sister William prepared the "crowning touch" as she made Sister Roberta and me the crowns complete with greenery – from the fallen pine tree for the Feast of Saint Lucy. Sister Philip and I re-enacted a Swedish tradition in getting up before the early rising bell and preparing hot chocolate and buns. We donned our white gowns, and paraded down the cloister corridors, our heads all aglow, with Rosario serenading us – singlng Sancta Lucia. I used to read about this to the children at Saint Mary's back home. I have always thought this would be a lovely tradition to carry out. Now I was a real "hot head" as the wax from the candles was dripping on my head. Rosario should have followed us with the fire extinguisher instead of her guitar.

Afterward, we went down the cathedral for Sunday Mass. It was the third anniversary of something called "Act Up". The police were everywhere. The Cardinal is always a target because he represents what is good and true. Thank God everything was alright.

We joined His Eminence afterward in the residence. Sister Lucy, on her feat day, presented the Cardinal with two eye balls that were in the form of inverted egg shells with eyes drawn on them. Then, cheesey as it sounds, we all sang, "I Only Have Eyes for You".

I cooked and served supper that evening. Found a mandolin recording of Sancta Lucia which I played while Sister Aquinas presented Sister Lucy with a candlelit (can't get away from those candles) cake. Mother Regina really appreciated the music piece. Sister Lucy opened her gifts then.

Recreation followed and then Compline. I am first cantor this week and I must say that I am improving.

Went to my haunt, the roof, only to find that the door was roped shut on account of the storm blowing it off its hinges. I am going nuts because now I can not go out on the roof and dance to my heart's content Whatever will I do?!

It is ten p.m. and 5 a.m. comes early. Let it not go remiss, that our dear Confessor did attempt to come in on Friday despite the ravages of the storm risking his welfare for the benefit of ours. God love him.

What happened to that little bird ?

The one I spied ---- during schola practice.

Did he fly away?

or, was he taken by storm?

Monday
December 7. 1992

My Dear Grandfather,

Hi Grampa! I went to Pennyslvania yesterday – well, really Port Jervis to speak at a Parish. Sister Christina and I were the only ones who went. There was Exposition of The Blessed Sacrament. The priest there looks just like that actor Chuck Connors. He met the Pope too. We had cake afterward.

We didn't have class in Monroe on Saturday on account of Sister Immaculata's grandson was getting Baptized by the Cardinal. The other Sisters went to Marycrest for classes while my group was privy to attend the Baptism of Sister Immaculata's fifteenth grandchild. It was a secret desire of my heart that I could be present. The Cardinal is very personable. The Godparents came in from New Jersey. They were emotional as was all of Sister's family. They left Rhode Island on this cold, snowy day. The Cardinal gazed at Sister Immaculata. He said something to her which she will never forget and I choose not to make mention of it out of reverence for both. I am convinced that His Eminence is aware of the great sacrifice this lady continues to make.

Father Jacob is coming tonight. He will give us a three-day retreat. He is actually a close friend of Helene's.

Tomorrow is a very big day here – The Feast of The Immaculate Conception.

Thank you for the stamps.

My friend Mr. Honerkamp dropped off steaks and all kinds of goodies for tomorrow's feast day.
It was great to see him.

Sister Francis shared with me that she had belonged to a religious order prior to joining this one. I felt sorry for her. It was hard for her, one to tell me, and two, with all the changes since Vatican II.

Had a nice letter from Cousin Francine.

Hope you are alright,

Lovingly,

Your little Virginia

****

A Grand Day

Wow! What a magnificent day! A day to remember .... a day to write home about.

After Lauds, Meditation, and Mass, we had breakfast and then did our duties. Then, at 9:30, we had our Holy Hours. However, I had many interruptions today as I was portress – but I enjoyed them. Then, at 9:40 a.m., we left for the big city. We got a flat tire down near the market place – the wharf. A mailman named 'Chesslie Scarborough' helped Sister Olive change the tire. This is second nature to her though she is unaccustomed to changing tires in a skirt. She is also happy if she has something to groan about.

While that made her day, mine was made upon entering the grande ballroom of the Waldorf Astoria. This is where Cardinal O'Malley holds his annual Christmas Charity party to help the orphan children.

There were balconies draped in garland and ribbon. Thousands of tiny lights were suspended from the center of the great high ceiling. The architecture was pretty and perhaps Greek, (or at least Greek to me). The stage was decorated with Christmas trees and big gold angels and a deep mid-night sky alit with tiny stars. A trio was singing jazzy Christmas songs as we entered. There were hundreds of well-dressed people in attendance: socialites, the former mayor as well as the current one. In the midst of all these benefactors was the lowly me who really just enjoyed the dreamy atmosphere – taking it all in. Is it real? Was it true? The chairs are posh and the tables are decorated fancily. For starters, there is a cream cheese and beet salad. The waiter was anxious to whisk away our salad plates so the next course of baked ham and creamed spinach with pine nuts on top and potatoes au gratin could be served. The rolls were delicious too. Just the setting and the silver were lovely. I should not always be thinking of food – cuisine in this case, I should firstly have made mention of the Naval Color Guard. A young man sang the Star Spangled Banner, and Sister Rose McCready gave the invocation. Then, as guests were announced, a huge spotlight would single them out from where they were seated. He introduced Miss Helen Hayes, the First Lady of Stage and Screen. She has always been a favorite of mine. It was exciting. Of course, the guest of honor was our host, Cardinal O'Malley. He looked regal with his long, red silk cape and sash. He is such a gracious and personable man. I felt honored and humbled to be a part of the community he founded. He also saw to it that we were announced. The atmosphere was magical; the lighting low.

I was too late for the Cardinal's reception line though he saw me peek around the corner to see if there was still time to greet him. I was so embarrassed so I made my way back to my seat. However, at the close of the gala luncheon, I did approach him...... on account I knew he was leaving for Rome in a matter of a couple of hours. I did not want him to leave without me having properly greeted him and thanking him for. I went to kiss his ring and he opened his arms and let his red silk cape enfold me. Shoot – Christmas was in the air. I even embraced a couple at the next table. What really capitulted the mood, was the Philadelphia Boys Choir which are comparble to the Vienna Boys Choir. In fact, they had just returned from a tour in Sydney. A slender little Black boy and a fair Irish lad sang "Requiem" - a piece by Andrew Lloyd Webber. If that was not enough, there was the awe-inspiring masterpiece - "Behold The Tabernacle". There were some Christmas selections. We all joined in singing "Silent Night' which is simply beautiful. The "Foundling" children relived Saint Luke's Gospel about The Greatest Story Ever Told which was read eloquently by Mary Higgins Clark. To see these children both moved me and broke my heart. I met two little girls in the foyer, and I asked if the older one was helping her sister. She said that the younger one was not her sister. Then it dawned on me. What did she know, or not know. It did not matter. I thought, how spoiled I have been to grow up with so many brothers and sisters - to feel such a strong sense of belonging; indeed, a sense of identity. That little blonde boy singing Requiem reminded me of my brother Georgie when he was little. So many emotions conjured in my mind causing my eyes to overflow.

The finale, that is, after our peppermint ice cream served festively in chocolate-shaped stars, was everyone, joining hands and hearts and lending their voices in oneness to "Let There Be Peace On Earth" - that was what drove me to go to the next table and share the wealthof the season.

On the way out, we were each presented with a costly bottle of Estee Lauder perfume which reminds me of dear Mrs. Keogh and also of my friend Fred Provonchawho worked for that company. Since Mrs. Keogh is not with us, I will give it to my sister Annie for Christmas.

There was a sharp contrast coming out into the cold streets where the hustle and bustle of the city swept over. The most disturbing to see was the poor, homeless and hungry. God help them. We have only to pray. We did talk to several homeless people as we gazed at all the shop windows.

Thank you Lord for giving me so much. May I never take for granted. Thank you Dear Jesus for a wonder-filled day as I await your coming.

All my lowly love,

Sister James Mariah

****

A CHRISTMAS MEMORY

It was Christmas Eve, 1978, in the small Adironack town of Ticonderoga. It was unusual because there was no snow.

Virginia's grandfather was not in the mood for any holiday cheer. He had just lost his 32-year old son that September. Nonetheless, it was that time when one would be thinking about putting up a Christmas tree.

"No!" was the grandfather's adamant answer to the teenage granddaughter who had asked if she could get a tree.

He only wanted to stay in his room and drink.

Virginia had an idea. She had gotten a Santa Claus outfit and she had persuaded the old man to dress up. He had a natural beard so he looked the part even if he was acting like Scrooge.

Virginia dressed like an elf with bells on her boots. Now they were off to spread good cheer. They went down to the big house which is really Gramma Burleigh's house where there is always a lot of festivity. Then, they went to George and Jane King's house on Iroquois Street. Mr. King worked at the Burleigh Pharmacy and Jane King was the secretary for the family doctor – Doctor Tom. Next, it was off to one of Virginia's favorite high school teacher's house – Mr. Royce. Mrs. Royce was making fruit cakes and it sure smelled good. Time just flew, and before they knew it, the bells were ringing for Mid- night Mass. No time to change; so they went across the street to Saint Mary's Church – which was directly across the street from Mr. Royce's house.

What do you know …. It was snowing! It was beautiful and moreover, Grampa was in the Christmas spirit. They sat in the back of the church as Father Salmon and Father O'Reilly celebrated the traditional Christmas Mass.

The joyous strains of 'Hark the Herald Angels Sing' could be heard as Santa and his little helper greeted people after Mass. They were heading home to a house without any decorations, particularly – no tree. But the snow seemed to satisfy, and the evening had been memorable.

They made fresh footprints on their way into the New England style home. The wood stove was starting to go out. Just as Grampa was going to get wood, Virginia exclaimed, "Look! A Christmas tree! Oh, where did it come from?!" There in the corner behind Grampa's rocking chair was a pretty Scotch pine tree standing in a cast iron pail leaking water on the hard wood floor. One candy cane adorned the tree. Why there were no footprints in the snow when they returned home. How did it get there? It did not matter. A miracle took place.

Around two in the morning, Virginia's mother and brother Karl stopped by. Virginia excitedly told them about the tree. They shared in her excitement. "An angel must have put it here!" Mother exclaimed.

Well, it was twelve years later before Virginia found out how it had gotten there. It was when her brother Karl died that she heard all these stories of magnificent things he did in an untold way. It occurred to Virginia, that he may have had something to do with this. She asked her mother about the tree. Now, it meant even more.

Indeed an angel had brought it!

****

VIII. Christmas Tree Mission: Sent on by Reverend Mother
or
"A Tree Grows in the Bronx!"

Sister Lucy and I were out to get a Christmas tree. Mother Assumpta said she'll never forget but a priest told her a long time ago, "Always give a person the opportunity to be generous…………." It was with these words that the two stalwarts set out.

After finding a parking space on the curb, two white-veiled novices popped out of the little car. The attendant selling Christmas trees was a young man named George. "Oh! That is the same name as my father an brother!" I exclaimed. He looked like he was ready to light a cigarette as if to say, "I know what they are up to." But he was real nice and he felt confident that his boss would make a donation of a tree. He should be back any time only he had not returned just yet from getting more trees. We would come back in another hour.

This time we came back with the van. It would have looked presumptious anyways if we had taken it the first time. George told us that his boss, whose real name is John – only they call him 'Charlie' on account that there's an uncle in the family who they call 'John', was there in the Italian deli. On the window there was a sign that said "Charlie's Cheap Christmas Trees". Charlie was on the phone so we stood watching the different people come in and order their subs or buy homemade spaghetti sauce. The coffee brewing sure smelled good, and there were some Christmas cakes, small ones, on a rack for sale. It seemed like Charlie was a real hustler. He was probably about 38 years old. The phone kept ringing off the hook. Then Charlie went out and gave one lady a tree and she promised that she would make him an audio cassette of something or other.

"I'll be right with you. You know, it's a busy time with lunch hour and all….."
"Oh, that's fine," we said. Afterall, we weren't paying customers, and a man has to make his living, and the economy is bad.

So Sister Lucy and I stepped outside and watched the operation. There was a big truck piled with Christmas trees in the back. One man was throwing them on the sidewalk and another man in his 50's, would then stack them.

"Hey, you don't throw them on the floor!" Charlie shouted. He seemed to take pleasure in impressing us with his set-up and how he was in great demand between the phone ringing and different folks from the Bronx coming in to buy their tree.

This short, dark whiskered man who appeared to be a Rabbi, came by. He stared at Sister Lucy and me. Then, after about two minutes, he said, "Merry Christmas!"

Now Charlie returned to us. "Now what do you want?" I've dealt with nuns before."

Sister Lucy said, "We need two little trees for the chapel, and …..."

"Wait a minute, first you ask for a donation, and now you are asking for how many trees?!"

"Okay," Sister Lucy backed down. "We'll take anything."

"Just a minute." Charlie said as he decided to tend to someone else at that moment.

All of a sudden, this white limousine pulls up and parks right in the middle of traffic. The driver gets out – probably wants to wish Charlie a Happy Holiday or something. But no, this is a surly-looking character. He was shouting at Charlie and one of his men on the crew using some very colorful language. "You're no good! You broke up my family …."

"Why don't you tell the nuns over here your story….."

The brawl worsened. George took two trees to shield Sister Lucy and myself though we could hear everything. That man went on, "You took me to court. You're a thief! You took one of my men, and whose side are you on?!" He was positively fuming as more expletives followed.

Sister Lucy and I kept our eyes down in keeping with custody of the eyes – only that didn't help our ears any.

"Okay nuns," Charlie embarrassedly came to us, "We're going to take a little walk."

So we walked around the corner. "Okay, what kind of a tree do you want? You mentioned something about two little trees for your chapel….." Then he showed us some small ones. I couldn't believe it when Sr. Lucy said, "I think they're a little too big….."

Then, she thought better of it. "Oh, we can cut them down. That will be fine."

So I carried them to the van. Sr. Lucy said, "he would die if he saw our tree in the community room back at the convent that has to be over twelve feet tall!" Here we were asking for not one, but two more.

Charlie went over and grabbed a six-foot tree. George put it in the van …. that is, after Charlie first tried to put it on top of the van only it was too awkward for him. He was only too accomodating at this point.

Sr. Lucy turned to me, "Get his address so we can be sure to write a thank you note."

As I started to go in the deli to get his address, I noticed three men with dark hair, long dark coats, black gloves and scarves step out of another limo and head into the deli. Charlie was back on the phone. Was he a "bookie" or whatever you call them. Boy, it sure looked suspicious. He wanted us out of there, and frankly, I didn't think it was such a bad idea. He was receiving some sort of summons from these men who definitely looked like "Mafiosa". Of course I wasn't going to say anything to Sister Lucy – she being from Sicily and all. Funny enough, she picked up on it too.

Charlie stepped out of the deli, the hustler to the end, and gave us the menu to the place in case we ever wanted his catering services. We shook, and I assured him that I would pray for him.

"Yea, anytime….." He was looking over his shoulders.

"God Bless you!" I said to him. "And Merry Christmas George!" and to all a good night!!

Christmas Eve Nineteen Hundred and Ninety-Two

The Christmas tree in our living room which was well over twelve feet high was decorated the old-fashioned way. It had ginger bread nuns, delicious apples with red ribbons on top, and white cut out doves; the tree was filled with "The Holy Spirit". Strands of popcorn and fresh cranberries also trimmed the pine tree. It was not an ordinary tree. This one, looked like it grew there – right in the living room – it was like "Jack in the Beanstalk" the way it touched the high ceiling. Objectively, it looked like the most beautiful

Christmas tree I have ever lain eyes on. My favorite will always be the tree I grew up with – the one adorned with my mother's ornaments. Some would be homemade, some were gifts from different family members and others I picked up in my travels.

Anyways, I made "wassail" on this night as the Sisters sat around and made the ornaments. We played Christmas music, and some of the sisters continued in the baking of the bread and cookies and candy for our benefactors.

I had not even so much as written one Christmas card yet. Frankly, I was finding it difficult to do so. Me, or I guess it is "I", who have trouble curtailing my pen in hand, and in fact, was given twenty stamps and twenty cards to send out – ah, reverse psychology works every time!, could not even get one card out. I just was not in the mood though I did feel somewhat carried away in the hustle and bustle of activity. Most of the sisters were fighting exhaustion, and I found myself forgetful of little things.

What I wanted to do most, was to relay a joyful spirit to my family and all those dear to me, but how could this be granted if I was not, or unable to cooperate. This would take more than David Copperfield, and yet I was still holding out for it on Christmas Eve – this late. Father O'Reilly's words resonated with me, "Yes, Virginia, there is a Santa Claus."

We loaded up three cars on this cold night, and made our way to Saint Patrick's Cathedral for the Mid-Night Mass. One of the streets was blocked off. And TV trucks were everywhere. A huge line of people were queuing up to get in the Cathedral were lined up around the entire block. In fact, His Eminence said that there were 12,000 requests for tickets to get a seat at the Christmas Mid-Night Mass. 5,000 could be admitted, and 3,000 could be seated comforatably. Imagine that, 5,000 people – the size of Ticonderoga!

Well, believe me, Ticonderoga was there, or if it wsn't, I sure was – both in my heart, and! Are you ready? In everyone's living room on the big TV screen! Here I was, sitting in the Sanctuary, in the choir stalls, right behind the Spanish Bishop and Bishop Sheridan, and

Bishop-elect Manselle. And didn't those camera lens zoom in on the ole' girl at the most strategic moment, that is, just as Baby Jesus was born, one He saved was borne into the hearts and homes of all of Ticonderoga – oh yes, the entire nation! I say this in complete humility because I think I looked kind of goofy. But my little sister Sarah said that I looked respectful and nice. I have to admit, the tempation was there, to lift my hand in the most discreet of waves, such as they do when they "sign" the Mass for the audio-impaired, and move my lips, "Hi Grampa". There was no time to get emotional - I would not do that to Ticonderoga, they were going to see me in my glory. "Isn't that how you do it Queen Elizabeth?" It was just unbelievable. Here I had not sent out any Christmas wish, and now my whole town was receiving a greater joy than any postman could deliver (sorry Tom Blanchard).

It started first at the big house. Uncle H.G. was the likely candidate to get on the horn, and call the folks. But 'lo and behold, Pa was not sleeping in his chair, but rather watching, one he calls "Pineapple", in amazement on television. Mom called Lizzy who had just gotten in from work at the nursing home. The minute she turned on the TV, she got her birthday present. Operators had a work-out at the phone company on Christmas Eve.

All vanity aside, His Eminence celebrated the most beautiful, solemn High Mass. A blind lady who works at Covenant House read the First Reading in brail. It was very powerful. Sister Margy read the Second Reading beautifully. The choir was magnificent and the drums rolled to "O Come All Ye Faithful" as the procession began. A world-renown soprano sang "O Holy Night", Gramma LaPointe's favorite, during Holy Communion. "Hark the Herald Angels Sing" sounded with trumpets and a thunderous ovation for the Cardinal who gave an eloquent message in his thought provoking homily.

Father O'Reilly was right.---

****

Christmas Day 1992

Sister Yvonne, from the other religious order who has been assisting here, did get me back. It seems Santa's elves put pencils in our stockings – not just one, but two. However, one was readily identifiable in that it had "Ticonderoga" on it. Sister Yvonne said, "One is to be used, and the other is to be admired." Oh, how we laughed.

Louisa is a sweet, young, childlike in her faith, lady in the parish. She is very inspiring. Each Sundy after Mass, she greets me with the biggest hug. Sometimes she will carry "the Gifts" up to the altar. I should tell you that Louisa has only one arm. But I feel as though two arms are wrapped around me when she embmraces me. She is very upbeat. I believe that she has a direct line to Heaven. I asked her if she would pray for me. She replied, "Oh, I pray for you every day!" as though that were a given. Well, that made an impression on me. I should be praying more like Louisa and for her and folks like her. God bless and keep her.

I miss my friend Angelita. I don't know what it was that propelled me to run over in-between Masses a couple of Sundays ago, but, I gave this dear old italian lady, who sits through several Masses, some Ticonderoga honey. She is the one who, a couple of weeks ago, pressed ten dollars in my hand during 'The Sign of Peace'. Anyways, on this day, I no sooner arrived, and the ambulance was pulling away with my Angelita. She was rushed to the hospital. I must find out more – the poor dear. Mother Mary enfold her in your Mantle.

My Sunday walk, my heart was broken as I encountered an old lady. Her name was Sarah Beaton. She only had a few teeth and she was dressed poorly, and she looked very cold. She was carrying a bag. I do not know how far she had to walk, but she would call a taxi from the rectory. She really was beautiful and gracious. She made my day – in untold ways.

Golly, I guess that I am really not talking much about Christmas – well, the spirit of it maybe. I got to go for the ride to bring the Cardinal home after dinner today which incidentally I cooked. We got to have wine with it too! But Boy, that Cardinal is something else. He said that was one of the nicest Christmases ever. Then, to see him get out of the car, and enter his residence on Madison Avenue – which was empty. One could feel his loneliness. God love him.

I met former Mayor Ed Koch after the Mid-Night Mass at the Cardinal's Residence. I shook his hand. He seems very nice.

I am forgetting a bunch of stuff as the bewitching hour approaches. The best was hearing from everyone in my family. Well, almost everyone. I did not hear from Henry but he did meet me at the train station when I got home in August. Father O'Reilly even called. Then to top it off, Father Halligan stopped by on Boxing Day. So much joy – I scarce can take it in. Then I was showered copiously with gifts from Gramma Burleigh and dear Mrs. Dechame. I really had to pace myself!

One last note, "Sister Mary of her Own Will" wanted to reiterate that "oat meal- colored veils" were fitting because the Cardinal brought a Nativity in which the Madonna is wearing an oatmeal colored habit. I wanted to say that there was gold trim on this Black Madonna too but I kept still.

29 December 1992

Was really complimented when four people thought that I had them for their "Kris Kringle" or "Secret Santa" as we call them at St. Mary's. Of course, I did try to throw a few people off by putting trinkets here and there. Rosario, however, did guess correctly. She was a joy to have and to do nice things for

because she is so nice and appreciative. I knew after two days who my "Kris Kringle" was. I was stumped after I received the first trinket because it sounded like Mother Regina's footsteps outside my

171

door. But then I knew that Sister Yvonne could have arranged that. But, when I received an Advent reading – fresh out of the computer, and with my name misspelled – I always think of Herb Winner when I see the word "misspell". He used to always stamp the word "mispelling" on his correspondence to me, his humor, but, "anywho" as my friend Mildred Ramsey used to say, whoa – I am really getting off on a tangent, but, as Mr. Cembalski can vouch for, I never was good in Geometry. - that is, until the second time around. Well, speaking of math, this girl put two and two together. It had to be Sister Yvonne as my "secret Santa" - that is "elementary" if you want to get back to St. Mary's! Not that it particularly had to do with the three proverbial "R's", but you see, she spelled, rather misspelled my name. She wrote 'Moriah' instead of 'Mariah'. Now there is a town right next to Ticonderoga called Moriah. That is where my sister lives and her Clint Eastwood – ish husband. But you see, if one is named after that driving element, then one must get the name right. If I may say, the Wind. - that which sends the stars a flying. Now, have you got your houndstooth cap and cape. There was another clue, I received bath gel from Germany. I had lived in Germany and this Sister happens to belong to an order that has a convent there. The third clue was, I received a bookmark on my bed with a sticker that was left on by accident. It said, "Sr. A., can you put this in Sr.J.M.'s room over the weekend…." A brilliant scheme I must say, considering that Sister Yvonne was to be in absentia for the weekend. Like the old fella says, you got to get up pretty early in the morning to fool this bird.

On The Feast of Stephen

Dear Grampa,

I am so happy that you saw me on TV on Christmas Eve at the Midnight Mass. Maybe Mom can make a copy for you so you can watch it again. I think she video taped it.

It was so good talking with you on Christmas day!

172

I am so happy that you got a chance to talk to Father Halligan. He is the most humble person. He stopped by today and he gave a beautiful card with a check for $250 to the Sisters. He was so cute when he said, "Guess who I received a phone call from?" He couldn't wait to tell me that he talked to you. He will come on Wednesday for Confessions. Then, on Thursday, we will go to Dunwoodie for the Cardinal's retreat. I will try to get an emergency contact number for you.

Also Grampa, you should be getting a parcel in the mail. Can you please see to it that the gifts are distributed. The presents are few and far between. Mostly, I am recycling stuff. I feel bad that I don't have anything for you, but there is a little "coin of the realm, as Miss Hall would say, for you.

Lizzy tells me that she is taking good care of you – as best she can.

Glad that Jane was pleased with the jacket. She does so much for you.

Mother A. said that visiting days will be cut back to once every three months during the canonical year.

I am enclosing some daily prayers for you Grampa.

Today, I walked to Fort Schuyler – approximately two miles.

Good news – we are going to have new habits. They will be just like I suggested – floor length, cinture, scapular. Our group of novices is so excited while the first group is less than ecstatic. They would not budge on this one. Sister Agatha is having a hard time accepting this. Then she likes trendy stuff anyway. She said that she gave her stylish wardrobe to her sister. She really does not like me.

You didn't have to send me that ten Gramps. Thank you though. I will send Sister Mary Agnes P. five. Say, if you see Sarah, can you have her pick me up some Pepsodent tooth paste from Newberry's. I have enough for now, but for next time. Karl always used Pepsodent too.

Received another beautiful letter from Mrs. Dechame. She is so kind to me.

Well, take good care Grampa.

I love you,

Little Virginia a.k.a. - Sister James Mariah

****

January 3, 1993

My Dear Grandfather,

It was so good to talk with you the other night.

Thank you for the mints, candy and the film. Am enjoying the 'Walkman'.

Had a nice card from Father O'Reilly.

Thanks for delivering my modest gifts. Did you send the twenty to Mrs. Grimes? I would like to send twenty to Father O'Reilly's sister too. The K of C sent me a check. They have been wonderful.

That is great that Mary has a son now. I wish she would move up North.

Heard from my friend Bill McDonald. He sent me a sand dollar.

Mrs. Dechame really outdid herself. She sent me a beautiful cream colored throw – woolen made by the Kennebec weavers. She aslo sent me a book on angels, some French chocolates, a fancy writing journal, that huge Panettone. Gramma Burleigh sent me a huge Harry & David Tower, some stamps and a check which I turned in.

174

This Monsignor Powers is a real character – impish. He does not miss a trick. He smokes a pipe and he walks with a limp – God love him. He is the one who whisked me in his office so that I could call you. I must send him a thank you note for that. I took his picture this evening so you can see what he looks like.

I think one of the Sisters has a battery re-charger so don't worry about sending me batteries.

Thank you for your love and support Grampa,

Your loving "Heidi"

11 January 1993

My Dear Grandfather,

I am supposed to be doing my duties now, but I have been trying to write to you since Friday. There has hardly been an ounce of free time and then, if there is, I find myself exhausted. I was supposed to have finished a paper on St. John's Gospel last night, but I had to cook on Saturday, and I cooked breakfast and lunch yesterday. Then, I prepared a coffee break for everyone on Saturday and Sunday. Plus, we had to unload a whole library of books from the basement – three levels up! We had to go through them and compile lists. Then, we had to take all the Christmas decorations down – which just about killed me. You know how I feel about Christmas. I like to keep the decorations up until the Feast of The Presentation. However, I have fresh greenery for my Advent wreath in my room. It is my third replacement of greens for it!

Then, between our regular schedule: Mass, prayers, cleaning duties, wash up after meals, classes and conferences – I just can't write the way I would like to.

We did watch a movie last night – St. Joseph Cupertino. It was an old black and white film though very good.

We got one to two inches of snow – really, the first snowfall to speak of.

I really miss the Parish Visitor Sisters. They were more mainstream.

Sister Immaculata went to Rhode Island. She needed to see one of her daughters. She received special permission from the Cardinal. Another one of the sisters accompanied her. We prepared tea for them when they got in and we had conversation. Then we had Compline which finished at 9:45 p.m. It was then, that I slipped out or should I say 'up' - I went up on the roof to look at the snow. Then I went to the office to do some typing but Mother Superior came in and glared at me. It is Grande Silence after 10 p.m. So I could not get my paper done. As it is, I am writing you this from the bathroom so I don't delay your letter.

Last night Maura set off the alarm. And is it loud!!! I thought I would have a heart attack. The police came within twenty minutes. The funny thing is, I got Sister Immaculata to answer the door with me. Here I was in my striped night shirt looking like a jailbird and Sister Immaculata had her cap on without the veil and the rest of her habit – looking very much like a warden and here were the police officers!

Then up at 5 a.m – Ugh! Hopefully, I can take a nap today. I have two morning classes. I think there will be mention of "Grande Silence" too!

Oh, did you notice that our penmanship is very similar?

I am glad that Aunt Karlene made it down for your birthday.

Yes, I did receive the walkman alright. Thank you. It is so nice to listen to music before falling asleep.

Had a nice letter from Father Salmon. Also one from Sister Damien.

If you could send me six airmail stamps for my overseas mail that would be great.

There is talk of going up to Brother Andre's Shrine – wouldn't that be something! Then we could stop en route and see you!

Gotta run, thank you for being there for me – I love you -

Sister James Mariah

****

There is a lovely light dusting of snow on the roof. Finally, it has arrived, and it is beautiful …. worth waiting for. After Compline, I went up on the roof and oh, the lighting was magical. It was like twilight yet it was ten o'clock at night. Everything was glistening in the bright night. I decided to christen the snow with some gleefully landed jetes and plies. Am glad that I am able to ply that door open that leads to the roof. Thank goodness I have no fear of heights.

Watching the film on St. Joseph Cupertino seemed like an appropriate way to end the weekend as I have been rather "klutzy" myself. It started, well, let me go back to the beginning of the week.

Sister William and I are the versiclerians. Each time I had the invitatory marked, she insisted that it was an alternate one. And, each time, she was wrong to the tune of five times – four of which were in a row! And, it probably would have been six times but I consulted with her the previous night in an effort to get her to agree on one. She never believes me. She and Olive are always undermining me. I was not going to argue even though I believed that I had chosen the correct responses. Sister William could hardly look me in the face all week as she must have felt sheepish about being in the wrong and insisting otherwise. That made it worthwhile even though Mother Superior was not pleased with what turned out to being a sideshow.

Then, on Friday, our general cleaning day, I decided to clean by only wearing my cap as I was mopping the corridors. In an effort to keep my veil clean, I set it aside in my room. Sister Dominic does the same thing because our group of novices does not have three or four veils like the first group. I was shaking the dust mop vigorously out the window when it detached and fell three stories down on the front walk below. A good therapeutic laugh ensued. A few moments later, Mother Regina asked me to track down Maura who happened to be on the first floor. She was in Sr. Yvonne's room. Sr. Yvonne had a sore throat so I offered to make her a little North Country remedy sans the whiskey. So I whisked down the stairs to the kitchen, me in my cap! Peter, the workman, was at the kitchen door. It never dawned on me that I did not have my veil on. I did have the rest of my habit on, but I was looking the part of the washer woman when I opened the door. I was in the midst of making Sr. Yvonne's hot lemon while another sister (from the first group) decides to tell me to show Peter what needs to be done which I hadn't the foggiest idea. So here I am going up and down the stairs with the kettle whistling. Meanwhile, Sister Lucy decides to correct me out of fraternal charity about me having only my cap on and not my veil – particularly because – there is a man in the house!!! Horrors! So I went to turn the kettle off, and two from the first group of novices looked at me disapprovingly, "Well, what do you know," I said, "Didn't even realize that I only had my cap on..." So Sister Indian Chief tells me to put my veil on. Should have stayed in the corridors. C'est la vie or is it c'est la guerre!!

Saturday, Patti and I are on for cooking. Sister Agatha leaves the bread basket in the oven. Toxic fumes are permeating everywhere, and once again, Father Euk is here to witness another breakfast catastraphe. It would appear that I am the culprit, yet I was the one to discover it. It was when I went to the laundry room to get the wash basins, that I detected a ghastly smell. It was the shellac from the bread basket smoking. Meanwhile, everyone at the table started to wriggle their noses and get up. They thought sure it was the Christmas tree. Father Euk was chuckling. The server, Sister Agatha, was staying in the background. It was kind of funny though I spent all day trying to air out the kitchen and clean the oven so I could use it for cooking.

Well, I probably shouldn't have laughed at that incident, because as I was pouring the coffee pot into the carafe, you know, that nice new insulated one from Denmark – well, it was just too close to the edge of the counter, and that coffee was too hot, and before I knew it – it was on the floor – the liner shattered. Another mess to clean up. With that, came the accompanying humiliation – having to tell the superior. One tries to do something good, and put the coffee away properly and she was not in a

good mood. Well, it could go either way. We were all in the process of moving Dr. Stanton's library upstairs, first, having gone through twenty-seven boxes of books and listing the titles and authors.

"Mother, I, uh, broke the good coffee carafe, but I am sure I can get another one from back home." She looked at me sternly, "That is too bad." "It was just too close to the edge." I explained.

Then I went to mop the kitchen floor. Mother Regina passed through, and she did thank me for letting her know.

I assisted with the boxes and Mother Regina asked me to prepare a tea break. She seemed impressed when I made her a single cup of fresh brewed coffee using the Milanta filter. It was hazelnut and I put brown sugar in for her.

Then it was time to prepare lunch. Patti was pre-heating the oven. It smelled to the high heavens. It seems something left over had spilled in the oven and now it was burning. So we opened all the windows. Patti is one of the new postulants. She is from Louisville, Kentucky. Patti said, "If anyone asks what we are doing, we will say, 'We are keeping the homefires burning, and picking up all the pieces.'" Oh how we laughed.

We put away Christmas decorations all afternoon and oh how I hated to see the tree come down. I was trying to figure out a way to avoid Mother Regina because every time I saw her, she had a different job for me to do. Patti suggested that I take the stairway before the

179

community room. Before I could take the third step, "Oh Sister James Mariah….." Mother hands me the creche and I burst into laughter. She seemed to enjoy the fact that I knew she was not only going to ask, but also receive. Of course, you can't squawk because she is a workhorse in her own right. She is also indefatigueable which is a word I have trouble pronouncing and probably spelling too.

Next day, did not realize that I was on for breakfast as well as for lunch. Made fresh blueberry muffins, bacon and fruit salad with a flavored coffee – a resounding success.

There was a conference after breakfast and we were supposed to have had our papers done for Monsignor Turro's class the previous day. But after the conference, I had to prepare lunch. And Mother wanted another coffee break for the afternoon. In between that time, I crashed for about an hour. Mother did not specifically ask for me to prepare the coffee, but she just assumed that I would. We were going to have the pannetone which Mrs. Dechame had sent, only Sister Lucy felt that since it was an Italian specialty that it had to have come from her family – so I did not say anything. So Sister Lucy and I put on the coffee break, yet I was to receive a further humiliation.

Mother Regina said, in her Southern accent, "Sister James Mariah…." what was coming I wondered. "I opened this letter because it said "Sisters for Hope" on it, but it has your name on the return address." I thought I would die. My face dropped. Everyone of the sisters in the room seemed to be engrossed in what was transpiring. Some went so far as to commiserate with me – share in my mortification. I could not even think who I had written this over-sized letter to, the one with a Christmas stamp on it, a flag stamp on it and an animal stamp on it. It was one I let slip into the mailbox en route to the airport. It was on a day that I had twenty minutes to pack and obviously, I was
not too coherent. Clearly the letter had not been approved to go in the outgoing mail. I had forgotten to label it but I had written it to my brother Thomas. I was writing to thank him for the twenty which was en route to Ireland. I also included the music to the song

"They Call the Wind Mariah". It was a confidential letter to my brother. That hour of rest was all undone at this point. I was a wreck at this point and the worst part was I still needed permission to re-send this to my brother. Haste makes waste…

That is why I had to laugh when we saw the movie on St. Joseph Cupertino. He was getting in so many pickles. Of course, he was innocent – big underLYING difference. Oh, I don't like that word!

Needless to say, there was no time to get my paper done and had not Mother Assumpta asked how everyone was coming along with their papers. That was done during one of those "prized coffee breaks" in which she turned to me, "What about you Sister James Mariah?" To which I replid, "Slowly, but surely – hopefully tonight by the deadline." Everyone laughed. Guess they thought I had not even started it or something!

X. Clicking Down the Corridor

Then, our first real snowfall. This is a follow-up to my previous mention of the snowfall, and that is because, Monday night, during recreation, Mother Regina said, "Do you know what I saw last night?" I could not imagine what she was going to say. "I saw two feet, and they were covered with snow. Who do you suppose they belonged to?" Well, we were all dying to know only I was the most surprised when she said, "They belonged to none other than Sister James Mariah!" I just about died. Had she seen me. Then it occurred to me that when I came down from the roof, I usually look down the stairwell to see if anyone is coming or is I hear any clicking down the corridor. But Mother was a fleeting this night. I thought we had just missed each other. But she was behind me – just close enough to detect my snow-laden shoes!

Of course Sunday night is hardly over. I went to the office to type my paper. It was after ten p.m. The door opened, and there, this night hawk, met a set of glaring eyes. "Am I making too much noise?" I asked. I could not imagine what I was doing wrong. Then came the retort, in a stern voice, "It is after ten o'clock." "Oh, I thought I was okay up until eleven." Nope, okay, I got it straight now. Meanwhile Maura is setting the alarm which happens to go off. It is loud and piercing – practically knocking me off of my chair. Sister Immaculata and I went to check it out. Maura had just opened a window while trying to shut it tight. We were all paranoid. So when 'paranoid' hit the hay, the door bell rang persistently a short time later. I looked out my window and saw a police car. Since my room has the enviable position of being closest to the door, it seemed natural that I would answer the door. Yet they keep reminding me that I am not in Ticonderoga anymore. I sure was not about to get Mother Assumpta. So I went to get Sister Immaculata. She had her habit on except for her veil – just her cap on. We both went to the door. We were getting reprimanded from the officer about the number of "false alarms" they receive. "Oh, I am sorry " Donovan, (I saw his name on his jacket)/ We will be more careful. God Bless you." He decided that he would not issue us a ticket. Just then, Sister Immaculata looked at me, "Do you realize how you look?" I was wearing my striped nightshirt looking every bit like a jailbird which I confes I often feel like. Sister Immaculata in her cap looked like the warden and here was the policeman. We got to laughing.

Gosh, sometimes I wonder how I am going to make it. You see, there is a 'church mouse" inour chapel. Perhaps, I should say, there is a "chapel mouse". She bears great resemblance to one Sister Mary Francis. She waits as long as two minutes after the opening prayer – that which can be agonizing for a bundle of nerves like me. The worst is waiting in dread. One knows that what is going to come out is a shrill, loud squeak that trails down to the very nether world itself. No one wants to offend. It is actually more embarrassing for the victims – such as myself. Could be others as I was beginning to wonder. Felt reassured when I heard Maura blurt out in laughter. Sister Lucy had to leave the chapel. Sister Agatha followed behind. Now my shoulders, which were in clear view of Mother Regina, were shaking up and down. It is so hard getting through the "office". No disrespect is meant for either Sister Mary Frances or The Good Lord, but my goodness, three times a day, and oh no….. next week she will be singing the Responsorial!

****

Humiliations and Aggravations for week of January 18, 1993

I suppose yesterday's Midday Reading would sum it up best. It seems either I am a nervous wreck, or, I am so calm, I feel as thoughI could fall asleep. In either event, the consequences are unprecedented. They all seem to preface their religious names with "Mother" in that other order from Connecticut. Mother Mary Perpetua and Mother Mary Philip were guests in the chapel along with the two superiors here and the 13 Sisters for Life. I really was fine reading Paul's letter to Timothy, and then it came, "that Christ Jesus came into this world to save sinners." Okay, but then my eyes scanned what I was to read next. And when I read, it is as though I am Paul speaking. It is very real ,,,, only, it caused a sudden and uncontrollable outburst of laughte; then a pause, and I half managed this truism, "Of these, I myself am the worst." I returned to my seat. Patti is laughing and Sister Francis Mary is in hysteria, and I am wondering if I am going to get in trouble.

Mother Superior didn't really say anything to me about it and I could not even bring myself to apologize. Some of the Sisters, particularly from the first group, were disgusted with me. "Haven't you got a sense of humor?" I tried to defend myself. " Are you so dense that you don't get it?" My blood was boiling. "It is the closest thing to a 'Chapter of Faults' - I make a public admission through the Reading." The usual balkers backed down.

Vespers: I start with a Reading from the Letter of Paul to the Ephesians, but Mother Regina knocks on wood. Evidently, I had the wrong reading, so I turned to January 25th – and I select the Mid-afternoon Reading to Timothy, woops, wrong again. I felt my usual pale face turning red. O God, please don't make me laugh. I can not bear it, but, I lost it. By the grace of God, I was able to regain composure, aand begin the Reading to Corinthians. The words said it all: "I am the least of the apostles; in fact, because I persecuted the church of God, I do not even deserve the name. But by God's favor, I am what I am." Then of course, I read the rest of it which is very beautiful. I did excuse myself before I started it and it flowed. Everyone shared in my embarrassment. "This favor of his to me has not proved fruitless. Indeed, I have worked harder than all the others, not n my own, but through the favor of God."

Mother Regina was quizzing us on Father Hardon's Catechism. She got to Sister Francis Mary, "Sister Francis Mary, what do we need in the world today to survive?" She asked in her Southern drawl. "Well, a lot of things – God's grace, a lot of faith, prudence, ... Did I hit it yet?" Well, she sent everyone roaring in laughter.

XI. The Hatfields and McCoy

Once again, Father Euk was at Saturday morning breakfast to witness one of my faux pas. Was serving blueberry muffins to which Sr. Yvonne asked if they were homemade. I replied, "They're the real McCoy – no Hatfields here!" Then Patti Horton spoke up, "Hey, my great-great grandfather was a Hatfield." I thought I would die – but I had meant no offense.

Sister Justin answers the phone. A newspaper firm is calling to see if we get a subscription. I could not resist, "Didn't you tell them that we are getting "The Times of Ti". I bet their paper does not have Arvila Mae Gibbs 104th Birthday in it!

Did I tell you about the time that Sister William was helping me make an angel doll for Mother Assumpta's community feast day. Well, we were waiting for the hot glue gun to heat up when all of a sudden, I hear that jingle jangle of the Superior's Rosary beads. Sister William turns towards me, "Quick, Hide!" I couldn't believe it because usually I am the first one to hide but I have been trying to be less covert. We are not supposed to be in anyone's room and here I was hiding behind the bureau in Sr. William's room. I could see that long white habit like a banshee that I hoped would not spot me. Then, Sister William starts to blurt out laughing. I had no choice but to reveal myself. Mother Assumpta looked very surprised. Now she knows that I am a sneak! Later, Sister William did explain to her that it was on account of her feast day.

It was a funny thing about that thermos that I broke. Sister Catherine only discovered it last night. We were in the laundry room washing dishes. "Oh heck," says I, "You didn't know that was broken? Shoot, that broke the day you and Sister Immaculata went to Rhode Island."
"Well, did they save the body of the thermos?" Sister Catherine inquired. Sister Immaculata was studying my expression. "Well, uh..." I said, "I don't think they did....." and precisely at that moment, I went into hysteria Sister Immaculata realized, (guess it didn't take a Rhodes Scholar to figure this out – only someone from Rhode Island!), that I had a more active role in the case of the missing thermos. I had to leave the room. I was bent over in laughter. Sister Immaculata was close behind. By the way, the "body" went out to the trash!

Good thing I noticed that one single solitary spoon before it went down the drain as I was emptying the wash basin. This one was covered in peanut butter. I exclaimed to Sister Immaculata, "And who had the peanut butter?" Oh is she quick – peanut butter was not n the menu for lunch today only since I was the server I thought that I would make it available- to me anyways." Then I quickly changed the subject, and said to her, "I have a consolation for you – for your missing apple, and I presented her withone of those apples rotting on the counter that we will be making applesauce with." We both laughed.

****

The Last of January Quips

Rosario cracks me up. She comes out with the most unexpected lines that send me roaring. I really enjoy her. She says to me last night, "Did you get your pencil? I put it on your pre dieu." "Oh, thank you..." says I, "But Rosario, you should have a 'Ticonderoga' pencil." To which she replies, "I do, but it is only to look at!"

185

Then one Saturday morning during a break from class, she asks, "Do you have an 'Empire Apple' for me?" She caught me off guard. There is a long-standing joke about Empire Apples and me in the convent. Grampa sent me a huge box of them. Mother Regina thought it would be nice to trim the tree with them – that was, until she saw my face drop. They are such good eating apples that I could not bear the thought of them hanging on the tree and not being savored while they were fresh and crisp.

The other day, there was one left-over fish shell. Rosario loves fish and rice. She asked if I wanted the last one. "No," says I, "It's got your name on it." She sits beside me in the refectory and announces that she has just eaten the 'R' and the 'O'. I had to laugh.

Last Thursday, I found Sister Immaculat awfully quiet. "Sister Immaculata," I said, "Are you alright? You are very quiet." To which she responded, "Yes, and that is because it is supposed to be 'Silence'." I gulped and then I said to her, "Sister Immaculata, I'll get the wash basins, and you carry in the wash cloths ----- just don't be dropping them on the floor. I don't want you to make a lot of raucous." We both chuckled.

The same morning I was in charge of hymn preparation. So I left the usual note "Good Morning Father Larry" - However, it was immediately followed by 'We Are The Light of the World'. He incorporated this in his homily. It struck a funny chord so early in the morning.

"Father Rinaldi's obituary was in The New York Times." Sister Immaculata said. "I wonder what the criterion is to get in The New York Times obits." I chimed, "I know one……….."

On our way into New York City, one noticed the new billboard with the crossword puzzle on it. "Papal cape …………...hmmm, that's 36 across, four letters."
"Oh, that's a 'cope'!" exclaims Sister Immaculata.
"A cope," says I. "You mean, a cope for the Pope?"
"That he washes with soap..." adds Sister Peter.

186

"Oh, I hope." says I.

"Nope." Sister Peter quips.

That's right, our Pope would not wash his cope with soap, or at least I hope, not; he might, I grope – at the thought. It seems someone would do it for him. Heck, it probably goes to the dry cleaners.... In which case, the Pope's cope would be hung on a rope. "Are we near the Cathedral yet?" Don't mope!

Sister Frances Mary can't seem to get away from it. She has Office of The Readings once again. Her friends, Puah and Shiprah and Raamses and the like are there to greet her at 5:30 in the morning. There is also Quoleleth who she refuses to pronounce – so she skips his name – giving new meaning to the Reading. The funniest was when she read about the 'Perrizites' only she referred to them as 'Parasites'.

Took a fit of laughter, as my friend Mrs. Grimes used to say, in chapel tonight. Sister Philip is trying out the descante on a new song with these extra notes and 'La's' that are not included. Sister Lucy got laughing too.

Getting back to Father Rinaldi – I was very impressed when I met him last April. He was soft spoken, and he would capture one's attention. One knew he had something to say. He was a very saintly man on this earth and now, we have someone in Heaven who will intercede on our behalf. He was raised in Turin in a large family of fourteen. He had a twin brother who was studying for the priesthood but he died before he could make his ordination. Many in his family entered religious life. Father Rinaldi came to America to the Salesian parish in Port Chester. He served there where the "Shroud of Turin" Chapel is. We went to visit there one day. There is an image exactly like the original – a replica. I is behind glass and there was special lighting. It was very powerful to see. Also, Father Rinaldi's uncle served as an altar boy with Saint John Bosco – in Turin where Father Peter Rinaldi died. One of our Sisters took his name in religion.

****

"Crash! Bang! Crunch! Pow!" I swear Sister "Mary Excelsior" - as in upstairs, above my head, is going to come through my ceiling. So much for the vow of silence. Boy, the spirit sure moves in mysterious ways.

****

She will not say which one -

but, says she

"My teacher is built like a box!"

****

On my way back from the mailbox,

I saw a hearse ....

It's name, "Porta Caeli" --- what else!

****

I think her favorite word is "presume".

****

At the break of dawn

a concerto of sounds rumble

in the chapel ....

to cover the cacaphony,

feigned coughs and rustling of pages are made

in the midst of the gastronomical overtures!

****

Letter from Sloan Wilson

Dear Virginia,

You really are a good writer, and I don't say that to many people.
You should nurture your talent and keep exercising it! Submit your
work to Catholic publications and to genreal publications. There
always is a lot of interest in the life nuns live and you describe it
with great wit, charm, and devotion. So keep up the good work!
The Church needs good writers. I know, because they tried to
recruit me, a
lost cause if there ever was one. But the religious life is a great
subject for those who are dedicated to it.
Affectionately,
Sloan
(Then, his wife Betty writes:)

I am so proud of you in so many ways. Most of all because you
remember the times we shared in Ti, and the memories which I love
about dancing. You remember my birthday and send wonderful
thoughts which make me feel important and loved. Sloan was so
impressed with your with your Christmas stories. I have passed
them on to Jessica. We didn't get up Northt his year, but when we
do, I plan to be in touch with you.
All mylove,
Betty

****

Sunday night, our group of novices put on a little skit about being in
the Canonical year.
It was I who came down with a severe case of "Canonical". I played
the outpatient who was a bit of a basketcase. Once again, art
imitates life – or, is that the other way around?

Am second cantor this week. Next week I will be first. We have learned some new chants with Father Sorgei. He is a dynamic teacher.

****

Does the towering Dominican loom

in the classroom?

"I presume......"

(she says).

Just finished Father O'Connor's exam. We celebrated with a little 'Lancelot' wine.

Mother Regina told me that Father Salmon will be coming this Thursday. He will be going to Santa Domingo from here. It will be so nice to see him.

Excerpt from letter from Ed and Dixie:

"With all due respect to you and the Pope and to anyone else interested, you will always be sweet and lovable Virginia or VA to us – no matter what you call yourself."

****

31 January 1993
Sunday Night

Hi Grampa!

I hopeyou are alright.

The Cardinal came Saturday. Six new young ladies interviewed with him.

Had a very nice letter from Betty and Sloan Wilson.

Tomorrow is a solemn retreat day as Tuesday, The Purification of Our Lord marks the official start of our Canonical year. Our duties will change . It will be tough – see the enclosed regulations. The letter writing is really going to be clamped down and phone calls will be few and far between. I can hardly bear I. I don't know if I can ask for an exception or if I even dare. Mother is fair but she does run a tight ship.

Well, you have Father's number.

I put this notice up on the bulletin board – it was a little joke for the card that Patti made for – It had St. Thomas Moore on it and he looked like a cadaver. "N.B. - Sisters, there will be calling hours from 2 to 4 p.m. for the card of St. Thomas Moore. Private Viewing. Rosary to follow. In lieu of flowers, fresh bees wax candles are requested". One of the novices was aghast – so I did not mention who posted it.

Mr. Honerkamp, the gentleman who I met at Basin Harbor, came by the other day. This time he brought us some delicious bagels and cream cheese. He is such a sweet man.

Tisdale is good calling you and keeping you in tobacco. Also, that was nice of Annie to bring you some bakery goodies.

Francine did come by with Donald and his wife and their two little girls. They are very sweet. Francine brought two bars of soap. She said that if I could not accept them, she would take them back. She also brought me a piece of "Mother's applesauce cake". I gave her a pear from the parcel Gramma sent me. I think a pear is a beautiful Christmas symbol. I accepted one bar of soap from her.

It was so good seeing Tizz and Rick too. Poor Gramma couldn't get through on the phone as the lines were so busy.

Did I tell you that I visited the Vatican Embassy? Met the Papal Nuncio. Wow! The art there is unreal!

Well, thank you for taking care of everything for me Grampa,

For now,

Love,
Sister James Mariah

****

The other day I was portress.

"Hello, Sisters of Hope ....: The portress answered the phone.

"Is there a man in the house?"

"No, not really,............ this is a convent."

"Oh, that's interesting. How old are you?"

"I am 33."

"Well, can you answer a few questions for me – on a vitamin survey?"

"Sure, I guess so -----"

"Do yo take liquid, coated tablets or uncoated tablets?"

"One-a-day plus iron." Says I.

"Okay, but in the last thirty days, have you taken liquid, coated, or uncoated tablets?"

"Well, I would have to say that they are coated because they are orange colored."

"Alright, but how important is it for you to have the selection to choose from in the store of different varieties?"

"Well," says I, "Not too important. You see, I just tell my Grampa to send me the 'One-a-day plus iron'. In fact, I just got some in the mail today, but I told Reverend Mother, on account I am improving on reporting the contents of my parcels – particularly, if they are 'One-a-day Plus Iron'. Do you think I should have told her about the mints? You see, Ticonderoga just got a new pharmacy and they were running a special on 'Mentos'. Now they are coated! Heck, and that little boost of sugar is just as good as taking a vitamin. Yep, like a shot of Geritol. Oh wait, I used to take Geritol – the liquid kind. Does that count? That was when I was touring and we had a really tight schedule. Then, I heard that it lowers your blood pressure, so I stopped taking it. So now, I am on the 'One-a-day" - Plus Iron that is.

"Well, you didn't quite answer my question, though I understand what you are saying. You see, I have to know if the selection is: a) very important, b) somewhat important, c) slightly important or d) not important at all?"

"Oh, okay, that sheds a little different light on the matter. I would have to say my answer comes under 'slightly important'."

"Okay, what about in the last six months …….?"

"Oh, a, Mother Regina,……. Do you need to use the phone?"

"Uh, Mam….. I don't think I will be able to answer any more questions. You see, my Superior has to use the phone. Thank you and God Bless you."

Later …………

"Sister James Mariah, what was that all about?"

Moral – Drink lots of liquids, get plenty of rest, and don't let your guard down!!

****

Excerpts from my journal:

Met a Mr. Burleigh at the Knights of Malta ceremony. He was bowled over when I said, "Hello Mr. Burleigh." He had driven through Ticonderoga and he had seen the Burleigh Pharmacy. "Oh yes," says I, "that was my great grandfather's establishment. Shook hands and then had to skip ahead to the Cardinal's Residence.

Saturday was Sister Aquinas's birthday. I am on for cooking. Will not have to bake a cake as Father Halligan has once again pulled through with a birthday cake. Sister Aquinas will be very happy.

Went to Monsignor Well's Rosary Vigil this afternoon at the Cathedral with Rosario and Sister Lucy. It was very cold out today. We seemed to attract illegal aliens – the poor and lonely type. The refugees were from Guatelmala. They could not have been more than twenty years old. Yet the girl looked at me pleadingly with eyes hardened to life. They did not speak English. Their country is in war. It is heart wrenching.

After the Rosary, this older, Irish looking woman came up to me, "Can I give you a hug?" Is this I in my older years? "Sure," I exclaimed. I gave her two hugs – one for her, and one for me. Her name was Rose Martin. People are lonely and they sorely need affection.

We headed back to the car. We passed the Drake Hotel. I wanted to go in and see that famed Bird Cage in the lobby. Mrs. Dechame had always told me about that. She had sent me a picture of it one time. But Sister Lucy did not think that was a "religious" thing to do. I guess I am too spontaneous and "unthinking".

Patti helped me in preparing dinner. We had chicken curry and rice, and green vegetables. Rosario was in Heaven on account of the rice.

194

Then, I set up the ice and cherry coke; made hot water for tea, and set out the cake on the tray for Sister Aquinas's birthday. I really get into birthdays so I was enjoying this. Even selected three of her favorite songs to serenade her with. She was to arrive back at the convent at any moment. I played 'Flower of Scotland' (Wolfe Tones), and a little later, "Kilkenny, Ireland" (Green Fields of America), and then, I asked everyone to stand in a circle in the community room. "Join hands," I said, and I played "Give me Your Hand" by the Wolfe Tones. It was a resounding success! To my great surprise, the evening ended with everyone dancing! I couldn't believe it! Thank you Dear Jesus!

On Sunday, I was sitting in the front pew at Mass. We were singing 'Here I Am Lord – I will go Lord'. I happened to look up. I noticed Monsignor Devlin, who is codgey wipe a tear from his eye. Just then, he saw that I had noticed. After Mass, he scurried back to the Sacristy. I approached him, "Hello Monsignor, I just wanted to wish you a Happy New Year." I gave him a peck on the cheek. Then, the monsignor, who is never wanting for words, was speechless. He usually says something sarcastic. I told him that we were going to the Cathedral.

Later in day, we went to Bishop Henry Mansell's first Mass as auxillary bishop here in New York. There were over 100 clergy in attendance including Monsignor Devlin who never mentioned that he was going. He is a humble man.

Officer Rudolf John Ostrande II is a policeman who is always at St. Patrick's Cathedral. He reminds me of Peter Sellers. He walks like him and he has that same dark mustache. He had sustained an injury on duty some months back. We had been praying for him. Today, he was not wearing his uniform. Rather, he was all dressed up in a pin-striped suit. One could detect the cologne of aftershave he was wearing. He had just been received by the new Bishop. I went to say hello to him. He asked me if it was a sit down dinner. It really struck me the innocence and humility of one who lives in the city and yet is not affected by it all. So the small town girl who fights worldliness, showed the grateful officer to the hors d'oeurves and finger food table. I suggested to him that he may want to sit, but if

195

he was more comfortable standing, he could do that too. I had asked him about his wife Connie and his children. He has a son named for him who is the third with that name. I showed him where the beverages were and I said, "You don't want to miss those nice pecan tarts over there." Another moment brightened my day.

Then, an Irish priest sang a song to me. It was something about Sts. Peter and Paul. This priest resembled Cardinal Cooke with his round face.

Can't help but be impressed with His Excellency Bishop Henry J. Mansell. He is solid, reserved and humble. God Bless him.

I saw Monsignor Middy whom I had met on another occasion. He was with another Indian priest – a Father Archie. Saw the ushers who are very good at what they do.

****

What's Up …………...Is Down at Saint Frances Paola Convent

No, it wouldn't or couldn't happen to anyone else …..only to me. Was wearing that sweater, ou know, the one of the bulky nature. Just so happened Sister Francis Mary was passing me the fruit bowl and didn't my elbow nudge my water glass, yes, sixteen fullounces of water, allowing my cup to spilleth over, yes, in the refectory - --- right beside Mother Assumpta. Sister Mary Pio was quick on the draw. She grabbed a tea towel and came to my rescue. God Bless her. Sister Mary Pio has a tendency to leave things undone though her heart is always in her efforts. Heck, thank goodness none spilled over on to the Superior's lap. Thus Mother Regina rang the bell, and we ll got up from our places to pray a prayer of thanksgiving, and
…………………….

"Sister James Mariah! What is this? I am drenched in water! Why look, there is even a puddle on the floor!"

I was as dumbfounded as she - and everyone else for that matter. I thought I would die. "I'll get the mop...." I suggested. Evidently the water from my water glass had seeped under my placemat and onto the many cascades of Reverend Mother's Dominican habit. When I returned, I offered her a solution with the hair dryer.

"Oh, no thank you. It'll be fine." She moved away from me.

For restitution, I did iron Mother Regina's other clean habit that was hanging in the laundry room.

Later in the week:

Mr. Honerkamp dropped off some soup, salad and rolls. It seemed I had waited a sufficient amount of time before sitting next to Mother Superior again. Maybe not. I mean that salad had cucumber slices the size of silver dollars in it. I decided to do like the English and make a cucumber sandwich with mine. I noticed that Patti was doing the same thing. She was sitting "kitty-corner" to me. Well, whenI went to take a dainty bite of this silver dollar size cucumber, it shot like a dart --- plop! Right onto Mother Superior's lap! This was during a meal of strict silence, save that of Sister Agatha reading the life of Blessed Theophane Venard in which most left most of the Sisters weeping albeit silently. My peripheral vision could not mistake that this piece of greenery clearly was on Mother Assumpta's lap. And then, it came............

"Sister James Mariah, did you lose something?" And she smiled in her genteel, Southern way.

"Uh, oh, ... thank you." I smiled nervously, embarrassedly, and Sister Agatha continued to read some more dramatic stuff. I could hardly contain myself. I burst out in laughter. Dear Lord, help me to get through this dinner gracefully! Afterwards, Mother Regina announced my mishap. "I could not have done that if I tried." She said. She did, thank goodness, get a kick out of it. Thanks be to God and from now on I am sitting at the end of the table!!!!

****

Monday
15 February 1993

Hi Gramp,
Just got your parcel – thank you for sending the thermal carafe. I tried to send Mom the video from Mid-night Mass last month. I set it in the outgoing mail, but It was a little bit later than when it was supposed to be for outgoing mail. I was reprimanded by Mother. However, later, she seemed to have a change of heart, and she permitted it to go out in the mail. Therefore, Mom should have received it long before now.

I am so glad you talked to Father Halligan. He is such a good and holy man. He said that you sounded great. His sister Betty is very sweet too. She sends me notes now and again.

I am enclosing a prayer for you on how to make a "Spiritual Communion". It is very powerful especially if you are not able to get to church. I was thinking Grampa, that I could discreetly ask Uncle H.G. to bring you Holy Communion if you like.

I am bell ringer this week, so I have to get up extra early. I am on for cooking twice this week and I have an exam on Thursday and a term paper due the following Thursday. This is not counting my job working in the laundry room. Plus, I am one of the cantors – therefore, I must learn the Lenten tone. Was portress yesterday and we went to the Cathedral for Mass for Black American History Day.

How are you feeling? It is okay if you write. I think the Superior wants to curtail it, but all last week, there has been mail in our boxes. So I am in a quandary. I do miss when I don't hear from you.

Am receiving The Times of Ti.

The Sisters seem to be enjoying the "Grandpa" mugs.

Father is so fascinated with the Fort and the Tattoo . He hopes to visit there one day. He would also like to meet you.

Yes, the valve on the toilet is working fine.

I will get to write to you again before long. Meanwhile, you take good care Gramp,

Your loving granddaughter,

Virginia – Sister James Mariah

****

From my journal:

It was a secret desire of my heart to see Miss Sarah Beaton, a poor, elderly lady who I met last November. I had not seen her since. We received an overstock of some blouses and I really wanted to give her some. Though I was portress today, and moreless confined to the house, Mother Regina did ask me to take an article of mail over to the Poor Clare Monastery. Who should I see on the corner but Miss Beaton herself! I was delighted. She was apologizing for having lost the gloves and the scarf which were given fomr one's having too much. That same day, incidentally, I had received a new pair of gloves in the mail. Thank God she did at least have some knit gloves and a muffler on. I told her to wait there. I ran back to the convent. I interrupted Mother in a meeting. "May I give a couple of those blouses to a lady who could use them?" "Oh, sure." She replied. I was thrilled. She really is good. I gave Mother Regina Tizz's address when she went to Maryland and Mother Regina tried three different places taking a lot fo time trying to find Tisdale. Unfortunately, she did not locate her. But that she tried and went out of her way, meant everything to me. She did not tell me this until four days after she had returned. I did not broach her on it either.. I could not imagine her not trying to find her knowing Mother Regina. But how selfish of me – the roads were not the best. I was perhaps expecting too much. It was like Mother to make that effort. She even let me take some blouses for my sisters. I ahd

199

asked her I felt kind of funny about asking with the vow of poverty
and all, but shoot, there were so darn many, and I would not be
greedy about it. I do, afterall, have seven sisters.

Today, Sunday, February 28th, we went to the Cathedral to Mass fro
American Black History Day/Month. What was disturbing, was, that
right during The Offertory, this thin older Albanian man came right
up to the altar and placed a letter in an envelope there despite all the
security. He was probably in his early 70's and he did appear
nervous. He was wearing an old suit though it made me sad to see
his tattered socks and worn shoes. What was worse, was that he was
in the Cardinal's line to receive Holy Communion, bu the he was not
able to procede as the police were clutching him under his elbow.
 This man had been, funny enough, sitting in my pew – not far from
me. The Cardinal had given the letter to Father Matt who was
assisting in the Mass. It seemed to be a plea – a sort of last desperate
plea to find this man's lost three daughters from Albania. The man
had put money in th envelope. The man seemed to be grinding his
teeth. He had a little red button on his lapel which led me to believe
that he was probably an usher, but this was not so. I admired His
Eminence as he announced this man's plea. He was asking the
Archdiocese of New York to help if they had any information. The
strange part was, that one was not sure if the man had lost his
daughters recently, or, if this had been a lifelong search. My heart
ached for him. I wanted to reach over and take his hand, but now he
was gone. Oh, the names of his daughters – this was the really odd
part. They sounded more like Richard Nixon's daughters – a
Patricia Nixon, a Julie (I think he said'Eisenhower') Nixon and I
forget the other name. It is sad. Only God knows and God please
help him.

Was in a really good mood today. Washed the aprons and tidied up
the laundry room. The Sisters set up the community room for the
two guests arriving today. Also, a friend of Mother Regina's came
for lunch. She had been in the city for a toy show. His Eminence
came too with Father Matt.

I enjoyed lunch. There were lots of laughs with Father Matt as he recounted his days in the seminary. The Cardinal even greeted me more warmly thanhe has lately.

Then, we went to Mass at the Poor Clare Monastery. Father Anthony from Nigeria celebrated Mass. Today marks one month of his being in the states.

I changed my bookshelf in my room. The bigger one makes the room appear much neater as I had crowded too many things on Helene's smaller one. Cleaned out my desk drawers too.

Later in day, after lunch clean-up, and the Cardinal's talk with us, I went over to Confession. I saw Vincent on the way in. It is always good to see Vincent. He is so friendly. Then, I see two black galoshes and red piping on a black cassock. It was undoubtedly my friend Monsignor Devlin behind the screen. Thus, I went to Confession. Met Mr. Connally on the way out. He is a real 'Ernest Hemmingway- type. It was nice to see him.

So what was wrong with my day. I don't know. Am still trying to figure it out. Well, firstly, Sister Frances was discussing who would come when Mother Regina leaves us. Of course, yours truly walks by commenting that we look very serious. Sister Frances says, "Oh, we are talking about you – nothing bad – just about ...."
"Gosh," I thought to myself. "Can't she just keep her yap shut."
Then I was mad at myself for engaging in the conversation to begin with.

Last night, and today, still feeling the effects of "bad vibes" from Sister Lucy. We went to the funeral home to see if they had any left over flowers for our chapel. Mr. Massey, the director was there. He said, "There's not a soul in the place!"
I said to Sister Lucy, "Unlike that delivery the last time."
"What delivery?" She asked.
"You mean you don't know?"
"No, tell me."
"Well, I don't really remember. It was probably nothing."
"Tell me." She insists.

"Okay, it was in a box."

"Oh, was it mints?"

"No, not exactly......"

"Books. Was it books?"

"Uh, forget it."

"No, tell me what it was!" She was adamant.

"Later."

"No, now!"

"I shouldn't tell you, but since you ask....... A body, er, at least I think that's what it was '"

"UGH!"

"Sorry."

So, during clean-up after supper, I rendered this account to Maura – precluding it with, "Sister Lucy, I hope you won't mind if I tell about our flower pick-up at Massey's Funeral Home." And so I told Maura. Sister Lucy was not amused. She can dish it out, but she can not take it. "It is all in fun, I mean no harm." Nonetheless, the repercussions have carried over into today.

Then, there is this matter of no mail. I did not even get my 'Times of Ti' this week. "Why is that?" Sister Aquinas asks in front of everyone.

"Well, I can tell you that it has nothing to do with publication." I replied rather dryly. Suddeny, everyone was bent over in laughter. I was between a pillar and a post, quite literally I might add. Here I had been leaning on the post, and to compound matters, Mother Regina, the "Pillar" of our community had just gotten off the phone – just in time to hear me murmer under my breath. I thought I would die. Next morning which was this morning, I found the latest edition of my hometown paper in my mailbox – that which I was sure to thank her for later rather sheepishly.

Am asked to serve the guests dining with Sister Agatha upstairs. Gladly. That is, until Sister "Nouvelle Riche" decides to tell me after I have made nearly a dozen trips up and down the stairs to bring back the Hungarian goulash.

"It would mean an extra trip, but do see how we are doing."

"Are you sure you could not take all you might like now? I suggested. "You see they forgot about Sister Peter William."

202

"No, take hers, but bring it back." Sister Agatha insisted.

Well, I am all for hospitality but this did not sit right with me. She is carrying on this "Ritz thing" a little bit too far. There was just enough for one serving for Sister Peter William. Thanks be to God, because it would not have been in my heart to go back upstairs.

Then, the Sister who is on dish detail with me, says that she prefers to wash the dishes. Now this is a new one on me. She would use cold water and soap if she had her druthers. Small wonder people are getting sick. I tactfully gave her the Octagon and a scrub brush and ran the hot water. I was drying greasy dishes. Even Sister Aquinas gave one back to her. If I wash, it is this Sister's favorite thing to do to me. She will give me back a pyrex lid with an otherwise undetected fleck of nothing on it. Oh, blessed submission............

Now I was on edge. Rosario loves rice. There are about four to five servings of left-over rice. So let's take a portion out for Rosario I suggested.
"No, you can't do that!" came the retort. "It's better for you to serve the guests." Sister Philip was adamant.
"Well," I declared. "The way I see it, there is enough rice for both the guests and Rosario."
Then, another from the first group interjects, "You can't do that!"
Well, that was enough for me to deliberately do that.
Then says Sister Scrupulosity, "Now you have to offer everyone a little bit of that rice because that is the spirit of Poverty."
What I felt like saying, I can not write here. I was still. Only I saw that Rosario had a good portion of the rice. The way I see it is if she grew up in the Phillippines, she knows poverty better than anyone of us here. Also, for her to give up a lifelong staple of her diet is a big sacrifice. If there is a little left over rice, she should have it. And as long as I am here, she will! I did ring the remainder of the "squabble dish" (best served cold) upstairs.
Just as I sat down to eat, Sister Lucy tells me to go upstairs to get the goulash. I obliged. She, Sister Philip and even Maura were malcontent with me.

Then, Sister Lucy announces that dish duties change tonight. Don't know what came over me, but the fact that Mother Regina was present did not make a difference. "The list says we do the current duties 'til the 14th, that is, through the 14th." I said.

"Well, we change all our duties on a Saturday." She rebuts.

"I realize this is done for all the cooking duties. However, she did not specify it for this new assignment." Of course, "Sister Schumzer" wrote up the new teams for the dish detail. She hardly rotated the people and it was rather obvious who she put with whom. Forget it............ Last evening I received a gorgeous and huge floral arrangement to my great surprise. It has yellow roses – Gramma LaPointe's favorite, they are also the ones that I got for Karl (my late brother). There were irises, exotic tiger lilies, white mums, carnations, tulips,and pretty little purple flowers with lots of greenery and yellow spider mums all in a big glass dish. This graces the foot of the altar. Patti says to add more water. Sister Immaculata says don't. I just add a glass. Tonight, some of the flowers are keeling over – like my spirit. "Didn't you put water in?" Patti scolds me. So I went and added more water. Now, I must go and pray. Oh, dear Mrs. Dechame sent me the flowers. She is very kind and thoughtful to me. God Bless her always and God rest her dear brother.

Father Halligan did not come today. He has not been feeling well.

****

Dear Sister James Mariah,

I just got your letter – thank you.

What is a waste basket among friends. You are welcome to it. (I had asked Grampa to send me a p ink waste basket that was in the cellar, but he sent me the wicker one that he uses.)

Your sister Karlene called. She tried to get a hold of you on the phone. I set her straight as to times, etc.

Helene called last night. She tried to get you yesterday. She thought it was visiting day.

Your knocking over the music stand reminds me so much of you around here. It made me laugh.

I hope "Boot Camp" is going better for you. God Bless you for what you are doing.

Aunt Peg is home now. I think she is doing alright. She dropped in before her surgery. Brought me a jar of jam and some brownies. She asks for your prayers.

No, I never got a prayer book but Father G. gave me a booklet that has morning and evening prayers.

You know for someone who is suppose to take the oath of poverty you really try to do too much.

One of the Sisters from Watertown told Sister Sharon that she saw you on tv. She said you looked great.
Sister Julian brought me a loaf of bread – delicious. She and I made a bathrobe for Karlene. We went through the whole procedure, stitch by stitch. Even so, I enjoyed her visit.

Don't worry about my walking. Anyone will tell you that damp and chilly weather will make arthritis worse.

Harry is the usual Horses -----s. He comes over for the paper. He says he will come at 9:30 but then comes much later. Edna is out chasing the cats. I don't know why because they can't catch a bird. I think I will make them wait later for the paper now. They drive me up the wall.

Not much new. I guess I am not the best writer.
I miss you so much.

Take care my best girl,

Love,

Gramp

I have to laugh. It seems I am not alone in my "mischief". During the storm, I went to check on my sidekick Sister Frances Mary. She was kicking her heels up listening to her radio, curled up in her afghan and hot pot was plugged in. It was good to just see her really relaxed. She cracks me up. She changes her room around on average twice a week. She always manages to put her dresser in such a way that her hot pot and electric toothbrush are concealed on the other side of it.

Promised a peppermint hot chocolate to my friend Patti. Told her how my little sister Sarah used to make them back home for Mom and me. I bring it into her and I notice that she is listening to her radio too. Then, the day before, I just by chance happened to pass another consort wearing headphones who I must leave "nameless" as I promised her I would not tell. I certainly do not set out to discover these things. Shoot, if anyone can relate, it is I. I am lost without my music and yet, I have really not listened to much since I have been here.

Sister Francis and I took a fit of laughter on Sunday night. All lights were out and I knew she was hankering for one of those crumb buns. I was waiting for the coast to be clear. Great minds were thinkin galike. Of course the challenge of it is fun for me. So we bumped into each other – I was coming up the stairs, and she was coming down. During the transaction, we managed to get crumbs and powdered sugar all over the living room carpet which set us in hysterics. So Sister Francis Mary takes her foot and decides to rub the powdered sugar into the carpet. I nearly died laughing. It was

Dorothy and me

also a time of strict silence. The reason for getting the crumb bun
was because tomorrow they would take flight to the Franciscans.

Figured they would not miss one. Heck, with a name like Saint Francis ....

Speaking of stairs, I am portress this Sunday, plus cook, plus bell ringer. In an effort to keep up with the clock, I took six stairs at a time. No one was in sight --- or so I thought, "Sister James Mariah…...."
Oh no, I thought to myself. I looked down the stairwell, and just like a Cheshire cat looking up at me was my Superior, "Uh, yes, Mother Regina --" She smiled and said, "Could you take this letter over to the Poor Clare Monastery, whenever." "Oh sure." If one was to interpret that, he could say that that was the Superior's way of letting the novice know she indeed saw her subject take the stairs in leaps and bounds.

Sister Mary Compulsive assists me with dinner. Honestly, I have never seen anything like this. She profusely washes a single green pepper in hot water for seven minutes – all while wearing rubber gloves.

Sister Agatha likes to throw around these $3.00 words interspersed with, "You people" and, "Essentially what you are getting is ----" or, "I get a sense of ---" or "Actually, it is quite wonderful --" or "I get a sort of feeling ---" or "The basic element is ---" or she maybe so inclined in her predicatableness to constantly interrupt and interject what she believes to be profound thought at the most inopportune time to prove that she dominates. It is either in class, or at a meal, (thank goodness for those silent meals!). Otherwise, she will disect a topic and then ask to repeat parts of conversation which should have been digested like the food on her plate! Such display of hyper hyperbole!

It is so, Sister Francis Mary and I have a mutual exchange society ranging from one party finding one of Eugene's jelly doughnuts on her pillow, to another, finding chocolate chip cookies left over from our brown bag lunch at Dunwoodie. All So much fun ....
especially to eat!

Sister Aquinas is always talking about her "docksiders". Patti says they will be in bronze yet. Sister Someone else says they will be in cement. Sister Frances Mary mumbles under her breath, "With her feet in them.........."

Incidents of March 7th – 14th, 1993

Monday morning while doing chores, Sister Frances Mary says to me, "I was talking to God this morning, "
"Oh," says I. "What did He have to say?"
She chuckles, rings out her mop, and seeks my approval on "her refectory floor." Then, she says, "Didn't you hear me?"
I said that I was not sure what all the raucous down the hall was.
She always makes me laugh. I do enjoy her.

Tuesday morning at breakfast, Sister Immaculata was saying how Jesus tricked Peter, James and John when they wanted to know where they stood with Him. That they would still have to do all that was asked of them. "He tricked me too." says her listener.

This week, during Mid-day prayer, Sister Francis is versiclerian. Therefore, she invokes the start of the second psalm which starts, "Hear me complain O Lord." I thought I would die. Maura coughs to cover up a laugh. Sister Aquinas even appreciated this one.
Maura leaves the Chapel. I regain composure. It completely goes over Siser Francis's head. Later she asked me, "Do I complain?" I told her no, and that she just told the truth about things.

I made Sister Francis Mary a hot chocolate and went for a walk out in the blizzard. It was a blast! The wind was actually buoying us several yards, a strong physical force thrusting us about. Hail stones beat in our faces. It was like the Psalms being brought to life. Oh, how we laughed and hooted and howled – all of a treacherous two blocks.

I have been much improved about behaving in Chapel where laughter, that is, untimely laughter, is concerned. Well, Sturday night we switched "hebs". Sister Immaculata is a natural alto. She just can not seem to reach those high c's and what comes out, which is every other word, is too much. It is slow and drawn out to compensate for not hitting the notes. I must say she thinks through each syllable, but oh there is a week ahead yet, and I am having great difficulty containing myself. Lord, make haste to help me!

Poor Sister Francis Mary. Today was not her day. She decided to use paper napkins in the refectory and hold off on the cloth ones until our company comes. The Little Sisters of the Poor are supposed to come for lunch the first of the week. Well, one sister who has nose trouble implied that she was taking liberties because the Superior was away. That set Sister Francis off. And why she gave in and went ahead and put the cloth napkins on, I will never know. Sister Immaculata and I went to cheer her up. Her spirits picked up somewhat. The funny thing was when we went down to the refectory for lunch, the napkins had been switched back to paper. I patted Sister Francis and said, "I see you switched them. Good for you." She says, "I don't know who did, and I am not making a big deal out of it." I agreed, "I don't blame you Sister Francis."

All last week, Sister Margaret wore a coffee-colored stocking on her left leg, and a beigh-colored one on her right leg. Some days, the coffee-colored one would be on her right leg, and the beige one on her left. All I could think of was one of those Harlequin clowns..............which reminds me, we went to a circus at St. Frances of Paola School. The kindergarteners put it on and it was more fun than a ....

It is pretty funny that Mother Assumpta is away and we have been taken by storm. Sister Peter William, a noted cat-lover, rescues a cat who is now in our basement on her heating pad eating sardines. She also manages to give "Blizzard", a name which Sister Lucy coined, a change of scenery in bringing him/her up to the community room. When the cat's away -------

We have been praying extra Hail Mary's for Mother Regina's safe return. Siser Francis says, "I hope she gets marooned for a week. Of course I don't want anything to happen to her – just want her to be marooned for a week." It seems Sister Francis was anxious about getting Father O'Connor's paper done by the deadline which is today – Sunday by Vespers. The majority do not have it done.

If cats are not being rescued, two are out looking for a homeless man to give him a lunch to eat. Disappointed – can not find him. His name is Paul. He asks for prayers.

Sister Francis Mary says she can not wait to see Mother Assumpta's face when she sees the cat. Well, when she called, someone's conscience got the better of her. She broke down and told her. Mother Assumpta also heard a man's voice in the background. It was Luke's. She does not iss a trick – not even on the phone over eight hours away!

It was so nice that I popped my head out the door only to see my friend Vincent. "Hi Vincent!" "Stay inside, keep warm Sister James Mariah!"

Oh, I did something different today. I read at the 8 o'clock Mass at the church. Monsignor Devlin had asked if there was a lector. I volunteered. Sister Margy said that she would about a second after I did, but she conceded and let me read. I figured it was a good opportunity. I was relaxed and was even told that I did a good job.

Saint Patrick's Day 1993

The way I feel about Saint Patrick's Day can almost be compared with to the way I feel about Christmas. That is, the feelings that are conjured are similarly at an apex. Though perhaps diffused differently. They are sentimental and more subdued on the surface at Christmas, but felt every bit as strongly as the passion I feel for Ireland. I think o fthe Seventeen Martyrs and the Irish Saints led by Saint Patrick. The poetry that arose out of the depths in their plight from the Potato Famine to the brutal oppression inflicted on them by the English. The original IRA and the "Troubles" in the North stir a fury within me. The music: the harp, the tin whistle, the bodran drums and the fiddles. Oh, and the dance – how I love the Irish dancing – the jigs. Then, there is their own distinct Gaelic language – which my dear friend is fluent in. The heather tweeds and the Aran knits are as earthy as the Emerald Isle's people. It is a people I have grown to understand, to identify with, and to fall in love with. One of my dearest friends lives in Belfast. Indeed I have Irish blood running through my veins.

Can not leave out my favorite Irish group – the Wolfe Tones! They are terrific. The thing is, if you go to one of their concerts, you automatically lose yourself in song, in spirit. You find yourself, stomping your feet, clapping your hands, singing along, and if you are lucky, dancing too! It is beautiful. I love the tenor John McDermott too. His singing is most heartfelt.

What to do – for starters, put on the corned beef and cabbage. Pick up some butter milk and bake some Irish soda bread. Be sure to stop up to Bunny Vigliotti's and get some Bushmill's or Jameson's. Get some Guiness while you are at it. It is good for the blood. Then stop at the Ti Market and pick up a Saint Patrick's Day cake. You may want to have vanilla ice cream with a little crème de menthe! Did you go to Mass? I know it is Lent, but the Good Lord makes provisions on this day so that you can celebrate. Did I mention Paddy Reilly – you have to listen to "The Town I loved So Well". Oh, I hear the pipes calling! Uncle John has a live Irish band this year. Would love to see Johnny sing 'Finnegan's Wake'. He also does a good "Mack the Knife". Not this year though.

We went to Mass at Saint Patrick's Cathedral. It was magnificent. The bagpipes sounded, and the procession began. The Cardinal had these beautiful vestments on that he only wears on St. Patrick's Day. The statue of St. Patrick was draped in Ireland's Tricolor and a garland of green carnations. Lots of people were wearing green and even fresh shamrock in their lapels. We sang "The Soldier's Song" and Ireland's National Anthem also, 'Hail Glorious Saint Patrick'! The pride of the people was just pouring through the air – like the rain outside – real Irish weather. Can't forget to mention New York's finest as most of them are Irish Americans; they were there

with "The Fighting '69'ers. Lots of dignitaries were in attendance.
We prayed for two officers who were killed in the line of duty. The
Cardinal also mentioned a remarkable woman, and, a close friend of
his, Miss Helen Hayes! The Mass was very beautiful.

The Cardinal officiated at Miss Helen Hayes's funeral. She was 92
and he is 72. He said he always had a passion for her. Grampa saw
it on TV and told me that. God Rest Helen Hayes.

Would have liked to have seen the parade firsthand, but we had to
get back to the convent. Mother Regina let me put my Paddy Reilly
video tape in. Then we decorated with the decorations that Mr.
Honerkamp dropped off, and to top it off, we had Father Halligan's
ice cream cake! We invited Mr. Gallagher over. I put some Irish
music on. I was in my glory. It is like the Christmas spirit only its
Irish fervor. Then I helped bake bread with Sister Yvonne and
Mother Regina. We enjoyed Sister Peter William's Irish soda bread.
Sister Margaret and Sister Philip fixed the traditional Irish supper.
Here is the best part – we got to have green crème de menthe on ice
cream. Sister Janice and I did the Irish jig. Sister Francis Mary and
I waltzed to the Irish Wedding Song. We opened the community
room window and hollared over back and forth to Father Paul at the
rectory – as though we were in some Italian neighborhood. Then,
we watched one of my favorite movies. Nope, it was not 'The Quiet
Man', it was 'Captains Courageous'.
MAUNDY THURSDAY

I made hot cross buns for the breakfast today. I made a hard sauce
of sorts to make the crosses on the buns. Tomorrow we will have
the rest. They were a big hit, only the crosses melted when the buns
were reheated. Baked bread yesterday with Sister Agatha and
Michelle, our new postulant.

Now I have just returned from Confession at the parish church.
Earlier, we went to Saint Patrick's Cathedral for the Holy Thursday
Mass. It has been an exhausting week – both physcially and
emotionally.

I had to laugh. At the Cathedral, Tom, the usher, (Quasimodo comes to mind), is a riot to watch in action. He is a fixture there. He is very comfortable in his position that which he takes very seriously. I enjoy watching him hook up his ear piece and talk in his remote "walkie talkie". He always seems to be mumbling under his breath. I really get a charge out of him. Mother Assumpta does too as does Patti and Maura. But poor Tom, he must suffer from arthritis. I noticed him walking up to the pulpit during the Chrism Mass on Tuesday. He was hunched over and he appeared stiff. The priests came in during the procession. I proudly watched Father Halligan. There was a priest from Newburgh, I t hink, and he reminded me of Cardinal Cooke with his round face. Sister Immaculata thinks he resembles the bishop from Rhode Island. Come to find out, he was Cardinal Cooke's secretary. Anyway, he is the one who sang "When Irish Eyes are Smiling" after Bishop Manselles's first Mass as bishop at the reception. On this evening, he was with a whole busload of school children. It was so cute because he did something that I could see myself doing if I were in the same spot. He filed in with several hundred priests. Then, he happened to get a seat at an angle where he could turn his head and smile, giving a big 'Hi' sign to the children. He was beaming. He wanted them to share in his pride or something. He is a dedicated priest too. He was explaining the different chapels and structures in the cathedral to the students. I recall Father Sorgie saying that this priest is one of the saints fo the diocese. I believe his name is McDonagh. Sister Immaculata was very impressed with him. Then, I met a Father Dugan who serves in Middleburgh. Come to find out, he is one of the original "Harlem 7". He had a lot to do with the evangelizing some 7,000 to 8,000 now Catholics in Harlem. He has a real humble manner.

I was really hoping to meet Father Bruce Jackson. He is dying of Cancer. I had written to him. He had been in the same musical group that I used to belong to - 'Up With People'. I was kind of ambling around in hopes of the opportunity. Sure enough, on my way to the parish house, I bumped smack into him. That is, of course, after I happened to notice Father Halligan. God is good. I said to this priest, "Hi, Oh, do you know who I am?" He answered, "You are Sister James Mariah, Sisters of Hope, and, you were in "Up With People". Wow! I could not get over that. He had received my letter. My postal workers always deliver .... well, almost always (private joke). We shook hands, I felt ever so glad to meet this priest. He was very upbeat, and yet, he looked drawn out. He appeared as though something supernatural brought him here tonight – a strength that was not his own. I was very moved on seeing him on the altar. Deo voluntis -------- I left with Sister Francis Mary and Rosario. There was a poor beggar shivering in the cold. I only had crumbled crackers in my pocket and a piece of cheese and a carrot. I put them in his hand looking into his weary, worn eyes which haunt me as I recount this.

Heading around the block, I met Father Dennis Dinan. Father Dugan was with him, one I had met earlier. I had met him before, or at least he looked very familiar. The first thing he mentioned was how we both have the same spiritual director. We really ought to have a "Father Halligan Fan Club". It is astounding to think on how many people's lives he has influenced. Talk about bringing souls to God and the rest of that bit in the Book of James, well, his namesake sure is there for those hungering for something greater than themselves. He went on to tell us how Father Halligan had preached at his first Mass. Father Dennis was very proud of this. Father Dennis went on to tell me how his father died on his ordination day. Yes, I do recall Father Halligan telling me that when we were at the Rosary March last June in New York. Father Dennis's father could not receive Holy Communion at his son's first Mass because the Lord was receiving him. He celebrated his first Mass at his dying father's side. Father Halligan preached at his first official Mass in a church. Indeed Father Halligan inspired him to follow in his footsteps. I told Father Dennis that I would pray for his father. He said, "Just remember, 'Cheap Frank'." Well, Mr. Frank Dinan can proudly look down on his son whom the Lord uses to confound the proud. He is a simple and beautiful man of God. As I was heading back to the other side of the Cathedral, I heard a voice singing the theme song from 'Up With People'. I looked up only to wave, (One last time?) to Father Bruce Jackson.

It was a great evening all around. Monsignor Devlin was there though I missed him. We did see him earlier in the day back in the Bronx. One of the Sisters asked him if the Cardinal talked to him.

215

He answered, "The Cardinal doesn't talk to anyone unless he has a mircrophone on." Then he laughed.

24 March 1993

Forgot to mention a funny scene at Mass on Saint Joseph's day at the Jeanne Jugan Residence. When Bishop Manselle was removing his mitre, his fuschia colored skull cap, came off in his miter. I noticed one of the priest on the altar chuckling to himself. I met this priest at the reception afterward. His name is Father Cawkins. He too had noticed me smiling at the incidence.

Flowers from the funeral home were delivered once again, or I should say that Maura and I went to pick them up. The laundry room is the catch-all and this is where the flowers end up until further use. I asked Patti if she had gotten all the flowers which she had planned on using. "Yes," she told me. So I proceded to discard them since the laundry room is my duty to keep clean. That's funny, me thinks, this arrangement looks good. I wonder if it was the same one that had been in the community room for the past two weeks. I hate to throw it out. Maybe I could use it to decorate the laundry room. Heck. I have got some stay fresh flowers which I will put in one fo these buckets. They will brighten up the room. Plus, I made a bouquet for my bedroom as well as one for Rosario's study room. Rosario is finishing her studies to become a medical doctor.
Later, "Sister James, did you happen to see that arrangement I made for Mother Regina's office?" Patti asked me.
"Uh,........" I had difficulty containing myself. "What did it look like?"
"Oh, it had yellow spider mums, and daisies, and..."
I lost it, "Shoot, I thought you said you were finished in there, and that I could throw away the rest of those flowers."
"What?! Do you mean to tell me that you threw out that arrangement?!"
"They went out about twenty minutes ago. They're history..."
"Sister James Mariah!"
"Yep, I eighty-sixed them."
"Mother Regina has been looking all over for her arrangement!"

"I'm sorry. I really thought it was that one that had been sitting on the hi-fi for nearly two weeks, and ...."
"Forget it."
I laughed some more. I couldn't help it. It just struck me so funny because I am the worst hoarder. I never throw anything away and here I was wondering about those flowers.

Two days later:

It is Patti's birthday. I surprised her and made her a maple walnut birthday cake only to be surprised myself, and learn that she hates that kind of cake. She did appreciate the gesture though. She is a good sport. She had asked me the other day if I had thrown out the basket that those flowers were in. I had not. Today, I decide to take a sprig from a plant which I call "the Karl plant". It is a plant which I received when my brother Karl died. Typically, I am not able to grow much, but this does seem to grow. I took a sprig off for Patti and arranged it in some soil in that basket. I wrote a noteti Patti, "Do you recognize this basket? You did not think that I would throw the bathwater out with the baby, did you?" She liked that. She is a lot of fun.

Speaking of the Jeanne Jugan Residence, reminds me of the first time we went there. Sister Mary Pio was driving. Sister Francis Mary refused to ride with her. Sister Immaculata thought, in her maternal way, that it would give Sister Mary Pio more confidence if we rode with her and acted casual. Myself, I thought, give her a chance. Was talking to Sister Immaculata afterward and telling her how I admired her for being so calm about the whole thing and how it helped me to act calm. She then told me that she was a nervous wreck but she did think it was important to give her a chance. I got such a kick out of that. She is pretty cool. Sister Mary Pio does drive alright – so long as others don't "backseat drive".

Saturday mornings I like to put out the 'Rice Krispies'. They remind me of Gramma Burleigh and the 'Big House'. The tea kettle would be on and there was cinnamon toast, oranges, and, of course Rice Krispies cereal. H. G. always put peanutbutte on his toast. Aunt Betty dotted her toast with butter strategically at each corner and once again in the center. Oh those were the days. Annie and Lizzy would start the breakfast at the big house and send me over to Mass with Gramma.

"Old habits die hard, (poor choice of words?), anywho, when I am on for breakfast today, I put out the Rice Krispies and I am sure to have an orange.

The other night while playing charades, Sister Francis Mary busied herself crocheting a baby afghan. She had no interest in our game – that is, until, Sister Agatha acted out "Ma" in "Sum – Ma" and started to make like she was rocking a baby in her arms. Well, Sister Francis Mary perked up then. She loves babies. It was so cute. She put her crochet hook down, and hollared out, "Baby! Mother!, Infant!, Toddler!" and the list went on until Siser Immaculata correctly guessed 'Summa Theologia'.

There was another funny incident at the 'Right to Life' Institute which we attended two Saturdays ago at Dunwoodie. Rosario was sitting next to me. She must have lost a button from her skirt. Of all people – poor Rosario. Well, didn't that skirt decide to slide down when I was introducing her to Monsignor Morkenhauser. He had a big grin on his face. He said, "I think you are losing something." Rosario tried to make like she did not hear him. She is trying to conceal the fact that she is mortified. I assure her that he must have been joking about something else. She says, "This must be the humility that Father Halligan speaks of." We did laugh over it. I was not even going to write about it but Mother Assumpta asked Rosario to share the incident at supper time. I figured it was fair game at this point – besides the fact that it was funny. I did find her a safety pin. I asked one of the Little Sisters of the Poor. She carries one with her. I think that is all she carries with her.

Only I would read from the Book of Joshua when the Lord is asking Moses or excuse me if it is the other way around, but "Does he remember the meat? Well, how about the cucumbers?" I thought I would die. I mean, I was really in a "pickle". I could not very well subsitute 'zuchini'. It was 5:30 in the morning. We had a guest staying with us and it was Sister Philip's last day with us. I

218

explained my dilema to Patti. She said, "Now, you know, you can't do it. You will be in hysterics, but, with God's grace you will get through it." She took me by the hand. "Now , don't come back to your predieu beside me if you don't do it." "Okay", I said. I only stumbled slightly and not until I got to the part aobut the melon. I was fine after the garlic. Then there was the part when Moses said, "Why don't you just kill me now to relieve me from my distress." I read that in all seriousness, though everyone in the chapel was trying to stifle chuckles.

26 March 1993

Today, we packed a picnic lunch and we went to Bear Mountain. On our way, we stopped at Maryknoll in Ossining. It was interesting to see the seminary there with its Chinese influence in architecture. We visited the chapel there. I made my three wishes that which my mother always told me to do upon entering a chapel or church for the first time. I also visited the crypt where the two founders of Maryknoll are entombed. What was fascinating, were the two dozen or more altars behind the crypt. These were for the priests and seminarians to celebrate The Holy Sacrifice of The Mass.

Then, we went over a couple of suspension bridges where my eyes followed a tug boat pulling a big barge as we rode through the mountains. It was nearly tw o'clock before we found a suitable spot to have our lunch. My lips and fingers were all pink colored from eating the red pistachios. What I really wish to express, is, one single, solitary experience which singled me out. Why – I do not know, but I was touched, and dumbfounded. As all the Sisters were walking back to the parking lot, amid patches of snow on the mountains, we passed a group of mentally handicapped adults. There were Blacks, Whites and Asians. They gleefully waved their hands up wavign at us. Then, one older looking man who had a hearing aid, and who was of short stature; a stocky build and looking a bit rumpled, approached me – stretching his hand out to me. I took his hand, and then, he planted a kiss on me. It was so sweet and affectionate and spontaneous. All the Sisters were looking at me.

No one said anything. Then Patti put her arm around me to share in the specialness of this gesture. You know, the little things ----

We stopped at Graymoor on the way home. Sister Francis Mary was in her glory although her good friend Brother Ray was no where to be found. I must remember to pray for Miss Margaret McDermott who gave me and aspirin and a glass of water. When I had retruned to see if I could get Maura some water, she kindly gave me her lst paper cup. Another lady names Frances gave me, rather insisted that I take her glass of juice as Margaret had told her that I had a headache. I could not get over that. God's goodness comes through His people. The next thing I knew, Miss McDermott was on the phone calling about the policy of getting some juice and coffee for the Sisters. I told her not to bother, but she did in her goodness. God love her. I thanked the kind ladies and caught up with the others in the van. Frances handed me two additional juices which everyone ahd a sip of when I got to the van. We prayed our Rosary and we were quiet on the way home. Wow! I can't believe I just wrote "home".

Was going to comment on Sister Philip leaving. Mother Regina told us on Monday morning. I was stunned and saddened. Some burst into tears. I just shared her pain. That poor girl suffered so much. I thought of her mother. She is a lovely person, who has had her share of a mother's anguish. I was just getting used to Sister Philip's quirks. She was getting to accept me too. I felt comfortable with her. In a strange way, I felt she looked out for me – like she cared for me even though I know that I gratedher at times. It was she who was responsible for having the Mass said for Karl. Now she was leaving. I was not aware of how much I felt for her. After Meditation that day, I fixed her a nice cup of tea with her 'Sweet & Low' which she likes. She was always impressed how I remembered that. When I went to her,I wept. She said to me, "Virginia, don't be sad. It is for the best." Then she hugged me. The next two days watching her at the meals, or seeing her pack, broke my heart. She held up pretty good though. The worst was seeing her in her street clothes. One everning, after Vespers, I went to my room only to discover some chocolates wrapped in cellophane and ribbon on my bed. There was also an Irish joke book, and a green, glittery shamrock sticker along with a small wooden Easter bunny pin on my bed. Sister Philip wrote a sweet message on a prayer card for me. The next day she would leave. I potted some of Karl's plant and I told her that I had a yellow ribbon out for her. I don't know what came over me, but I saw her mother looking forlorn. Her father seemed nervous. He cut his finger while loading up the car. I am not the nurse that his daughter is, but I ran and got some band-aids and Bactrine. Sister Philip's parents were very good to me. They made me tapes of my favorite Irish songs – some of which were hard to get. I hugged them both tenderly and then their daughter. She was rather consoling me. I didn't think I was close to her yet there was something there. We both entered together. She told me, "Virginia, never change. Just be careful with the sweets around Mother Regina." She was crying. Father Rinaldi, please watch over your spiritual daughter.

The Blessed Mother on the stairwell landing has been moved to the refectory. Sister Francis Mary says to Mother Regina , "I can stand on that little table, and you can put flowers by me, and then walk by and touch my feet. And I'll give you my blessing." She does come out with some good lines though the Superior is not always amused.

Sister Francis comes in the laundry room, "Virginia, do you smell something burning?" "Oh, Sister Josephat just had an empty frying pan on the burner with the gas turned on high." When Patti discovered it, she looked disgusted, "I guess someone meant to put water on for tea but got mixed up."

Well, my Crucifix that Chrissy gave has been moved out of the refectory. Mother Regina was cute because she came to me and said, "Sister James Mariah, may I see you for a minute?" I thought, oh no, what is she ging to say to me. Then she says, "How are you at detachment?" I could not imagine what she was getting at so anxiously, I muttered, "My music?"
"No"
I tried to think what else, but then thought better of it. "What are you asking of me Mother?"
"Your Crucifix."

221

"Oh, I already reconciled myself to that. That is okay." I knew that one she got in Chicago from some Jim Isaacson was going ot replace mine which my dear childhood friend Chrissy had given me. I know one can not nor should not compare Crucifixes, but I could not deny the great beauty of this one with brass bordering the wood, and a sterling Corpus. All the Sisters took a hand in polishing it. I thought that was very beautiful. I also thought that Mother Regina was very considerate of my feelings in approaching me. I really had not expected that. I appreciated that. She even hugged me. Sister Aquinas, who likens herself to St. Joseph the Carpenter, will find a good sturdy nail for the one Chrissy gave me. She will hang it in the office as it was duly noted, that I spend a little time in there – such as now as I pen my thoughts.

Sister Francis Mary was funny at supper last night. She said she was talking to Father Halligan. "This time we were talking about spiritual things ….." She gives herself away every time. She is innocent like that. Father celebrated Mass with us yesterday. It was so beautiful.

March 30, 1993

Remember those dolls we used to get at Christmas. I can still smell the fresh vinyl or plastic, or petroleum on them. This Christmas, Patti's family sent us new covers for our Office books. They have that same smell.

We have a lovely new postulant. Her name is Michelle. She is a very sweet and pretty girl from Chicago. Her family are real nice too. They are sincere and simple folks. Michelle's brother Garrett is 21 years old. He sang a couple of songs that he had written accompanied by his guitar. He is very talented and modest about his gifts. He was cute as he asked the Cardinal if he ever knew Bishop Fulton Sheen. The Cardinal enjoyed his freshness and suggestd perhaps a better way to phrase the question wouold be to say, "Did Bishp Fulton Sheen know him."

The Cardinal is very quick with his quips. There was talk about a "Jack Daniels", a patron I believe. A little later in the conversation there was mention of a sizeable donation, and how it would be allotted. He dryly, and almost inaudibly said, "Jack Daniels."

This evening, March 30th, we went to the Franciscans of the Renewal for Vespers. This was followed by Holy Hour and then supper. I think we were all edified if ot put to shame by their austere lifestyle and rule of poverty. Or, as Sister Mary Francis said, "It is to be admired, but not imitated." Really though, these Sisters are a lot of fun. I sat with Father Bob Stanion except I kept calling him "Father stan" - inadvertently. Finally, he corrected me. Father Bob's trademark is kissing the ladies' hands. Sure enough, I presented my hand before leaving. He got a kick out of that.

Small world – I happened to know people who Sister Joan knows – from one of the many retreats I have made. Brother Peter sat beside me and he knows two of my acquaintances – one from Ti and another from Port Henry.

It drives Sister Agatha up the wall because I seem to know people wherever we go.

It is Grand Silence and Maura is ironing on the second floor. Herself passes by to discuss the day's events. "Oh no! Quick – be quiet! If you make me laugh, I will kill you!" The Superior is coming – clicking down the corridor. "Hide behind the door!" One had the distinct feeling that the Superior wa holding out in the hallway waiting to catch the likely suspects in action. Finally, a door closes. Maura checks to see it the coast is clear. Quietly, herself emerges, stops off in her room, and makes her way to the stairs, and there upon bumps head into the Superior letting out a silent shriek while throwing her arms up in the air. "Oh, Hello Mother..." Had to have warm milk and a hot bath to calm the ole nerves after that one.

A certain party who left the fying pan "frying" on the stove, leaves an empty tea kettle on the flame the next day. The end of that story is - the crackpot cracked the pot and the whistle that once blew is all blown to pot!

End of March

Friday night at the Stations of The Cross, took a fit of laughter upon noticing Sister Francis Mary in hysterics. She was watching the altar boy, a husky lad with blonde hair about ten years old. He had freckles and chubby cheeks. Well, he was just a swinging that incense burner like a batter with his bat ready to hit a homerun. It was too much. It was like a pendulum swinging and it was hypnotic in its "yo yo" effect. The smoke from the incense took our restraining laughter to the rafters.

If that was not enough, Rosario substituted for the regualr organist. The bellows let loose on the pipe organ. The flaps or shutters by the huge pipes swung open almost as ferociously at the incense burner was being swung. It was only Rosario's second time playing the church organ. She is very petite so it is difficult for her to reach the pedals which control the sound. It gave new meaning to the dirge. It was LOUD!

The Floating Bowl – The things one does to entertain himself. It happens when I am drying the dishes in the refectory. I seem to be the only one who notices or at least who takes such great delight in this natural phenomenom. This is how it works. Assorted dishes which have just been rinsed, are placed on a tray. I will call it Tray 1. Whence dry, the preceding are then placed on another tray, thus, Tray 2. Somewhere, in between this daily process, which occurs three times a dy, one of the assorted d, or aishes, more specifically, a bowl, or a glass; at least they are the ony two types that I have seen this phenomenon take place in – well, anyways, (Or anywho, Hello Mildred Rippon of Randolph, Vermont! This little invocation is said in the tone of Lloyd Lindsey Young, jr. or sr.), what actually takes place before the onseer's eyes, is; the inverted dinnerware, breakafstware, supperware, what have you, and/or glassware floats on Tray 1 which has at this time accumulated a small amount of rinse water as it readies for final drying in the assemblyline so to speak – or so to write, but who is trying to be right. It is just like magic. One minute, you could be drying a plate, the unbreakable Corelle which passes the Sister Mary Pio test every time! And the next moment, you find yourself entranced at a freshly washed bowl (i.e. - depending on who filled the wash basin: determining factors of not enough Octagon which is really in a recycled "Joy" container, and water temperature as well as degree of friction used in actual washing process are to be considered) floating in water on Tray 1 as though it were one of the very apostles testing Our Lord on the waters! It is especially neat when it happens with the glasses. You see, they are 16 ouncers! Did you ever see an inverted 16 ouncer take off on you. C'est incroyable as they say somewhere.

Speaking, rather writing, okay, so I am typing, of such phenomena, call it science, today, after breakfast, I reached for one of those water glasses. It was only a 12 ouncer. The Ricotta cheese lid was stuck to it as though it were in a vacuum. I even showed Sister Margaret. She thought I flipped my lid .... woe, did I say (write, type) that? One would think with all those carrots she eats, she could see it more clearly.

My friend Sister Francis Mary decides to read from the Cardinal's "Way of Life" during breakfast. All is fine and well until she comes to the part about the maggots on the dead person's body in India (the part about Mother Teresa). When everyone is eating oat meal first thing in the morning and hears that, one is caught off guard.

Pattiis rather humorous. The Sisters were talking about Tom, the usher at the cathedral. Now he is a man who enjoys his job. Of course, he takes liberties. He is given to kissing all the Sisters but he is harmless in the way that flies are. One of the Sisters says that Tom got married laster year. Patti retorts, "Certainly not for the first time!" "Yeah, and his wife is a lawyer." says another. "What?!" a third registers shock. Then Patti sings, as only she can do, "Beauty and the Beast....." right at the dinner table. Mother Regina was trying very hard not to laugh.

Later, at recreation, we all sat around the community room table playing a card game called "PIG". "Patti, are you going to play?" asks one. "No, I just thought I'd look at the troth from here."

Telephone rings, "Hello, Sisters for Life - " Your portress answers. "Did you get your free copy of The Times?"
"Wow! A free copy of The Times?"

225

"That's right," A distinctive Black woman's voice said.

"Well,now," Herself ponders, "I don't rightly know. But I think I know someone who might know. You see, Sister Aquinas is our big periodical reader. Of course "The Times" is a daily, isn't it? That would come under a different category... or maybe you would just say 'newspapers'."

"Mam?"

"Oh yeah, I'll go ask her."

"Hello....."

"I'm still here...."

"No one knows anything about us receiving a free paper. Did you want to send us one?"

"Well, here's what I am gonna do. I am gonna send you your first week's paper free, and then -"

"Second thought, we do get that paper ...... but thanks just the same. God Bless you"

CLICK

APRIL 1, 1993

About that food we had at the reception at the Jeanne Jugan Residence. Well, Sister Francis Mary and I went over to the parish church on the day of the snowstorm/blizzard to scout out the wedding situation. There were four brothers video taping each other with their arms wrapped around each others' shoulders. They were making sport of the weather which was worth commenting about.
 Then, there was the groom's parents, a nice Italian couple who were real friendly and taking everything in stride. They were saying, after of course Sister Francis Mary put the question to them, that they would probably go to their house afterward and have bologna sandwiches. The reception was supposed to be at Marina del Rey, but it got called off on account of the severe storm. Sister Francis likes to have a cause. She seemed satisfied with the input and felt confident that she would head the conversation at our evening meal in the refectory. Several days later, on the Feast of St. Joseph, my partner in action was putting a major dent in the strawberry platter at the Jeanne Jugan Residence . This is the home, or one of the homes, of The Little Sisters of The Poor. Sister Eva was marveling at God's Providence when she told us all that these fancy hors d'oeuvres and

226

pastries that were donated by Marina del Rey. It seems this was the food for that aforementionnend wedding!

How about condiments. Sister Francis Mary kept walking past me as she was setting the table mumbling under her breath, "I have got to fill those sugar bowls......" Once again, The Little Sisters of the Poor have shared their bounty with us; this time, in the form of sugar, but we took our lumps well. Here was a ten pound bag of the granulated sugar that was so hard you could have docked a boat to it. Solution – one grates it. Or, one grates Sister Francis Mary, and takes a chip of the ole block and fills the sugar bowl in block form. When serving tea, one simply says, "One lump? Or two?"

Now that we are discussing food, here is one for you. Patti is the victim in this situation. She is at one of the homes for unwed mothers in a very run-down section of the Bronx. It is predominatly Black and Latino. Patti is teaching basic living skills to some young Haitian women who just came off the boat. She was looking in the fridge for something to fix their breakfast. She spots a big bowl covered in foil in the fridge. She is thinking perhaps there is some fruit or yogurt. "UGH!" It was a live octopus! Patti said it was like something out of "20,000 Leagues Under the Sea". She said it looked like all these black snakes crawling out of the bowl. The tentacles really got to her, but I guess the Haitians really like it.

So then we go to The Franciscans of Renewal. What's on the menu, but Father Bob's doctored-up octopus!! It was too much! I myself had an experience with octopus but I will leave that for now.

How about Sister Francis Mary receivng a personal card in the mail telling her that her special order wedding gown can be picked up. She loved that. She was a blushing novice explaining that one to Mother Regina.

Remember when you were little and you used to make angels in the snow. How about when you made them – when you were not so little.... On that note..................

PALM SUNDAY

After Mass at the cathedral, on Palm Sunday, I overheard this man say to a sister who loves to sing, to my chagrin, and everyone else's, "You have a lovely singing voice." I thought I would die. She said, "Oh, thank you." It was plain it made her day. She has one of these "church lady voices" that sing an octave higher that what they are geared to sing. It also sounds like a quart of milk may have been imbibed beforehand to wash down the chocolate bar she must have eaten. This proud Sister relays in the car on the way back what I was afraid could be lethal particularly since I was sitting beside her.

"Did you know that I heard something today that no one has ever told me." This is where I am wondering if it ever occurred to her to wonder why. Then, she pleasingly, goes on to say, "This man said I hae the loveliest voice." If I had not witnessed it, I would have sworn she had made it up. Then Patti pipes up, "Was that the man with the hearing aid?" I had all I could do to maintain 'til we got back to Throggs Neck.

When we got to our corner where the convent is, and where the traffic directing lady usually is, one says, "Well, she is not here." "No" says another, "Not at noontime." Then another adds, "That is when she goes home for lunch." Sister Francis Mary chimes, "And what does she have for lunch?"

Later, I bumped into Anne, the street crossing guard. She is a Scottish lassie. She told me that she was looking for a Blessed palm which she did eventually find. She said, "I am not Catholic, but I have been putting a palm behind my mother's picture for thirty years." That is very sweet.

Holy Week

Monday of Holy Week, I was the reader at the evening meal in the refectory. Sister Yvonne gave me a book - "The Passion and Death of Our Lord Jesus Chrisst". I was reading the part about the Agony in the Garden. Some parts were poetical. I was very much focused, and even eloquent. I can control my emotions except for bouts of laughter. Other times, I am nervous and stutter. But this time, I forgot myself in this most powerful reading – this sublime prayer. "There was no man's shame and confusion, no man's agony of sorrow and repentance, that Jesus did not share in that dread hour in

228

the Garden of Gethsemane. In that hour Man was atoning for what man had done; God was laying on Him the iniquities of us all; and the human self which was at once one with men and one with His Father in heaven. It was a strife whose misery we can not hope to fathom; we can not see it even in shadow; but we can understand enough to realize the torture that could drag forth the cry: ....." I broke down and sobbed in front of all my Sisters. My voice choked as I uttered,

"O my Father
if it is possible
Let this chalice pass from me."
It was the cry of God Suffering, the cry of the broken Son of God; yet, too it was the cry of the Man of infinite strength. He prayed to the Father for relief but only on conditions. He prayed for Himself, also prayed against Himself, for His Father was greater than He:
"If it is possible
If Thou wilt
Not my will
But Thine be done."

I could not read anymore. In doing so, I was praying in anguish. Only now, do I dare look at where I left off:
"The refrain is constant and unceasing. It is repeated more often than the prayer. The practice of His prayer through life revealed itself no less now; for how many times He had looked for one thing only:
'I came not to do my own will
But the will of Him that sent me?'"

GOOD FRIDAY

(A day no letters were mailed)

The bishops all sat stiffly, removing their mitres agiley in hopes that their skull caps would not not come off with them. To watch them grimace and pat their heads was comical.

Today at the cathedral, a little girl with huge brown eyes and little brown hands looked at me. She took her little hands and touched my shoulder. She was like an angel. She was wearing a pretty, pink dress. There was a partition between her and me so I was hardly expecting this gesture. Then, in front of me, was Sister Agatha's little niece Kaitlyn. She kept poking me. I winked at her and she was trying to mimic my wink back in her contorted sweet face.

Then, she would take my program and hide it and show me her "boo boo" on her knee. She took her hat off and flung it around. She pointed to her sash on her frock informing me that it is silk. She was adorable. I was reminded of life during The Passion.

Afterward, we all greeted the Cardinal. He called me 'Virginia'. Second time that I recall him calling me that. He used to always call me "Heidi". On other occasions, he would say tome "They call the wind 'Mariah'." He is not wearing his ring today, so there was no ring to kiss. One is never sure exactly how to greet him as one does not want to appear "over familiar". I usually wait for him to make the first overture. It was a semi-embrace today and that is how I reciprocated.

XII. Patti the Proculator

Then, the agony in the kitchen with Patti as the proculator and postulant ... a real dish today. It began last night when I was unaware that I had been put on a second day for cooking. Then, I learned that I was cooking with Perfectionist Patti. I got the flour to make the pastry shells for quiche which I understand real men don't eat and I don't blame them after today. Well, it seemed like all the white flour was all gone except for a smithering. So I got the wheat flour out to use. A wheat crust would be nice with a vegetable quiche. My proculator informs me that I am using wheat flour which I had already carefully measured. As a sidenote, I never measure anything. I use a pinch of this, and a doplling of that and it always works out fine. I have been trying to give up my will here in this regard. Patti found a bag of white flour so I switched and used that. We were pressed for time so I did not measure. We had choral practice and we were leaving for the cathedral within the hour. Sister Mary Pio was working on the spinach filling managing to use

230

umpteen dishes, pots and pans. It did not go unnoticed that I had dispensed with the measuring utencils for the crust. My pastry was scrutinized. I was told that I would probably have to throw it out and start again as this texture was not right. A lot of time would be necessary to improve it. This is, of course, after she tells me to mix it right in the pie dish and not in the mixing bowl. I obliged at Patti continued to get disgusted with me. The crust looked fine. I was then directed on how to flute my edges. Mine evidently did not have that "Mrs. Smith" look. I acquiesced on all counts. Sister Mary Pio filled the pie crusts with the blended spinach, ricotta, onion, mushroom and egg filling. I baked them and took them out of the oven forty minutes later. The crust was golden and they looked picture perfect. We were now out the door and on our way to the Good Friday Service. It happened during "The Fourth Word". Patti looked at me and asked, "Did you put the quiches in the refrigerator?" I whispered, "No, it was piping hot…." Well, what was she thinking about this whole time. I can not help but think that she wanted to teach me a lesson. Perhaps she finds me too casual. We returned to the convent close to six o'clock. I went to put the quiches in the oven to reheat them. "Lo and behold, there are no quiches on the counter. Patti seemed to take pleasure in watching me scout around looking for them. I happened to lift the lid on the garbage. There they were – two beautiful looking quiches in the trash. Then, I got the summons read to me about Salmonella and leaving things cooked with eggs out. "Do you know how they raise chickens now?" She asked me. I said, "No, I get my eggs back home from Chilson Hill. My friend Nancy raises chickens. They lay the most beautiful big brown eggs. In fact, I will get a double yoke quite often. My yoke is easy, my burden is light?
This was not the reaction she was expecting. She storms out of the kitchen first giving directions to Sister Mary Pio and me on cooking that tortellini that took New York – that is, the Franciscans had a run on it. Patti returned, "Don't feel bad about this Sister James Mariah because you can be sure that you will never do that again. Believe me! This is how you learn. Next time, you will refrigerate it."
I told her that I was sorry, but I really can not say that I felt bad about it. I mean, I would have eaten it and I still would have served the quiche. In Spain, when they make tortilla, they leave it on the shelf. They don't even refrigerate their eggs. If you were to go to

the store and buy a Freighofer's coconut custard pie, you would find it in the bread section. It would not be refrigerated. I don't think it was a big deal. I would do it the same way all over again even if I had not gone out. There is no heat in our kitchen besides. It was a shame to waste all that good food which hard work went into making. Patti came in to the kitchen giving me orders left and right. It was getting funny at this point. After a day of meditating on Our Lord's Passion, nothing could disturb me. At the same time, I felt drained. She was not about to let this drop. Was in the laundry room folding dish towels when Patti comes traipsing in to tell me that bread is the only thing you can leave out. You even have to refrigerate a cake. "Really?" says I, "Wow, that is interesting. We should all have a class on this."

Went over to The Stations of The Cross afterward. On the walk back, I felt someone's arm on my shoulder. "Sister James Mariah, how would you like to be in on a surprise?"

"Yeah, sure." I couldn't stop grinning because I knew this was a cross for her and she was desperately trying to make amends. This is what I will be doing – tomorrow, I am entrusted, (encrusted?) with the kitchen. I have been given carte blanche to make butter cream frosting for, are you ready, and Easter bunny cake. Yippee!

Later:

I had just set the alarm when my subject managed to set it off when she went into the storage room. I was able to reset it before the whole house woke up. Then the phone rang enquiring about the false alarm. Patti was thanking me profusely.

Next day:

Maura waxes the stairs, Patti falls down them. Then she reads in the Cathlic New York paper that the Haitian women she was working very closely with all have AIDS. Patti learns that she is serving breakfast with me all next week. Now she exclaims, "I will die for sure!"

XII. Easter

On Easter Sunday, an arrangement of red sweetheart roses arrived for one Sister James Mariah. Sister Francis excitedly comes down to the kitchen where herself is preparing the breakfast. "Go on up! Someone sent you flowers!" She was cute caught up in the

moment. "Go see who they are from." I scurried up the stairs.
Sister Lucy helps me with the wrappings. There is a notecard in a small envelope. Slowly, almost like I don't know if I can bear to see who thought of me, I take out the little card which says, "Sister James Mariah – Love, Grandpa".

EASTERTIDE

Received lots of mail including an Express Delivery letter and two parcels. One was from dear Mrs.
Dechame. It had two colorful tins of Brazil Rainforest snacks.
Then, there was a large assortment of Piccadilly English Teas: Earl Grey, Ceylon, Lapsong, and another one which is a man's tea. It smells like 'Grandpa's Pine Tar soap'. I love it! She also included some of those creamy pastel melt in your mouth snow capped butter mints. Georgie used to always get them for Mom from the Fannie Farmer Confectionary shop. Mrs. Dechame also sent a little book called 'Joy of Prayer'. It is a lighthearted little book and I am looking forward to reading it. To top it all off, there was a pretty cotton night dress trimmed with silk blue grosgrain ribbon. It is lovely. I was almost afraid to ask Mother Superior permission to keep it. But ask I did and she said yes to the dress! Of course I covered the $70 price tag. It is so pretty. Saint Hyacinthe should be my patron as I heard she had a passion for silk and nice things.

The other parcel was from home. To anyone else, it might be uninteresting, but, if you are like me and you are in the convent and you like to open mail, then one can appreciate its contents. There were a couple of large tubes of Pepsodent tooth paste – my favorite kind. There were some neutral colored knee socks – I never cared for the nylons. There was a tapestry designed scrap book and a jar of Pond's cold cream. Don't have much time these days to work on my scrap book let alone go up on the roof for reprieve. Now I must find Mother Superior again to report yet another package.
Meanwhile, I am brushing my teeth, sporting my new knee socks, and hoping to fill a scrap book.

In the car, on Tuesday, on our way to Connecticut for a picnic, Sister of Great Importance, a.k.a. Sister Agatha, used the word "actually" a total of thirty-seven times! I lost track of how many times she said "sort of" which she uses as an adjective, no I guess it would be an adverb: e.g. - "It was a 'sort of' quaint little cottage that we stayed in. 'Actually', it was quite lovely, and you should have seen the crocus." I thought I would croak!

We went to Whethersmith's or was it Wethersfield? We were picking up some books that the Jesuits were discarding. We stopped at Sister Yvonne's house on the way back. The sun came out and it was nice to get the fresh air. We made ham sandwiches and we had soda or 'pop' as Patti calls it. I never drank soda back home, but it is a treat now when I can get it. We went to see the creche at the Benedictine nuns, but it was locked. One of the Sisters went to fetch the key. Meanwhile, Sister Mary Samuel, a Dominican Sister from Nashville, who came to visit us for Easter, spotted a trampoline. It was in this outdoor theatre. It reminded me of Michael Whitney and how he was in summer stock in Connecticut. He suggested that if I were seriously interested in acting, that I should get started in summer stock. Next thing I know, Sister Mary Samuel is jumping high on this trampoline – her habit flying! Shoot! This looks like fun. So I got on next. It took me back to my gym days at Saint Mary's:

knee drops, quarter turns, seat drops, leaps in air, v-jumps, and semi-twists. It was a blast! Then Mother Regina gets on stage and starts us in a "Rockette-style" dance. Patti does a soliloquy and Sister Samuel pretends she is "Thinker" posing on a big rock. She is alright. Then I see Patti with a huge stick with a Y-shape on the end. She pretends she is putting out a feeler for water. One of the Sisters now returns with a Benedictine nun and a key. Alas! The Creche! It is unbelievable – real stepping back in time with intricate wooden, hand carved figures. Each face has a distinct personality. The Bethlehem sky is azure with stars alit. A Christmas pageant is held here every year. In fact, this is where that movie "Light of the Stable' with Loretta Young was filmed. A nun who used to be a movie star lives here too. Her name is Sister Mary Hart. She starred in a movie with Elvis Presley. After feasting our eyes on this Nativity, Sister Francis Mary and I go for a walk. We were headed in the wrong direction. We got a good work out. I flag a truck down to get directions back only to take another wrong turn at a "T" in the road. I hail another car down and we just make it back to the Mercy

Sisters' house. There we caught a ride with Sister Lucy. Patti and Sister Immaculata were also in the car. "Don't worry. I know the way. Sister Francis and I got lost enough that I think I can direct you right now." I said. Sister Lucy says, "That's a relief, because we only have four minutes to get there." "No problem.....'

"You see, you take a right where the road turns kitty-cornered ...."
"Yeah, there is, just wait – you will see it."
"That isn't kitty-cornerd!" Patti shouts, "That's what you call "Four dog-legged!"
"Oh, really? I never heard that expression."
"Sister James, just get me there." Sister Lucy says nervously.
"Okay, just head up this hill. You see, when Sister Francis Mary and I got lost, we saw this nun in a white car heading up this way. It had to be one of those Benedictine nuns. For a moment, I thought it was some kind of a shiek or something."
"Sister James, I don't want to be late for Office." Sister Lucy impatiently says.
A car passes by and Sister Immaculata says excitedly so as to contribute in a beneficial way, "Hey, there goes a car with a nun in it!"
"Huh! You're right!" I couldn't get over it. "That's funny, it is going the opposite direction. Gosh, Sister Francis, remember the last time we saw it, it was heading up this very hill. Shoot – it looks like the same car."
"There's a passenger in it." Sister Immaculata added.
"Well, I'll be. I would bet you a dollar to a donut that the little Benedictine nun who I mistook for some kind of a shiek went to pick up a passenger...."
"To bring to Vespers!" Sister Immaculata concludes.
"Precisely."
Sister Francis Mary is in stitches. Patti is singing "Get me to the Church on time -" and Sister Lucy is having fits under her breath.
"Okay, so then we would have to turn around. I was right in seeing one of those nuns from the place where we are going."
It is very quiet ...... " Gee, uh, Sister Lucy, I apologize about the little mix up.... Sister Lucy?"
Sister Francis was funny because when we did turn around, she shouted, "Follow that nun!"
Now in Chapel, at Regina Laus Abbey, we prayed Vespers.

I sat next to Sister Immaculata. It seems that she has not quite got her bows synchronized with everyone else. Either she will extend her rpofound bow during the Glory Be, or, she will start during the last strophe of the Psalm. When we say The Lord's Name, she will do a very pronounced bow which draws all heads to her predieu. Other times, she will remain sitting, when our side should be standing. The best is when she falls asleep in chapel and her book rolls off her lap after her snoring has awakened her.

I saw my dream house right across the way. The architecture was unusual. It was a muted white color and it had gables. It has a front porch too! Then we returned to the other convent of Sister Yvonne's order and enjoyed a baked chicken dinner with wild rice and salad which she prepared. I was very happy for Sister Immaculata as she was craving strawberry shortcake and that is what was being served for dessert. The only drawback, was that one of the Sisters in the original five, has a habit of picking her nose. I tried to offer it up during Lent, but now it is too much. Another one, constantly picks her eyelashes.

Poor Patti. Really, everything I write about is so mundane and nonconsequential. Then, something tragic happens. Yesterday, Patti received a phone call from her sister. Her brother's 24 year old son was killed in an auto accident. He was trying to swerve from hitting a deer, and a car came up behind him. His car flipped over and he was killed instantly. He was her brother's "fair-haired son" as he was affectionately called. He was deeply spiritual too. He has a sister who is a senior at school and another one who is in the eighth grade. Patti was able to get a direct flight home yesterday to Kentucky. Made grasshopper bars for her to take but did not get them out of the oven in time. We all went into the Chapel and prayed a Rosary for Patti and all her family. God grant Albert the happy respose of his soul.

12 April 1993

Too many thoughts are escaping me. It is now 10:00 p.m. Profound Silene has been extended until 10:15 p.m.

There is an image in my mind from the Easter Vigil Mass at the cathedral. It is of the flame at the foot of the Cross – giving light – warmth.
The Cardinal does the Asperges. A droplet on my cheek – the cleansing.

Had trouble getting to sleep Friday night. Was thinking about when my sister Annie and I would go down to the Ti Market and pick out a cake mix and some frosting. The strawberry one comes to mind. We would bake it and have it for dessert after our Sunday dinner. It was a nice memory to revisit.

Was also thinking about that monsignor at the cathedral. Patti says his hair sticks out like a flying saucer and that he must use "Miss Clairol" or something. He is funny to watch. There was this socialite lady with a big beehive hair-do, auburn colored carrying all these roses into the parish house. This monsignor is coming behind her carrying her big fur coat and her pocket book. He notices Rosario and me sitting in the waiting ara, and he says, "Holy Mother of God, they never told me it would be like this in the seminary."

"Mr. Wilfed P leau has arrived. " The portress announced.

Sister Francis Mary ....
My friend Sister Francis Mary! She motions to me to come to see her "secret " in her room. She proudly shows me a big poster of babies on the inside of her closet door. She loves babies and lives for them – much the same way my Aunt Betty does. Then, she giggles like she has gotten away with something, and says, "You better not tell a soul."

One time, in the car on the way to Marycrest for class, little foil wrappers are heard crinkling. Sister Francis Mary has one cheek bulging - appearing like a chipmunk who has just squirreled away her supply – thinking she has gone undetected.

The other day at Dunwoodie, during the Cardinal's reflections, Sister Francis Mary slept. When she did wake, she took three of those same chocolate candy kisses like she had in the van earlier and she

237

placed them on my lap. Next day at the Cardinal's Residence, she says to His Eminence, "Oh, I enjoyed the talks immensely. They were lovely."

The subject of a possible house in the Boston area came up at supper this evening. "This is as far North as I go." Says Patti. I added, "Boston is actually closer to Ti than New York."
"Sister James, you are in New York – at least physically. Though spiritually, it is evident that you are in Ticonderoga."
We were talking about being homesick. "I am not homesick. And even if I was, you would not know it." They all disputed that and picked on me with all the "Grampa" mugs in the cupboard.

Aunt Jane called tonight. The simple fact that I got to take the phone call concerned me. She was upset. Sheila Cross phone from Birmingham, England. Her husband Tony died of a massive heart attack. He was only 58 years old. Dr. Tony Cross served with Aunt Jane in the Solomon Islands for more than twenty years. They came to Ti to visit on several occasions one being on my last home visit.
 They have a son Peter who is about seventeen years of age. They took me to the School House Restaurant when I was home. They are lovely people. Sheila is a nurse. They are very humanitarian.
 Before flying home on my last trip abroad, I visited them in Birmingham. They took me to Coventry Cathedral and to Kennilworth Castle where Shakespeare used to stay. They were very kind to me. They took me to an authentic tavern where we had "pub grub". I saw the famous 'Lady Godiva' statue. I made a key lime pie for them. Peter made pop corn and we watched a movie when I was there (Driving Miss Daisy). They were always going to Third world countries giving medical attention to where it was most needed. It is hard to believe.
I talked to Gramma after. It was so good to hear her voice. We talked about a lot of things. Gramma inferred that some of the family would be down for the next visiting day.
I have been granted permission to write to the Cross's. God rest Dr. Cross.

17 April 1993

The terminator came the other day. I was delegated to show him which rooms had the ants in them. When he came to my room, he was explaining how he ants send out a scout to find food and drink, and when the scout hits mercury so to speak, he sends for the troops. "Yeah," your man says, "You only need a crumb for him to make the scene." Then he looks in my waste basket, and says, "Now see, you got crumbs in here." I thought, my goodness, where else is he going to look. Mother Regina hears a man's voice in the cloister and apprehensively comes out of her room. "It's just the terminator Mother." I told her.

When he got to Rosario's room, he was eyeing her Easter basket. I told him if he goes out by way of the kitchen, I could give him an Easter egg. Meanwhile, he was explaining all the possible theories on how ant, centipedes, and sewer bugs can get in a house.

The other day on my was to the river, my constitutional which is really unconstitutional in that I hardly ever find time to take my walk let along go up on the roof for some fresh air, I bumped into some school girls. They stopped and asked, "Are you a nun or something?" It struck me funny. "Well,sort of," I replied. "I am studying to be a Sister." They seemed interested in the attire of a sister and in what such a one does. I was happy to tell them. The odd thing is, they all attend a Catholic school, but it is run by lay teachers so they are unfamiliar with religious.

THE JAR OF JELLY BEANS

Easter week, all the Sisters pooled their jelly beans into a huge mayonaise jar. Sister Francis Mary said we should have a contest to see who can guess how many jelly beans are in the jar. She even volunteered to count them. I guessed 816, and Mother Assumpta guessed 856. I had a feeling that we were both close. Of course the only hint we got from Sister Francis Mary was, that it was deceptive. I took this to mean that there were probably more in there than met the eye. She had masking tape wrapped four ways around the jar. I tried to figure out a quarter of the container and then multiply it by four. Maura guessed 700 and something jelly beans. The correct number was 742. Maura wins. So came the retorts, "Sister Francis Mary, are you sure there are 742 jelly beans in there?!" She proudly replies, "Yes, because I counted them twice."

Longing to hear music, I took my walk. The pipes were beckoning me. A couple of blocks over a young man was playing 'Amazing Grace' on the bagpipes.

17 April 1993

Some people sure like to throw their weight around. The Superior is away, so we have an "acting Superior" who is very abrasive. I know she has had her own personal trials to contend with, e.g. - health, but she just grates me. Besides her over use of the word "actually", she is very pretentious. Yesterday at lunch, she declares, "Perhaps someone wishes to have half of my grapefruit. It is, afterall, of the distinct ruby red variety." I will take those "silent" meals please.
Then, she goes on to describe her ailing 'Aunt' which rhymes with 'font'. I have Aunts (ants) and my Aunts are killer Aunts, thank you very much! Then, she mentions putting flowers in the vase which is of course a "Voz". They are not from the Orient, but they are inexpensive vases from the funeral home. I just can't stomach her.
God forgive me. She is very bossy and she undermines every thing I say. She refuses to address me with my religious name. She thought she was going to die after a lump was discovered which was benign. I gave Sister Agatha a medal of Saint Peregrine and only then, and it was very hard for her to get the words out, did she call me by my religious name. I guess God is going to use her to help me grow in virtue or die a martyr.
Yesterday, she was a real jerk. Here I thought I had forgiven her for depriving me of doing the Irish jig with the Wolfe Tones when I singled her out to come with me. Then, I am portress again on Friday. Fridays, we have Exposition of the Blessed Sacrament and Confessions al day. Therefore, the answering machine is supposed to be left on – that which I was not aware of. I did have it on for Father's talk and
for the end but not in-between. That of course is when the phone rings. I answer it. I have to report all the calls to the acting superior. I had to interrupt her prayers to relay the message. This really

ticked her off because she did not want to talk to this woman on the phone who by the way, was schizophrenic. Sister Agatha was a psychologist before entering. She told me to give the woman (I wasn't sure which one) the information that she wanted. I had to return to the Chapel to get the phone number which Sister Agatha tells me is in the office. I looked but I could not find it. So I had to go back and tell her. I was trying to do my duty while she was growing very impatient with me. Finally, I did get the number and assistance for the caller. Then it is my turn to go to Confession. A great feeling of peace overcame me as I came out. The phone rings again, and I answer it. I tried to be quiet. I then go to my predieu, and the wicked witch of the North, south, East and West presents me with a note indicating that the answering machine is on. I turn towards her and whisper, "Oh, do I leave it on?" She frowns at me and directs me out to the hall.

"Let's not talk in chapel." She demands. I certainly was not looking for any conversation. She continues, "You know, you have a problem with silence. You really have to work on it. And why didn't you have the answering machine on?!"

"I did not know I was suppose to have it on. I am sorry if I broke silence." Though I could not imagine how I had.

No, she could not let it drop. She went on with some more banter. I appeared submissive but I felt bruised and misunderstood. I had all I could do to regain my peace. Here it is 36 hours later, and I am still feeling the effects. God help me. It is difficult. I meant no disrespect in the Presence of The Blessed Sacrament as she would infer. She derives great satisfaction fo squelching someone who is happy and free and to remind that someone of who is in charge. My faith was tried and I had to go to my room for reprieve though I know I should have sought solace in the Presence of The Blessed Sacrament. I did return once I got hold of myself. This is where one has to balance his emotions with intellect and act spiritual. I am reminded that I am human, and nothing without the grace of God. I state my human feelings which I am not proud of; the paradox of that statement, is that it is pride-filled. I don't know how I am going to make it. I dread the thought of her being the Superior. It is a liklihood. I have to have faith in The Holy Spirit. Could she possibly get hit with a good dose of humility?

Last night during Compline, Sister Margaret picked up the candle beside the Mother Mary statue for the vigil ceremony. She got a piece of eucalyptus caught in it from the floral arrangement at Our Lady's Feet. All of a sudden, like she was waiting for some koala bear to attack it or something, she bursts into laughter triggering a chain reaction. I loved this. Poetic justice. Was not everyone then being disrespectful? Would everyone be reprimanded? The giggles lasted throughout the 'Salve Regina'.

Then, today at lunch, Sister-in-Charge says, for effect only, "Isn't it wonderful to laugh in chapel?" Such hypocrisy. Not only that, but several other Sisters went to Sister Agatha's predieu during Exposition to ask her one thing or another. She neither scolded them or had them step outside the chapel. She could hardly look me in the eye today. But I looked her in the eye when she recounted two occasions when she had to leave the chapel on account of laughter. I don't object to that. It is just a case of calling the kettle black. As long as she is the center of attention and she is running the show, then she is happy.

ROSARY CONGRESS

What a beautiful weekend! Father Larry who offers Mass in our Chapel each weekday has really put forth a lot fo effort in organizing The Rosary Congress. It was held this past weekend at eh Crdianl Spellman High School. The Image of Our Lady of Guadalupe was there for the occasion. This one was touched to the real Tilma in Mexico. Miraculous phenomena has been associated with this one. The atmosphere was intense – filled with prayer. There was Exposition of The Blessed Sacrament throughout the weekend. The Sacrament of Penance was readily available. Father Groeschel opened the Congress with a theme of praying for The Church – and for those hurting in The Church; for those who serve and those who are served. It was very good. This gal from Denver, named Slyvia, sang the Rosary. We all joined in. It was very beautiful. There was a man named Mr. Vaccaro. He handed out long-stemmed roses to present to Our Lady of Guadalupe during each "Hail Mary". Sister Francis Mary got to bring up the first one which was only fitting as it was her birthday. I brought up the last one. She and I were the only two Sisters who received this honor.'

242

I met so many interesting and good people. I thought to myself, "If this isn't 'The Church Militant'."

Various people spoke. They shared their testimonies of healing, conversion, or other great stories of witness. People were deep in prayer – praying with all their being. Joy, tears, sharing, comraderie, and laughter – these are what one left with, and then one did not want to leave or have it end. It was such a feeling to be lost in The Presence!

I met a Brother Robert who had a birthday the next day. He will be 54 years old. He has these thick plastic framed glasses and he has huge dimples. He is short and he has a thick head of hair just starting to grey. He is from Syracuse and he is of Italian ancestry. He went out of his way to meet me in the foyer of the Cardinal Spellman High School. I shook hands and introduced myself. He said, "Sister James Mariah – you know, I never heard that name 'Mariah' until two years ago when my great niece was born."

"Oh really? That is interesting."

"Yes, 'Mariah' means "Gift of God"." Brother Robert continued.

"Oh, I had not heard that, but I like it very much."

He went on to tell me that his little niece has something wrong with her pancreas. He turned serious and asked if I would pray for her. I said that I would.

All seriousness aside, Brother Robert is a character. He said to me after lunch, "Hey Sister James, what did they do? Did they stop taking them young? I see you got a "whitey" in there – a regular Gramma Moses. How old is Granny anyways?"

"You are terrible Brother Robert! Well, she is a grandmother and don't you now that white light up the face."

"Something must have lit up." He laughed. Then he asked how old she is.

"She is not that old Brother Robert."

"Hey, don't be telling her I said that." Sister Immaculata just happened to be the convenient target. He was enjoying himself more than anything. Later, he asked if he could get a photo with me in it. Then throughout the day whenever he passed me by, Brother Robert would say, "I am going to tell Mother Assumpta on you." Should mention that Brother Robert is a good person. He works with alcoholics, drug abusers and the homeles. Soon, he will be working with those afflicted with AIDS. God Bless him.

243

I was starting to head out the door for lunch when a lady came with
the singer and asked if Sister Francis and I would like to be her
guests for lunch. We had a bag lunch in the car and it was absolutely
killing Sister Francis Mary to admit it in the face of this much more
lucrative offer. Her conscience got the better of her, so we
graciously declined. On the way out the door, Sister Francis
himmed and hawed and stewed how she would be around in case an
invitation for dinner should arise. Or, at least she would make it
come her way. The funny thing was that Sister Immaculata forgot to
make herself a sandwich that morning. Sister Francis, right on cue,
escorted her back to the cafeteria to scout out that offer that was
made earlier. Sure enough, she is sitting pretty in the cafeteria with
a rose at her table. The two ladies, along with Sister Immaculata,
were enjoying cookies and soda. She is too much. Oh, and she got
to bring up The Gifts during The Offertory too. I think she still
thinks it is her birthday.

On my way out the door to get my picnic lunch, I met a man – a
John Murphy. His is a very tragic story. He is a parapalegic –
paralyzed from the neck down. He broke his neck as a result of a
trampoline accident when he was fifteen years old. He must be in
his early forties now. He has turned this tragedy to The Lord. He
gives a powerful witness carrying The Cross. He does not mope or
feel sorry for himself. In fact, he is rather triumphant about the
whole thing. He has a good sense of humor and he prays beautifully
– powerfully! He carries a True Relic of The Cross which he invited
us to venerate. I kissed it, and touched my medal to it as well as the
garnet stone Rosary which Chrissy and David gave me when I
entered. Then, I gave him a big thank you hug. I could only admire
this man. With his paralized arm, he patted my hsoulder. He and his
wife have adopted four children. He had one of his care givers with
him. Her name is Cynthia. She is a lovely girl with dark curly hair,
brown eyes, and olive skin. She appeared to be in her late twenties.
She had stopped me, and extended her hand, "I overheard you say
your name was 'Sister James Mariah'. Your name means The Holy
Spirit."

"Really? Wow! That is beautiful!"

"Yes, they call the Wind Mariah and The Wind is The Holy Spirit".
Then she said that she would like to talk with me later. She said
that she felt drawn to me.

I went out to have my sandwich. Mary Jane (Sister Peter) joined us. She looked very well. I had not seen her since she left. She had good coloring and she looked rested. Still, she had to have felt lonely.

A Sister Anne Marie from the Parish Visitors in the Bronx was on the grass with a group of us. The funny thing was, she told me that "Mariah" was a very old and special name for Our Blessed Mother – one that was not much known about. I could not get over this. All, in the course of fifteen minutes, three different people interpret my religious name with three different meanings. I also met my share of "James" - all of whom are praying for me, and I for them. That was a fun day.

Then Father Sorgei did the healing service. He read the Gospel, and he spoke mightily. He processed all around with The Monstrance – The Blessed Sacrament. We sang and prayed and then so many people went up to get prayed over and/or to be anointed. There was a child in a wheelchair. At first I thought it was a boy with short, dark, wavy hair but it was a six year old girl named Melissa. She had a tube in the back of her head. She was all bloated – filled up with fluid. It broke my heart to look at her. She looked uncomfortable. Father Sorgei and Father Larry were laying hands on her. I felt compelled to go to her. I put my hands on her too. She was crying. Her mother and father were shedding tears too along with her two cousins – Steve and Jennifer. The father's name is Paul and the mother is Dariah. They are of Spanish descent. Melissa had just turned six the previous Monday, but she was way beyond her years in suffering.

On my way to the washroom, I met another family who had given testimony. Their baby girl was healed when doctors did not hold out any hope. Today, the baby's three year old brother was "slain in the spirit" – the innocence and receptivity of a child. I met all this family's extended family including one of the "James" - Mr. James Mallon.

Sister Francis Mary was in her glory because Father Larry said that a veil was good for a dinner and tonight was Italian. We all went into the dining area. I met Mr. James Mallon by the rolls, and later had dessert with Mr. and Mrs. James McGraw. At this table, a fellow named Marty told of his conversion story on his trip to Medjugorie.

He had a zealous look about him. He was probably in his mid-thirties; tee-shirt and jeans and very likable.

Earlier in the day, I met a homeless woman, a Pat Ninevah or something like that. She was intelligent but you could feel her sense of despair. I felt totally helpless in this situation. She had heard of Ticonderoga, but she kept saying, "The Almighty God had things in store for her." and that she attended "The School for the Homeless".

She also said that she was interested in religious life, and/or Catholic shelters or homes for the homeless women. She grew up in the turbulent sixties. She was sipping some tea from the styrofoam cup and she was wondering what the suggested donation was. I said, "Not to worry, I am having tea and I did not put in anything." I said that upon meeting her before I realized her plight. I felt bad then because I saw the dignity she bore. She did not want it if it ws not free for the taking. I watched Pat go to her cart. I offered her the soda and cookies that Sister Immaculata had given me. I assured her that she was doing me a favor if she could take them off my hands; plus the fact that they are oatmeal and no one should turn down an oatmeal cookie.

Getting back to Mr. James McGraw – he sent me some beautiful photographs he had enlarged of Our Lady of Medjugorie. He gave them to Mother Regina to give to me. He also include one of those little blue Pieta prayer books.

Now I must set the alarm for Sister Lucy and turn in. I am two weeks behind in writing down my thoughts, but tonight, this all came back to me vividly because it was such a special event. Thanks be to God and His Holy Mother.

The Agony and the ....

It happened. I predicted it. It came as no great surprie to anyone, and I believe it was vocalised sooner than had been intended because I called it in the face of the Superior who may very well have mentioned it to the Cardinal. The idea was for all the Sisters to visit Mother Seton's Shrine and pray to The Holy Spirit on what was

246

clearly already established. This is not to doubt that the Holy Spirit may have worked previously – only we did not go through the motions of what we ought to have. I believe that this was somewhat to do with me along with the timeframe was tight. Any one can pray any time for any thing under the sun. Right now, it is taking every ounce of faith I have to believe that The Holy Spirit is going to raise up one to take the helm. It was all a ruse. It had been established hitherto. It was rather obvious because Mother Assumpta would soon be leaving us. Her commitment will have ended. She came, she saw, and yes, she conquered. The other faction is/was Mother Yvonne Mary. She assisted Mother Regina, but now, she would be gracious and bow out – in effect – pass the torch. She will adhere to the Cardinal's wishes, but in her heart, she would just as soon return to her community in Connecticut where she is Superior. Ultimately, the Cardinal would like the community he founded to get off the ground – indeed, to become Pontifical. In order for this to take place, the community must be self-supporting, and have their own Superior. Ideally, this would happen while the Cardinal is still the Archbishop of New York. Enter the Cross. Enter Sister Agatha who made the comment in my presence, "Oh but to ride on the red tails of the Cardinal."

All week I have been in turmoil over my speculations which incidentally were right on the mark. I have been made aware of my own weakness. Is this so that I will only look to my God? Pray tell me... because I have been seriously questioning whether or not I can submit to one whom I find most unfair and inconsistent. Personally, she can not stand me. Admittedly, the feeling is mutual.

One has to believe in the power of the Office, and separate all else. One has to believe this is the voice of God and give up one's will, complying in humble obedience – being totally submissive. What is worse, is that in Father Gambari's book on the Vows which we are studying, one, that is – me, has to take my Vows to the Superior, and only then at her discretion – with her approval. I would rather die.

Of course I want to take them. It I truly desire to be holy and if I really love God, then this is the ultimate tst of that love. And for my God, I shall die of love because I am not here for myself, or for anyone --- only for Him. Then, Please God, my soul will be spared through it all. Please God have mercy on my family – rid me of this festering inside. I will to love, I will to love, I ....

Thus it was, after the Entrance Mass of our latest postulant, Sophia from New Mexico. Sophia is a lovley gal of 31 years of age. She is of half Columbian and half Austrian descent. She looks like she could be a contestant in the Miss Universe Pageant. It was kind of anti-climatic in that her ceremony had to be precedented by the Cardinal's announcement of the new Superior-elect ---my nemesis Sister Agatha. I sat through it motionless, fully aware before Mass began, that this was coming. Everyone felt it coming I sensed. Interestingly enough, everyone was still – almost expressionless.

When I was reading the Petitions during Mass, I happened to glance at Sister Agatha. Her face was writhing in pain trying to contain herself for the pending announcement – that which has been her goal. All made worthwhile – her goal accomplished.

Accomplished? Then it came back to me, that paper that she left in the laundry room. It had "Goals for the Sisters of Hope". It was typical for her to leave that lying around as she is high-strung and does things hastily. She is neither calm, nor approachable. She talks in a condescending manner to me. She squints her eyes as she can not look at me straight in the eyes. I sat in front of her when His Eminence made this most dreaded announcement. I met the Crucifix with my eyes, and through this struggle, I literally felt grace pour through me in spite of having these mixed thoughts and feelings. Then the Cardinal said, "Well, do I hear an Amen' or ----"

So everyone clapped. It was not spontaneous. We had to be prompted. I mean I know what to do, but I could not even will to do it subconsciously. However, at the Cardinal's command, I joined in the applause.

All I could think of was when Grampa called on Sunday evening, and she was not going to let me talk to him. He evidently put up an argument. She said, in front of everybody in the community room, He is a little confused, isn't he?" And how I wanted to say, where is the compassion such as I showed you during your trial? What about when your sister called at a random time and I ran and got you so you would not miss the call. Have you forgotten? Now I had to exit the chapel and wish this person well. The Cardinal gave her a big hug. Mother Regina did too as did the Cardinal's attorney. I suppose Father Matt congratulated her warmly too. The two sisters in front of me laughed, a release?, and then they went through the motion of a hug. Myself – next, I refused to be phoney. I would be

248

cordial – but, no more, no less. No words came out. I simply looked Sister Agatha straight in the eyes, and gently went through the motion of a semi-hug at best. Later, I was to learn, that my reaction disturbed her. It was also noted by the keen eye of the Founder as well as by Mother Regina. I did not stick around to "ooh, and aah" either. Rather, I went to help with dinner. I was not scheduled, but I figured they can always use an extra hand. I was solemn, and no words came out. Mother Regina came to me, real surprised that I would know how to conduct myself – she being cognizant of my feelings. "Sister James, I am real proud of you. It is God's Will." Then, she sort of hugged me. I nodded at her, and again, said nothing.

I got through dinner. Why is it, I wonder does anyone else not notice that no one sits beside this particular Sister except for Rosario who is as non-threatening as they come. Sister Aquinas will sit next to her and cow tow to her – predictable in her flip way. Then, she sits on a corner which does not leave room for another person. I wonder what others are thinking – what I have dared to say to the Superior, and only then, because I was desperate. I can not say regrettably because that is exaclty how I feel. Later this evening, Sister Agatha comes along while I was washing dishes – trying to act in her new role. She tries to pat me on the shoulder which was very unnatural for her. I feigned to be receptive. "You seem a little sad these days.?" She tries her psychology to win me over as my serene reaction has baffled and perhaps even embarrassed her. I hesitated.

I had no desire to confide my feelings to her – especially, since she is the cause of them. Deep down she knows or surmises as much. I was not about to say, "I am less than enthusiastic about you being the Superior." Though that is what I was thinking. For her efforts, insincere as they were, and a little late at that, I said, "I have been concerned about my grandfather." She could understand that and that is always a true statement. It gave her the courtesy of being left off the hook.

That night after Compline, I did turn around, and rest my hand on her shoulder. I do have a conscience. It is arduous – damn arduous.

Next Day - Mother's Day

After Mass, Mother Regina wished me a Happy Mother's Day. I wished her one too. While not mothers in the natural sense, we take on a spiritual motherhood. This is particularly so in our charism to save unborn babies and be a maternal comfort to unwed mothers and to anyone in need. Helene sent me a Novena of Masses for Mother's Day. Then Mother Regina said to me, "I've got something to tell you. Well, I am going to tell everyone, but I'll tell you first, so don't tell anyone. Go on up (in the office) and call your mother, and wish her a Happy Mother's Day...." She looked at me. I just knew I couldn't. I mean, if I was sneaking the call, then I could. But with permission, on this particular day, and feeling the way I felt – I thought sure that would come through in my voice. I did not want to do that to my Mother on Mother's Day. She looked at me, "Sister James, you can do it. Go on up and call her." Out of obedience, I complied. As I dialed, I cried. Thank God – the line was busy. Perhaps later and then I could regain my composure.

Just before we left for Connecticut, we would be going to the Dominican House in New Haven . It is opposite the Yale campus. We would also visit Father Malady in Cromwell, and then to North Guilford to see the Dominican Nuns there. They have the old style Rosary Beads that we would be getting to go with our new habits – to wear cinctured to our waist.

I tried to call home again. Oh shoot, Rosario is heading for the phone. Not sure what three minutes means to her if it is anything like the way she does her laundry. If so, forget it. I must interject this tidbit about Rosario. Patti said that any time you hear the washing machine shaking up a storm, you can be sure that Rosario is doing laundry. She packs it jam-full and then she will put it on the small load cycle. She mixes everything in – darks and lights. Whether it is because she is from the Phillippines or the fact that she is in Medicine, I do not know. This week, I separated her colors and I used two separate machines for her laundry. I put her delicates in a lingerie bag and I hung them up to dry. Rosario is a very private person, so she just chucked everything into the dryer – including what I had just hung up.

I tried again with the phone to get my mother. Mom answered,
"Happy Mother's Day…." I managed.
"Oh what a lovely surprise!" Came that beautiful voice on the other
end.
"Do you know who I am?"
"Oh yes, Little Virginia – and how did this happen?" Then I told her
how Mother Assumpta let us make three minute calls to our mothers.
I tried earlier but the line was busy.
"That's what happens when you have eleven brothers and sisters."
She chuckled, and, as a release, so did I.
I explained that I was on my way out the door but be sure to wish
Daddy a Happy Birthday for tomorrow.
"Oh, couldn't I just put him on -"
"Hello Pineapples!" I was afraid to say anything because one thing
about my father is that he is very intuitive. He can pick up on
anything.
"Hi -"
"Are you manning the switchboard today?"
I laughed – very hard.
"Get your buns up to Ticonderoga!" Daddy had a way of diverting
any possible emotion that could pour forth. It was good to hear his
voice.
"Happy Birthday Father – a little early, but did you get my card, that
is, my makeshift card?"
"Yes, I did. Thank you very much." Then he asked about the
Cardinal, and he said, "I love you."
I was looking out the window pretending to see if the cars had pulled
out yet. I heard the words, and yet, they were too painful to
confront. But I did mutter something to the effect of "Same here -" I
hung up.
Hmmm – I was wondering. My father asked me to come home.
Strange.

Father Jacob and me

Seeing Helene's good friend Father Jacob was a nice consolation of the day. It was at the Dominican Church, Saint Mary's in New Haven, Connecticut where Father Jacob is currently stationed. All of the Sisters were making their way to the washroom, and at the last moment, I went too. Everyone had gone to the church when I came out. Father Jacob seemed to be waiting for me. "I'll walk you over." He said to me.

"Oh, that would be very nice."

He asked me how I was doing. He told me about Helene and how she had met my sister Mary in Florida. He told me that soon the children would be baptized. Helene would make sure of that. I rejoiced on hearing that - how the Lord put Helene in my path and how He is using her now. The timing could not have been better.

We attended a Gregorian Mass. They sure have the freshest smelling incense. Father then gave us a tour of the church. This is the birthplace of the Knights of Columbus. The founder, Father McGiveny is entombed behind the altar. Father Jacob gave me further literature on him and the history.

I was joking with Patti about the necessity of having a bag at the Rosary Congress – for picking up free calendars and holy cards. Sister Sharon used to carry a bag when we went to book reviews. My friend Bill McDonald, who I used to work with at Basin Harbor, used to call me "the bag lady". He gave me a beautiful tote bag with a Currier & Ives picture on it. He also sent me a sand dollar and wrote me a nice letter recently.

Patti cracks me up. The other night, in Monsignor Smith's class, she is slipping off her shoes in her stockingless feet scratching her feet – or, rather the bookrack under her desk was.

Sister Francis Mary gave me a month's notice as to what kind of cake she wanted for her birthday. "All good people are born in April." She declares. She may be right. Father Halligan is born in April. Speaking of which, Sister Francis Mary did the funniest thing. Father Halligan is noted for buying these incredible and costly ice cream cakes on birthdays, feast days, and holidays. Sister Francis said that she did not want Father doing that, spending all that money on her. She said, "I would rather have a Mass." She wrote Father a letter to arrange it. She has the right idea. First, she was afraid that Father would miss her birthday as he was going to be away on that particular Friday. Incidentally, she had me make her a white cake with chocolate frosting. I also asked Sister Yvonne if we could get a new mop and give it to Sister Francis for the refectory as she is always saying how she wishes she had her own mop. Sister Francis was presented with a new mop with a huge bow, (from the funeral home), on it. I put a note on it: "This is Sister Francis Mary's mop". She loved it. She loved the attention more than anything. She is very childlike. She just wants to belong and be loved.

With that year older, came the more "set in her ways" disposition. I was painting in the basement when I discovered a great big broken bulb which needed to be disposed. There was an empty box in the kitchen which I retrieved to put this in. Sister Francis comes out, "Hey! What do you think you are doing? You can't have that! I just put those there and cleaned them out!" She was shouting. "I am sorry, I was....."

"Well, wrap it in newspaper!" She snapped.

I then went to make lemonade. She says, "Don't you think I can do anything. Get out of here!" It was as though I was one of her first graders from way back when. She hauled off and spanked me. Next time, believe me, I tried to avoid her, I asked her about her sister who was scheduled to have an operation. I had made the mistake of praying for her during the petitions on the scheduled day. Sister Francis announces, right during the Office, "She didn't have the operation." Then she scowled at me. This morning she warns me, "Don't be praying for my sister!" The funny thing was that Sister Lucy had mentioned her at Vespers this evening.

Later, Sister Francis asked me to go for a walk with her. I think she felt a little guilty though nothing was said.

Wanted to mention how Father Anthony sang this beautiful song about a mother during the homily. He sang it acapello. It was very sweet – and unencumbered – coming from Nigeria it would be that way – natural.

"You people." It is always "you people". It is never "Sisters". Sister Agatha addresses us thus.

Have learned to sew. Would not be a bona fide Sister if I did not know how to sew. Am working on the sleeves of our new habit. I sewed them all wrong. They are being ripped out. Mother Regina showed me a flat stitch. She says in her Southern accent, "Oh Honey, this is all wrong, but, it is okay." She says things nicely.

Was sitting beside her at dinner the other night when Maura passed around a plate of assorted cookies. I could not decide which one to take. I had already touched the one shaped like a pretzel. Was wondering if I could get away with putting it back and taking one of those Lido shortbread ones that has chocolate in the middle. My arm went back and forth in hesitation, but thinking better of it, I settled with my first choice. This was not lost on Mother. She patted me on the back reassuring me that the right thing had been done.

We have all been busy cleaning. We break for Mid-day prayer only to read, "My soul lies in the dust" and "O Lord, hear me complaining" (when prayer imitates life).

One thing I do not like, are big boiler rooms with all these pipes. Sometimes I have nightmares about them and being trapped therein. Here I was, perched in-between a maze of pipes, painting in the basement. Something seemingly of no consequence except Sister Agatha was close by with her acid solution. She told me to wash the outlets and the switch plates three different times. She reminds me of one of those types whom I would have been stuck with as a nanny in an au pair situation – ridiculously demanding. Maybe I will adopt Bishop DuBois as my patron. He said they could bury him right under the door step because the Irish bishops walked all over him when he was alive.

Now I must lock up. As bell ringer, I will lose twenty minutes in the morning.

May 15th – Ordination at Saint Patrick's Cathedral

The Sisters of Hope received an invitation from the Rector at St. Joseph's Seminary for the Ordination Mass of eight new soon to be priests. I had only seen one Ordination in my life. It was in my hometown parish of St. Mary's. Bishop Brzann celebrated it for Father Bucaria. What stands out in my memory, is how Father Bucaria lay prostrate on the marble altar floor. I was thirteen at the time. It was a lengthy ceremony but I knew I was witnessing a great Sacrament.

I flagged down Officer Klosterman and we got a good parking spot on this day. Coincidentally, Maura's brother Mark was parked right in front of us. Maura was elated.

Words like 'powerful' and 'beautiful' seem trite to describe what we witnessed. Eight young men processed in the cathedral with their vestments draped over their arms while joinging the choir in singing 'All Creatures of Our God and King'. I thought of Father Dinan as we learned that one of the incumbent's father was taken to the hospital with a heart attack. This young man was of fair complexion with fine brown hair. He had sensitive blue eye and he was slight in stature. I hope his father will be alright.

Watching the 'Laying on of Hands' by all the priests in th Sanctuary was a sight to behold. The Cardinal and the Bishops, and the Rector, Monsignor Powers embrace each of the neophytes. Monsignor Powers is brimming with pride with his proteges.

We went to get blessings afterward from the new priests- depending on the length of the lines. Sister Francis Mary just "bulldozes" through the crowds. I went to three of the new priests, one being Reverend Michael H. whose father was takento the hospital earlier. He was scurrying out of the cathedral now.

This was indeed very special and wonderful to be present at this Ordination of these fine men. Happy, Holy Perseverance.

May 25th, 1993
XIII. Sister Francis Mary!!!

I am ready to clobber Sister Francis Mary. As much as I love her, and she gives me great writing material, she drives me up the wall at times. She will ask me to go for a walk when I am exhausted and she has an ulterior motive. I am merely her appendage so that she can go over and talk to Father Paul. When we get there, she is oblivious to the fact that I am there, and she completely excludes me from the conversation. It is kind of a left-handed compliment in that she trusts me. Can always count on Sister Francis for humiliations. She usually makes jokes at my expense. "You should hear about her sordid love life!" Father Paul had a meeting with a young parishioner. Sister asks him, "So how did you make out with that young girl?" Then she turns beet red and erupts in laughter. She has me making applesauce muffins for breakfast now because Father Paul will be here and those are his favorite. I don't mind as I enjoy baking. It is just when a short walk turns into an unplanned hour visit, it gets tiresome. She did the same thing to me the other night. She springs it on me. Father Paul is leaving for his new assignment so it will be hard on Sister Francis Mary.

Sister Francis is my sewing partner. She was saying how Father Halligan said she failed to mention her age on her birthday, and out of humility she should own up to it. She told him to mind his own business as he was getting too curious.

The other day, Sister Francis was recounting a story about her teaching the first graders. She said the Religion books were a little graphic when it came to Adam and Eve. She said to her students, "Alright class, time to take out the crayons and color your favorite outifts on Adam and Eve so they don't catch cold." She added that some had Adamin a tuxedo and Eve – in, a, well, an "Eve"-ning gown!

Sister Immaculata got me going during Compline last night. She is usually very controlled. Sister Francis Mary is heb (short for hebdomadarin) meaning that she is in charge of intoning the Psalms. She starts with this dragged out, mournful sounding "God, Come to my assistance." I was convulsing in stifled laughter after Sister Immaculata started to lose it. Mother Regina was even having trouble maintaining composure. Mother has moved me in front of her now.

Sister Yvonne has departed us. I am sorry to see her go. She was very good to me. I found her very approachable and compassionate. She would take the time to listen. For some reason, some of the Sisters did not care for her. She gravitated towards me knowing that I would accept her. She had my name at Christmas for the 'Secret Santa'. I enjoyed her sense of humor. I asked permission from Mother if I could do a farewell dance in Sister Yvonne's honor. Sister Francis said, "It better not be long." I danced to a piece by Nana Mouskouri called 'Sweet Surrender'.

The next morning, in my mail box, I found a card from her with a tile cross on a piece of sanded wood. A Celtic cross was embroidered on it. She had written that a Benedictine nun had given it to her on her Perpetual Profession. I was very touched by this gesture. I washed her apron for her that which I used to wear when she was away. She told me to keep the apron. I am sentimental and I appreciate this.

We had our first visiting day of the year last Sunday. Grampa called. He sounded sad. Tizz and Ricky and their boys came for visiting day. Aunt Betty came. Oh how I missed her. She is great. She presented me with some ragweed which was cute especially since I am allergic to it. Gramma Burleigh came. Georgie made it and Annie and her daughters, Francine and Mary, came too. Mom,

Sarah and cousin Joseph came along with Aunt Mary and Uncle Mike and cousin Michael. Later in the day, my cousin Tom McDonald and his sweet fiancee Linda surprised me. Jane and Alexandra were planning to come but Alexandra got sick. Lizzy did not feel well either. It was great to see everybody. Sister Yvonne made it a point to meet my family. Father Halligan arrived with his lovely sister Betty. It was so nice that my family could meet them. My oldest brother Georgie is very dry. He does not miss much. He says, "Hey Virginia, how come some people around here are in 'plain clothes'?" One of the former sisters had just passed by. I was trying to shush him and it did not help matters that Annie was laughing. Then, without missing a beat, he adds, "What did they do – take the razor away too." Grampa joked about nuns getting a mustache in the convent.

It seems all my family, including Gramma Burleigh, took a fit of laughter during the May Crowning outdoors. Mother Regina was reading a prayer when a DC-10 flew overhead making her voice inaudible. When it was time to join in on the hymn, Uncle Mike was seen showing where the number had been cut out of the misalettes. More laughter ensued. I guess I come by it naturally albeit misunderstood. Maura's family has a good sense of humor too.

Bob was waiting out in the van. I tried to get him to come on inside to get something to eat. He said he was not taking any chances with the van. I assured him that it would be safe. He did not want to chance it with the TV and all the other features it had. He said, "Yeah, well it's also safe in Gramercy Park on a Sunday afternoon in front of a Jewish synagogue." That is where he went to have his lunch.

I helped Joseph put some stuff in the van. Patti says to everyone in the family, "This Sister James has got her own general store. You know, she has the most hard to find things you can imagine - - - like shoe laces with Elvis presley on them!"

"Well, my general store just got depleted. However, a new shipment has arrived."

Everyone laughed.

We observed ole Bob in the van with his shoes off, sliding door open in the van. Whooo Doggie! "That's okay Bob, you stay there. We got the trunk. On second thought, you want to put these in there Joseph." More laughter. It was a good day.

Now it is May 25th. I am exhausted in every way. Had a card from Wanda yesterday. It was sent from Salzburg. Her husband Wolfgang has died. She said she could feel the strength of my prayers. She said that she would call me when she returns to St. Thomas. She has a beautiful Faith. She is relieved that Wolf is out of pain. Wanda has suffered a great deal in life. It seems my best friends in life are those who have overcome the most severe odds.

Received some distressing news tonight. Mother let me take the call. It was Grampa. He apologized but he said there was a little emergency. Prayers were requested for Uncle H.G. A specialist from England was going to operate on him on Thursday for malignant colon Cancer. He is only 61 years of age. This is not his first bout with it. Gramma Burleigh prayed fervently and a previous surgery was deemed successful.

Sometimes one wonders if it is not better to go through life with someone to share the joys and sorrows. One could draw strength from the other. Both would be free and happy. No rules to break, write all the letters one wishes, see your family whenever you wanted and eat globs of ice cream cake! One could still be good, attend daily Mass and pray. The praying would be free and fervent and those joys would be offered to the Almighty as well as the sorrows. I guess one would not give the same kind of witness as in religious life. That is supposed to be a response to a higher call. Only, if that call can not be answered perfectly, would not one be better off in the noble vocation of the married state. That is a sacrament too. The holiest people I have met are not necessarily in religious life – enter my mother, Gramma Burleigh. I need some supernatural strength and graces. I am weak. God forgive me. I desire consolations.

I have asked permission to attend my cousin's wedding which is literally twenty minutes from here. Of course this is out of the question. My other first cousin is getting married, and again, I am not permitted to attend. These are the sacrifices that we must make.

We had the instructors from Dunwoodie for dinner the other night. Monsignor Smith is dry and witty. He resembles Fred Astair. His expressions crack me up. He refers to his sidekick Father O'Connor as 'James the Less". He was talking about how American Airlines cut back one olive on their salads and saved over $40,000 in one year.

Everyone ended up getting sicker than dogs. It began with Mother Regina last Monday. She had to leave chapel. She caught some wicked stomach virus. Then, it went through the house. I too was among the missing. I hated to leave Holy Hour, but I got dry heaves and cold chills. The best was Rosario.. She was sitting at the refectory table on retreat Sunday. All of a sudden, it was like Mount Vesuvius erupting! You should have seen everybody gag and make a beeline out of there. It was funny or ridiculous is a more apt way to describe it. We were all sick. Poor Michelle, Patti said half the parish must have her in the throes of agony. Patti herself was groaning in discomfort all night. I was bringing some ginger ale up to one of the Sisters when I saw Rosario coming out of the shower. She was apologizing for the incident while chuckling about it at the same time. She is cool.

Sister Josephat was very excited about the prospect of receiving her bike that her folks were sending from Ohio. She was sure to tell the portress to look out for its arrival on Monday, Tuesday and Wednesday. She said, no less than four times, how her folks sent $5.00 to have someone in the neighborhood assemble it. Patti was getting tired of hearing this. She boldly says, "Look, they could not pay me $505.00 to put together your bike!"

Was drafted to cook in the kitchen today by one Sister Francis Mary. She thought that I could take Sophia's place since the latter was working in the basement. "Sister Francis Mary, be careful with those lids on the cans as you open them." Just then, she had cut her thumb on a can of tomatoes (Pope – no less). She had a good gash. It bled profusely. I had her run it under cold water. It kept bleeding. I summoned Maura to help. Maura put gauze around it. She ended up going to the doctor's to have stitches and a Tetnus shot. Patti made her a blue fabric heart for valor. Sister Francis said later that she was going to have Dr. Cahill come and help sew the new habits as he did such a fine job with her stitches.

Next night – 26 May 1993

Sister Francis Mary was sitting across from me at supper. Suddenly, Rosario, who was sitting beside me, crouches down – her head completely under the table to fetch an orange peel. Rosario uses all this movement accompanied by panting and other audible noises. Meanwhile, Sister Immaculata is overcome with emotion while reading about Saint Elizabeth Ann Seton. The combination was combustible. Sister Francis would look at me and then convulse in laughter getting me to do the same. Mother Regina was not about to have the reading end either. The agony and the ectasy was to be prolonged. Rosario gulps her milk too. She is very loud. Maura laughs too. It triggers a release.

May 29th

Am in a much better frame of mind tonight. Am having a bout with hayfever, but am handling the fatigue that goes with that and our lifestyle pretty well. I am greatly relieved that Uncle H.G.'s surgery went well. He has been such a mainstay for the family since Gransieur died. He is a good and generous man who does things in a quiet fashion. The surgeon, a Dr. Creed (I do believe) did the surgery. It was an eight hour operation. Grampa phoned to let me know.

Last night during Vespers, Sister Margaret lets out a big hiccup. It was unexpected. Mother Regina was even laughing. These are the moments that carry me, that make me happy – giddy, or crazy.

Sister Francis washes the linen dinner napkins with her personal laundry. "I don't know how everyone would feel if they new that my underwear was washed with their dinner napkins. I am not going to tell them either."

"Okay, I say we 'coffee pot' it." says Mother Regina. That is one of her favorite expressions which she will never quite tell us what it means. She uses it with a context clue, so I am able to figure out its

261

meaning. I like that expression. It is a favorite of the Nashville Dominicans. For example, if I say, "What do you think I am going to write about next?" The reply might be, "See if you can coffee pot it". It might be an epic about Sister Francis Mary, or a tale from Ti – you get the idea.

I will not expound on Madame Pompadour who sits like a peacock beside the Cardinal. Now there's a couple of birds for you. I am not into birdwatching. If I was, I would say that the peacock is really a greedy blue jay. Besides, Mother Regina says that if they did not like a person in Scripture, they did not write about them much.

Sister Francis Mary is in charge of the storage room. She has posted a great big sign in there with an eye ball on it which reads: GOD IS WATCHING YOU. KEEP IT NEAT!

Last nights reading was from the Book of Tobit – need I say more. Thankfully, Sister Mary Pio was doing the reading. This was during the Mass which His Eminene was celebrating for the reception of our two newest postulants: Cornelia and Leila. Sister read, "Because of the heat I left my face uncovered. I did not know there were birds perched on the wall above me, til their wrm droppings settled in my eyes." I thought I would die. Maura did too. Sister Mary Pio did not flinch or should I say finch. She deserves credit for that one. I was caught off guard. Can't get away from these birds. The funny thing is, I was supposed to read that same reading for Tuesday morning's Mass. However, the parish priest was unable to make it. He called and I was saved by the bell so to speak.

Speaking of droppings, we set out our red checkered table cloth the other day on our way back from Connecticut. We got our sandwiches, chips and lemonade. Patti blurts out, "UGH! There is a doggie – something here!" Sure enough, there was. We had a lot of leftovers that day from lunch. Later, we had a Mexican dinner. Patti puts a bowl on her head in the kitchen and she parades around singing, "A coo coo karacha ". She makes me laugh.

We were talking about folks that live in the hills of Appalachia and such. Mother Regina was telling us how her Dominican Sisters brought a box of grapefruit to some people in the mountains. They

262

returned a month later to check on them. One of the Sisters asked why they had not eaten the grapefruit. "Sister, we boiled them and boiled them – but nothin' doin." They had never seen a grapefruit before.

Mother Regina was also telling us how one of her Sisters was reading from the Song of Songs – the part about the 'gazelle' - only, she pronounced it 'gas -sel'.

Sister Immaculata was portress the other day. I said to her, "Sister Immaculata, I just want you to know that I wil be accepting phone calls today; and furthermore, on each and every day that you are portress."

"Beam me up Scotty." That seems to be the catch phrase around here. I think Father Larry used that in one of his homilies. It just means that we are ready to go – to what God has waiting for us. Father Larry has the same hairline that my brother Karl had.

Leila, the new postulant from Texas, is cute. She has been working hard in the basement all day today. I said to her, "Leila, you are incredible!" Then she smiled that big Texan, and said, "You want to see something incredible, ...Look in the mirror!"

Went on a picnic yesterday with The Little Sisters of The Poor to their most beautiful, whitewashed Spanish-style house (estate) in Flemington, New Jersey. I saw two rabbits. Patti and I stayed behind, and Sister Margaret and Sister Mary Pio headed for the Blue Army Shrine. I was glad to stay in the pretty and prayerful surroundings. My hayfever was acting up. Perhaps I will see a deer. I ambled towards the meadow, and not more than several yards, was a beautiful, graceful deer. She looked at me and I at her for at least forty seconds. Then she fled, a white tail in a thicket of greenery.

Now I must turn in. Sister Aquinas is anxious to lock up. I offered to lock up for her, but she is not receptive to that notion.

PENTECOST SUNDAY

Today we went to Mass at the cathedral for Pentecost Sunday.
Mother Regina and I made our usual stop to the parish house for the washroom. Since the earlier Mass was still going on, Sophia and I decided to venture outside the cathedral to see what we could see (reminds me of that song - 'The Bear went over the mountain....').
The Cardinal was going to Confirm twenty young adults who are mentally handicapped. Sophia and I went over to one named Adam. He told us that he would take the name 'John' or 'Sean' for the Cardinal. He was very concerned about the Cardinal's health being that His Eminence was recently hospitalized. He said if we see the Cardinal, to be sure and ask him to pray for him. Adam would be praying for His Eminence too. Adam told us that he has a brother named Brian who is also mentally challenged. He has a sister named 'Virginia' and a brother named 'George'. "Oh, that is my baptismal name – Virginia and I also have a brother named George, the same name as my father." Adam took my hand. He was very pleased. He is 22 years old but he appears much younger in his innocence.
Adam's last name is 'Hughes' or as he told me, "H-U-G-H-E-S!"
The Holy Spirit is sure going to descend today.
At the High Mass, as the Cardinal and his entourage processed in, the Cardinal stopped in the aisle to talk to Adam. This made me very happy. When His Eminence confirmed Adam, I learned that Adam's father died recently. His mother is in poor health which is why Adam has come to live in an institution. Adam has been placed in one of the Archdioceses homes for the handicapped. The best part was when Adam went up to get is picture taken with the Archbishop.
Adam gave the Cardinal a big hug, and exclaimed, "I love you Cardinal O'Malley!" It came right over the microphone. It was priceless! The Cardinal smiled the broadest smile ever.
Something else happened at the Cathedral today. Tom, the usher, spotted Mother Regina. He went over and planted the biggest kiss on her. She was aghast. She did joke about it later. It reminds me of the time Queen Elizabeth visited Florida. Some well-meaning woman went up to her and kissed her. The Queen was gracious. I appreciate people who let their heart rule - more spirit of the law than letter of the law.

XI. Flight of the Mattress

On Monday we received our new assignments as well as our new room changes. Well, poor Sister Francis Mary – this was not her day. It started off with her setting off the alram at 6:25 when she opened the laundry room door before Sister Aquinas had reset it. That was enough to jar anybody but of all people – Sister Francis Mary. The next thing I know, I see this trail of white spots dribbled throughout the corridors and two flights of stairs. It was like a trail of bread crumbs being left for Hansel & Gretel. Sister Fancis was using every conceivable solution to blot up these white stains against the brown wood, and the granite staircase. I thought it was bleach. Come to find out, Sister Francis was trying to clean a spot on her habit, and, for whatever reason, she reached underneath a table in the corner of the laundry room and used a bottle of hydrochloric acid. We had been using it in the basement – probably when we were laying down the new parquet floor. Sister burned a hole through her habit and it went right through her under garments. She was lucky she did not burn her skin though she said her fingers "stung" all day. Of all things! But wait, there is more. Sister Francis Mary was desperately worried about giving up her "Beauty Rest " mattress in the course of changing rooms. So what does she do? She scouts out all the possibilities. Meanwhile, Michele has moved into Sister Francis's old room quicker than she would have liked. No time to switch mattresses. She was going to involve me in on this transaction which entailed getting one mattress from the first floor, and carrying it up three flights of stairs. I suggested the one on Mary Jane's bed which was on the second floor. The cloister was very much under surveillance all afternoon. Finally, and immediately, before Vespers, like two stowaways, we brought down the old one from the third floor, and we got to giggling. We were sliding that mattress down each flight of stairs. Here it was flopping down the acid stained stairs and we were just hoping and praying that we would not bump into any "watchdogs". It was hilarious – slapstick energy trying to fulfill a mission. We then had to clear everything off of Mary Jane's old bed. Sister Immaculata had been storing all her wares in there. The second floor was the riskiest because that is Mother Regina's floor. Sister Francis was also concerned about Sister Agatha on the third floor – right across from me! Well, we managed. We were just as giddy going up the stairs as we were coming down. It was so much fun especially since we did not get caught! I love how Sister Francis scouts me out. When we were finished, she says, "Don't you tell anyone."

This was also the day in which Father Salmon and "The Little Bishop" from Brazil came. We affectionately refer to His Excellency as "The Littel Bishop ' back home. They celebrated Mass on this Memorial Day which was also The Feast of The Visitation. The Canon was in Latin. It was beautiful. Sister Immaculata let me take her place in bringing up the Gifts for the Offertory. I had no idea she was going to do that. She is very thoughtful. Father had a big smile when I presented them.
Then we had lunch. Patti made hot dogs on the grill. It was too cool and windy to go outdoors. We enjoyed our hot dogs inside with potato salad, beans, fritos, and a Mexican refried bean dip. The Little Bishop especially liked that! To top it off, we had a patriotic 'Stars and Stripes Forever' cake and popsicles too. Father Salmon declined on the popsicles but Bishop da Silva enjoyed a blueberry one. Father Salmon went on to describe the ones he had as a youngster. It was ice cream on a stick covered with chocolate, and then there was another kind that was a flavored ice. I asked Mother Regina if we could sing a couple of patriotic numbers for our good priests. Rosario got her guitar out and we sang America the Beautiful, and Sancta Lucia for the Little Bishop. It was the closest we could get to Portuguese for the bishop. We sang The Battle Hymn of the Republic which is a favorite of Father Salmon's. We capped it off with God Bless America which is his real signature song. Father Salmon has a special connection with Kate Smith – he helped bring her into The Church. Father Salmon was in his glory. He went on to talk about the Irish writers. I could feel Thomas Moore coming on. With that came 'The Vale of Avoca'. Yep, just like John McCormack himself, Father was taking off in his rendition of "The Meeting of the Waters". Everyone was spellbound. Father said no one had better laugh. No one did. It was beautiful.

3 June 1993 – St. Charles and Companions

Just finished Father O'Connor's final exam. The incentive to get through it was that I could come down to the basement and write. I thoroughly enjoyed his class. Am looking forward to "Patristics" come September. My essay was on The Real Presence of Christ in The Eucharist.

Yesterday, Sister Aquinas was referring to Sister Francis Mary as a human pin cushion. She has all these pins sticking out of her and pins to spare (spear?). Speaking of pins, and needles, Sister was not at lunch yesterday. She went to Dr. Cahill's to get her stitches out. Mother Regina said that Father O'Connor had sent over the exam but no one knows where it is. "Okay, who has it under her mattress?!" Mother queries. "Could blame it on Sister Francis – she is not here." Mother Regina looked at me, taken aback. Then she chuckled.

Patti and I found "Our thrill on blueberry -" Patti dropped one of the blueberries on her plate onto the floor (otherwise known as Sister Francis Mary's Refectory floor). I leaned over to retrieve it. Then, one of the blueberries from my plate rolled on the floor. I fetch this one too. I put Patti's inside her napkin ring and I said, "Okay, Corral!" Then she put mine in my napkin ring. We both laughed. Then I had an idea. We had just moved into our new rooms. Wouldn't it be a nice gesture for Patti to find a blueberry sitting on her bureau. We are not supposed to have anything on our bureaus. 'Lo and behold, one single solitary blueberry sat on Patti's dresser. A little later, Patti said, "Sister James, I think you have a special delivery letter in your mailbox. I went to see and I saw something blue in there – and it did not require a letter opener!

XII. Sister Immaculata

10 June 1993

Sister Immaculata and I cooked together on Friday. It was strange because I called her by her Baptismal name of Diane by accident which I have never done. I signed us both up early for Confession since we were cooking together. The phone rang at one o'clock. I said, "Is everything alright?" She only smiled at me. I did not pry. As we were going into chapel, I took her arms and she looked straight into my eyes. She has such pretty, soft blue eyes. What was she thinking. She looked like she had been crying. She also looked peaceful but her demeanor was always calm exteriorly. I asked her if she wanted to keep her slot for Confession or switch with me. She did not. In the afternoon, I went down to fix a cup of tea. I noticed Sister Immaculata talking with Sister Aquinas. I offered them both a cup of tea. "No one makes a cup fo tea like Sister James Mariah." Sister Immaculata stated quietly. Sister Aquinas did not want one. I brought her some homemade chocolate chip cookies and offered her some milk. What is going on. One can not help but be in tune to other people's feelings around here especially when living in such close proximity.

Poor Sister Immaculata, she prepared the bulk of the supper but she did not really seem to mind. Other times, she would have felt the pressure. During clean-up, she motioned to me, "Can I see you a minute." Her tone was serious and my stomach was turning. We went into the laundry room. Sister Immaculata put her hands on my shoulders – and then, it came. Before she could finish, I blurted out, "You are not leaving are you?!" Then I fell apart – in her arms and I uttered, "No". My heart was broken. I could feel it coming on. I knew it was for the best. It was not too long ago that Diane broke down. She was in the kitchen. When asked if she was alright then, she said, "No, can't you see, I am not."

Diane had suffered terribly pining for her family. How could I ask or expect her to stay. Had I not been blessed having her in my life up until now. She said she was dreading telling me. She must have known how much I love her. It was awful during Compline. Poor Sister Francis Mary – she was doing the Reading, "Do not forske me, my God......" And she broke down. This is one time I did not laugh. I was sitting beside Mother Regina desperately trying to keep in check. Then, I felt Mother Regina's arm on my shoulder. I managed to smile – grateful for her compassion.

After choir practice, we went up on the porch. I could hear the bagpipes in the distance. It seemed significant. Sister Immaculata and I used to sing "Going Home, Going Home". Only, this time, she was really going home. Thank God it is only to her family on earth while there is still time. Her family also made a great sacrifice. I had no interest in soda or cookies this night. Sister Immaculata came over and sat beside me. We looked at the picture of her grandchildren. I love her little granddaughter Margaret whom just made her First Holy Communion. I said good night to Sister Immaculata gently and maybe superficially so as not to be pained.

The next morning at breakfast, Sister Immaculata sat beside me. It was nice. We laughed and joked. She always appreciated my cornball humor. Then it was time. I was going to get this over quick. I wrapped a bottle of violet splash cologne in pretty floral paper and a lavender ribbon. I put this on her bed with a card I made. It had a picture of a bear looking up at the moon and the stars. We had just gazed at the full moon the night before. She came to my room to get me when I was on my way to the roof. Great minds were thinking alike that night. In the note, I had written, "Remember the stars, Remember the Moon….. Remember me." She told me that she was going to see Gramp. "It is hardest saying good-bye to you." She was the mother, and I was very much her daughter pouring out my heart in her maternal embrace. God love her.

Mother Regina invited His Eminence to lunch on Monday. I think she did this to preoccupy our minds as the void was palpable since Sister Immaculata left. Also, it ws one of those rare days in which the Cardinal happened to have an available time slot.
The Cardinal came with his attorney Alice who is a very attractive and nice young lady. We went out to the sidewalk to greet him after of course one of the Sisters buffaloed her way ahead of me. I was reserved but I did lean in to kiss his ring. To my chagrin, he had his arm out to which I gently reciprocated. Lunch would be up on the third floor where the porch is. Mother Regina asked me to ask the Cardinal if he would like some tea. I was waiting for him to finish his conversation with one of the Sisters and as I started to ask him, realizing that he was not finished with his conversation. "Excuse me - " he then broke his conversation, and almost compassionately paid heed to me. "Would you like a cup of tea Your Eminence?" "Yes" He simply said. I was not going to get too excited. He always says, "Horses and troops first." I felt kind of logey besides the fact that I

269

had to go down four flights of stairs to get the tea and then come back up them once I got it. But tea I got. I boiled fresh water, got my "I love Grandpa" mug out of the cupboard. Then, I was overtaken by an inspiration. While I was waiting for the water to boil, I took a magic marker, and printed "CARDINAL" on a piece of paper. I afixed this over "Grandpa". Now the mug said, "I Love My Cardinal". Gosh, I must have been desperate. I nonchalantly brought the archbishop his tea setting down the mug. He noticed it immediately. A broad smile came over his face. I hardly looked to catch his reaction, almost, like I didn't care. I don't even know why I did it. I guess I was bored. To further add to my chagrin, he then said, "Only Sister James Mariah would do that. That is why I love her the most." It was real quiet. I was more surprised than anyone. I think he said it for effect or because of the prevailing mood. Then, he turned toward Mother Regina, and he said, "They're just jealous because you didn't think of it." He always razzes her. I still can't believe he said that. I am writing about it, pondering it, but in a way, I hardly took it in.

XIV. Feast of Corpus Christi – 13 June 1993

Wow! What a day! I am proculator in the kitchen while Patti is on her home visit. In addition, I was cook along with my cohort Sister Francis Mary who accuses me of being bossy in the kitchen! Today, I am portress too, but it is generally pretty quiet on Sundays. I would prefer it to be more busy as I enjoy those rare moments on the telephone or jabbering away with some wayfarer at the door.

Sister Francis Mary made the fresh fruit compote and I poached the eggs for breakfast. I put out some raisin buns which Mr. Gallagher had donated. Then I fixed a potato salad for lunch. And prepared a meat platter with lettuce, cheese and tomatoes for lunch. We were going to have a picnic outdoors on account of an aspirant and her mother coming to visit. She just graduated from Steubenville and she is hoping to enter shortly. I made lemonade, iced tea, and, served sherbet with cookies for dessert. I did not want to have too heavy of a meal on account we were going to a dedication ceremony and reception at the Franciscans of the Renewal in the South Bronx.

Yesterday we attended a Silver Jubilee celebration. We have really been going to town in the culinary way. We need a couple of good fast days. Now, I am just returning from the dedication Mass and Blessing of the Saint Anthony Shelter founded by Father Bob Lombardo. The school building was blessed too by His Exellency Bishop McDormack. There was this cute little elderly Irish priest named Father Fitzpatrick. Father Groeschel said that he was voted "Puerto Rican' of the year. It was a beautiful gala celebration.

There were lots of red, white and blue balloons. The police blocked off the streets. The neighborhood was alive with their car radios blasting Spanish music. The young Black people were dancing or "jiving" as they say right in the road. When I came out of the friary, I showed them how I do it. They laughed. It was so much fun. It is important to be one with them.

There was a slight beeze coming in the church on this very hot day. We hardly noticed the heat. We processed with The Blessed Scrament around the block. It took on an added significance because Corpus Christi fell on the 13th which is typically the Feast of St. Anthony and here the St. Anthony shelter was being dedicated. After the Benediction and Reposition of the Blessed Sacrament, we followd Bisop McCormack and the Franciscan Friars up to the clssrooms and Chapel for the Blessings. Then we went to the courtyard and enjoyed this great Italian ziti dish with meatballs and a tasty Marinara sauce. There was chicken and rice, and eggplant parmesan; big rolls, cold beverages and lots of coffee brewed plus desserts coming out our ears. There were tortes, and pies, donuts galore, and if I have not made you hungry yet, imagine double chocolate layer cake trimmed with cream roses! The fellows serving desserts were picking on me after my third trip to the dessert table.

Mother Regina seemed to enjoy me trying to be discreet as I made the rounds to the various tables. "Sister James Mariah, where are you going?" "Oh, just getting a hot touch for my coffee." Then she smiled at me and asked me to get her one too. She was having a good time.

I looked up to see one lone solitary red balloon drift into oblivion, over the barbed wire on top of a cement wall. I could see an apartment building – commonly called "the Projects". Out of one of the windows, I could see this man hanging his head out the window watching the party down below. I wanted to attach myself to that balloon and sail past his window saying, 'Come on down. You are invited too.' Surely he would have been welcome. How lonely he must have felt.

Father Bob showed us the new building in which work is still being done. It is incredible what one man has done; what one man can do, by the grace of God. This otherwise tawdry neighborhood is gradually getting a face lift. It truly is inspiring. This place will house 65 homeless men. God Bless them.

XV. You Take the High Road.......................

Yesterday, we went to Germantown, New York – nearly half way to Ticonderoga! We went ot the Carmelite retreat house in honor of Sister M. Therese Suzanne, O. Carm.'s 25 years of Religious dedication. She is from Scotland. This was another grand day. Her cousin came over and I loved hearing her accent. Her name was Shirley. Monsignor Turro was there. It was nice to see him. Sister Aquinas was especially pleased. The remarkable thing about this Sister Therese, is, that she is stricken with Multiple Scelerosis, that which she did not have when she entered. She carries her cross beautifully. She is modest too. When we arrived, Mass was due to start at eleven and we were cutting it close. This cute older nun says, "Oh, do you want the restroom? Don't worry, you have lots of time. You have three minutes." Three minutes in the convent is a lot of time funny enough.

Mass and all was very beautiful. One of the Sisters sang acapello in Gaelic "Ag Criost An Siol" - for the Communion Meditation. Another Sister spoke the translation as she sang. It was magnificent. Then, we all processed behind Sister Therese singing "Be Exalted, O God".

The most wonderful dinner awaited us in the refectory. Scottish music was playing over the loud speaker. I have that same tape – Lake Lomond. That is where Sister Therese is from. How did she ever get through that song! "You take the high road and I'll take the 'lo ....."

The reason we got to attend this special event, was because Mother Regina had taught a novice mistress class in Kentucky. This Sister happened to be one of her students many moons ago. I am very grateful that we could come to this. We had chicken, mashed

potatoes, gravy, turnip, salad, rolls and even wine. There were chocolates on the table and fruit cups on pretty silver doilies. There was soda and a big beautiful cake for dessert; and, strawberries and ice cream scooped in perfect round balls in a big glass bowl. The chocolate scoops looked like baked potatoes in the dim lighting.
 Noting my enthusiasm over the desserts, Sister Francis snaps at me, "Behave yourself. Dont' act like your mother never fed you!"
Sister Matthew and Sister Mary Gabriel gave us the grand tour of the place. It is gorgeous! It is on 87 acres of unspoilt land in the Catskills. There is a lake probably very much like Lake Lomond in Scotland, nestled in all these mountains. It is panoramic. During the tour, Sister Francis Mary seeks out an easy chair, plops in it and says her standard line, "I'm staying here. You can come back for me in a week." She says that everywhere we go. What is amazing, is how she is like radar finding these Lazy Boy chairs.
After we learned all about the foudnress, Mother M. Therese Angeline, we visited her grave and said a few prayers there. She was quite a woman. She has a lovely countenance. She died at age 91 on her birthday. She would give her medicine to the foreign missions after receiving it from her doctor. She did not like taking medicine. One time, when Sister Mary Matthew was giving her Milk of Magnesia, she took the spoon and flipped it in the air.
 Today, in the heritage museum there, one can spot some 'Milk of Magnesia' on the picture of 'Our Lady of Sorrows'. Incidentally, that is the same picture I have in my room, that which belonged to my paternal grandmother.
I was very taken with everything I saw about this community. They seemed joyful, and each retained her own personality. They wore a habit. It was a beautiful blend and refreshing to see. Then, I found out that they get four days off a month, or they have the option of taking a month of a year. They can even go home for a week at the end of their novitiate. Gosh, I didn't need to hear that....

Feast of St. Barnabas – 11 June 1993

Just went for a walk with Mother Regina around the block to see the rose bushes and to see if we could hear the bagpipes.
Sister Francis Mary, I don't know what I am going to do with her.
 She says, "Thank God Sister Immaculata took that chair with her. It

273

was falling apart. I would have been embarrassed to bring that old thing."

The other evening I went into my room. It had been raining out and my window was open. A gentle breeze came in. I could smell the dampness on the hardwood floors. It reminded me of the "little green camp" or the "brown jug" as we call it. It was Aunt Mary's camp but now it is Uncle Sherrie's. c I thought of the fireplace, and the charcoal being readied for the hot dogs and hamburgers; the marshmallows. The lake was in full view in my mind's eye – with a light drizzle of rain sputtering on it; the smell of rain on the paved road. There was the Flag day party that Karl always had there. It is amazing the memories that can be conjured by scent alone.

I do enjoy Mother Regina. Last week we were sewing before going to bed in an effort to get the habits caught up. Then Mother says, as she was fixing to retire, "Work! Get to work! Work hard, and don't stop until you are finished!" She was pretending to be a slave driver knowing full well it was an impossible task and that we were all exhausted. That is what made it doubly funny. She does have a good sense of humor. I feel that she is comfortable around me and I have grown comfortable with her. She seems to appreciate me more lately. She gives me more credit and respects me more.

After returning from the Focolare Family Fest in Caldwell, New Jersey on Saturday, I had asked Mother if I could take a little thirty minute nap. This was on the day that Sister Immaculata left. It was a rainy afternoon. I came downstairs to sew, an hour and a half later, and Mother says, "Why Sister James Mariah, that was the longest thirty minute nap I have ever heard of!" My face reddened. She does not miss a trick!

Sat next to Patti at that Focolare Family Fest. None (nun?) of us were really into it. There was a huge video screen with translations tht were louder thatn the English language on account it was being televised worldwide. We were going to be on TV all around the world. The thing was, we had all said good-bye to Sister Immaculata earlier, and it was a rainy Saturday morning. There were huge crowds of families from every ethnic background and religion. Their main focus, is the unity among people of a God, but not necessarily Christ. This part was unsettling though the

274

ecumenical approach is good in itself. People coming together for a common good – that is a good thing. Some of us felt punchy, and emotionally drained. Sister Francis Mary had a splitting headache because it was so loud. This woman from Australia is spotlighted on the mega screen. It struck me funny. She had these bangs that made me think of Captain Kangaroo. This was too good to keep. "Patti, doesn't she look like Captain Kangaroo?" This sent Patti roaring. Then I passed this tidbit to Leila who in turn passed it to Maura who passed it to Sister Aquinas. We were all laughing like crazy. Then Patti started to get these chest pains. She got up and went out to the foyer. Some lady brought her in a room with all these children. She had her lie down there.

I did meet a nice lady from Columbia. She had a stunning daughter, a brunette of fifteen years of age named Julia. The mother's name was Grace Cordoza. She and her daughter had traveled from New Bedford, Massachusetts to attend this family fest. I got Sophia, whose father is Columbian, to meet them so she could converse fluently in Spanish with them. Grace, as she told me to call her, also has a son named Danny but he did not make it. When we were singing "He's Got the Whole World in His Hands...", she got all teary eyed. She was using her dress to wipe her eyes. I gave her a tissue.

Getting back to "Captain Kangaroo". If I were doing a study off the record, I would say people have the most intersting reaction to him – his character. He is a personage who provokes a reaction in everyone. For example, Mary Jane's father knew him, Bob Keeshan, personally as he did his banking at the bank where Mr. Adams worked. My brother Karl met him in Albany a few years ago. He got his autograph for my little sister Sarah. Growing up, my brother Thomas and I watched him every morning at eight o'clock. Then, on our picnic with The Little Sisters of The Poor, the Sister who I sat next to on the bus, told me how her sister worked for the Captain Kangaroo production company. She knew him very well. Patti said that her father never let her watch that show because he thought it was "stupid". Most people can relate to Captain Kangaroo.

Sister Francis Mary is always picking on me about licking stamps in Purgatory. Maura says that would be Heaven for me. Then they will be chocolate flavored stamps!

18 June 1993

We received our new habits today. I sewed practically all of my own habit. I made the sleeves on all of them. They are striking: a navy blue scapular and capelet, over a long full white tunic like what the Dominicans wear. It is a 13th Century pattern, so you can not argue success. The other one was a simple tan colored long sleeved cotton top and and matching midi-skirt. The top had a button in the back and a little white collar that also buttoned in the back. It reminds me of a top that a dentist would wear. It was plain albeit practical while this one is makes a statement. Though, as Mrs. Keogh used to say, "It is hotter than Dutch love" today and these are being put to the test. If the Shieks and Arabs wear similar long layers in the Middle East where it is desert climate, than they must be good in the heat. Not so sure about those turbans. We wear a much lighter veil. We also have a navy webbed belt to cincture our waist and attach our Rosary Beads. In-between each bead, is a small silver rose-designed bead. I voted for this one because it reminds me of Gramma Burleigh. Gramma has a full Rosary like this. Anyway, I love the new habit, but then I have always had a flair for the dramatic.

I can't wait for our four postulants to come back from their home visit. I really miss them. I get such a kick out of Maura. She is missing us too. She called us on the Feast of Corpus Christi to wish us a happy feast day. She also came to the Cardinal's Mass where His Eminence blessed our new habits and our Rosaries. It was good to see Maura. Father Halligan brought us an ice cream cake. Since I am in charge of the Kitchen, I decided to save the ice cream cake until Thursday when the postulants return. Also, Rosario has a birthday on the 23rd, the same day as my oldest sister Elizabeth. My brother Georgie's is on the 22nd and my brother Thomas's is on the 28th.

On this special day, I prepared baked fish, rice, garden fresh peas and salad with my brother-in-law's famous dressing. The dressing is a blend of fresh lemon, olive oil and sea salt. It is simple but makes the salad taste so fresh. I made a wine sauce for the fish. The Little Sisters of the Poor gave us a chocolate cake and a lemon cake for the occasion. That was dessert served with hazelnut coffee. This was my first time serving in the new habit. Some of the Sisters said that I "flowed" in it. Wait, is that vanity?

On Father's Day, we went to the Cathedral for Mass in honor of His Eminence. We did the same last year too. The postulants baked bread with Mother Regina the night before which we presented to the Cardinal at his residence after Mass.

Mother Regina is really something else. She worked non-stop on our habits giving generously of herself. She would not even come down for meals. She even gave up lunch with the Little Sisters of the Poor. She would not allow any of us to sew on Saturday. Rather, she insisted that we all go out and take a walk while she stayed working on our petticoats and aprons. Then that night, in the sweltering heat, Mother made bread with the postulants. She came down late to the kitchen to put the risen dough in the oven and she waited for it to bake. She is incredible. I kind of felt sorry for her because I think she is getting run down yet she is as gracious as can be. She even did something unusual for her; and that is, she broke out in laughter in the chapel. It must have been a release for her. I have grown very fond of her. I took her up a pink lemonade as she was trying to get caught up on slews of letters. She looked at me so appreciatively. She turned to me and said as I was leaving her office, "Sister James Mariah, I want you to call your grandfather." She gave all the Sisters three minutes to call our fathers for Father's Day. Ashamedly, I had already called my grandfather, albeit 'Collect'. I called my father instead and he said that it made his day. When we were at the Cardinal's Residence, there was this man in his early 40's there with an attractive blonde lady of the same age. The lady had her daughter in tow with two of her daughter's friends. They had all brought the Gifts up during the High Mass. This was a surprise to them. The lady, whose name is Maureen, did not go up as she was worried about her hi-heels. The man, Noel Speare, was talking to me afterward. He told me how on April 12th, He had put on the score board at Shea Stadium, "Maureen, I love you. Will you marry me." I can appreciate that one. Mr. Speare then told me that he had a ring in his pocket and that he would pop the ole question officially – in a matter of minutes. He was a little nervous, but he had a good sense of humor. They both work for Eastman- Kodak. The next thing I know, Noel is giving me the big OK sign. I go over to meet them and congratulate them. The Cardinal is blessing the ring. Then, they asked me to join them for a photograph. It was fun to be in on it.

Then, I met a Mr. and Mrs. Genereaux, French of course. They have a daughter Emily and a son Wayne who is a Mercedarian Brother. They were celebrating their Golden Anniversary. God Bless them.

XVI. New Habits (die hard)

Later in the week – June 1993

Monsignor Robertson and Sister Catherine Q. stopped by. They had lunch at the Poor Clare Monastery. They decided to stop here to see us in our new habits. Both were present when I entered as a postulant. It was so nice to see them. The Monsignor has been through so much with his heart and all. He has a high pressure job as Vicar for Religious in the Diocese. Recently he has been assigned to a parish in Yonkers. That is near where he grew up. I am glad he can serve there. He seems to have a soft spot for me. He has been stationed at St. Peter's where Father Halligan is. Father will miss him and Sister Catherine will too. Today he looked well and he was in good spirits. God love him.

There is something about Sister Francis Mary. Last night, as I was getting ready to turn in, she comes out in the hall, "I was looking for you Sister James. Come, help me fix my door. It is stuck." Well, small wonder with the high humidity. Her door was jam shut. There was no budging it. We were both pushing it with all our might – she in her night shirt and me in my new habit. We got to laughing. "Sister Francis Mary, why does stuff like this always happen to you?" She did not know, but she agreed it was true. She said that if she has to use the bathroom in the night, she will just go around and go through Sister Immaculata's former room.

Speaking of rooms, The Lord sure knows how to satsify the secret desires of my heart. I am in perfect earshot of hearing, almost daily, the bagpipes. It is generally during my study time. I can not get over it. If one were going to pick a room specifically with this in mind, this would be the room to pick.

About Jim Crawford, that shoe salesman at Harry's, he says if you have narrow feet, you have to go down South to buy your shoes. "All the Southerners have narrow feet." He went on to say. I was telling that to Mother Regina. She was more interested in getting the habit adjusted on me. "Sister James Mariah, if I can get this habit to look good on you, I will have succeeded." She is always repinning my collar, or fixing my pleats on my tunic, or pinning my capelet. My headpiece drives her up the wall most. I wore a metal band under it today and it keeps the veil in place. "There, you look like a million."

Monday we had a Father Tom and a Father Philip prepare the Sisters an Italian dinner complete with ante pasta and Italian ices for dessert. When I was introduced to the main chef, I thought his confrere said his name was "Francis Fini" or something like that. Sister Aquinas is always talking about a priest named 'Fini" who wrote a poem about St. Joseph. I showed Father "Fini" the kitchen. Well, I think he was about to "fini" with me having addressed him no less than six times as such.
"Oh, do you prefer I call you "Father Francis?"
"No, No, my name is 'Franchesfini'!"
"So why does Father Tom keep calling you Father Philip? Oh, that is your FIRST name. I get it now."
I played some Italian hymns with dinner. They sure live up to their names whatever they are. They are good cooks!

This morning, June 22nd, (Georgie's birthday), Sister Yvonne came for Mass and breakfast. It was very nice to see her again. She looked like she lost a little weight. I made a nice breakfast – one of the liberties afforded as proculator in the kitchen. Mr. Gallagher dropped off some sweet rolls and I scrambled some eggs with cream cheese. Sister Margaret put on the bacon. We had toast from the homemade bread that the postulants baked. Then we went up to the porch to sit and "shoot the bull" as we say back home.

Isn't it funny how there is always one member of the local church group such as at The Holy Name Society, who wears the big gold medalion which he was honored with on his 25thyear of serving. He wears this with pride. He feels a real sense of belonging. One can't help but share in this pride. One also enjoys seeing his face beaming. He has his Sunday best suit on and leads all the other members in the Rosary. He walks around like he has the run of the place. He comes up to me twice during Mass, reminding me to be sure and go ahead of his group to Holy Communion. Then we follow
the Procession over to the statue of The Blessed Virgin Mother. He oversees everything giving directions. His name is Mr. Donald McHugh. God Bless him.

During a meal of silence, Sister Josephat lets out a big hiccup. Sister Francis Mary giggles.

We went to get new shoes for our new habits this past week. Sister Francis Mary retrieved two pairs of shoes that she had stashed away in her trunk. She was hoping to get them dyed black. "Why should they buy me new shoes," she says,"Thee shoes cost $65.00. I am trying to save them money. I am going to keep them even if they can't dye them. When the novelty wears off, I will just wear these." She stated this at least a half dozen times. Then, when we get to the shoe store, she says, "Well, as long as I am here, I might as well get something for Sundays." Then she says, "If my new habit is too long, I am going to take it up. I will wait 'til Mother Assumpta is gone."

Sister Francis Mary has been on the postulants' case about breaking dishes. Only, this morning who should break a milk pitcher but Sister Francis Mary herself. She said, "I guess this is my humility for getting after the postulants for breaking things." Then she says, "Quick, get rid of the evidence." Poor Sister Francis Mary, she cuts her finger in the process. Then, she raves and rants, "How am I going to tell Mother Regina. I don't care. I am not even going to worry about it. I am just going to tell her." Then, as I was taking the Superior's lunch up to her, Sister Francis Mary says, "Are you going up? Let me go up with you. I want you to be with me when I tell her." Then, she goes on about, "This teaches me. This is my humility. This is good for me because I was getting after the postulants about breaking dishes. Of course they have been clumsy. They have been breaking more dishes around here." Next thing I know, I see Sister Francis Mary in her white tunic, laying stretched out on her bed like she was St. Joan of Arc or something. She was half asleep. She was portress on this Saturday and she did not want to get too comfortable. Then I see Leila, one of the new postulants, bringing in a "replacement pitcher". Sister Francis Mary goes to her trusty trunk to reimburse her. She must have had sent Leila on an errand to Frank Bees. She does not even notice me pass by as she is so dazed.

About that store run, I think the novices were all a little disgusted with me. Of course it does not take much with them. They accused me of being attached when I refused to pick out a pair of shoes like theirs. Maybe it was because I had seen too many of those shoes in the nursing home where I used to work. We all had to get black shoes. I thought the shoes were all ugly. I would not have minded getting the same as theirs had they been good and sturdy. If figured if they were going to spend that kind of money on shoes, I might as get a pair that fits the requirements that appeal to me. And I did. I went again, two days later with Sister Josephat and Sister Agatha. This time we went to Harry's shoe store. That is where Mr. Crawford waited on us. He is a very good shoe salesman. He knows his shoes. His own pair are from Denmark. "The Danes make great shoes." He says. Jim Crawford has an uncle who is a Christian Brother on Staten Island. He is Brother Augustine. Then he said, "Boy, you nuns are really testing me today." I knew the moment I walked in the store which shoes I wanted. They are not the soft black leather, but rather the nubuck which I prefer. There were some nice European 'ecco' shoes there, but I was mindful of the vow of poverty. I got the American made ones. God Bless America

19 June 2020

Was saddened to learn of the death of Ronnie Donovan's father. He and his father always went to Mass together. They used to sit right behind us. Ronnie is like a brother to me. He is my brother Georgie's best friend. He lives across the street from where I grew up. He loves good Irish music. He served in the Navy. He was stationed in Spain. We used to enjoy sharing stories about Spain as that is where I traveled while touring with a musical group. Ronnie used to come up and visit Grampa a lot too. All my brothers' friends did. They are just good people.

It is funny how Sister Agatha gets 'carte blanche' when it comes to writing and mailing out letters. She knows that a letter with seven pages will go for one stamp, but anymore than that, then it tips the scale. "I don't know, I get this sort of wonderful sense of reconnecting which really is quite lovely. God gave me this before my vocation so I could be near my family." She says using a lot of words to say nothing. Then she wolfs down her food, talking with her mouth open, and uses her bread to somp up every last poppy seed on her plate. If she addresses us, which very seldom she does, she will refer to us only as "You people". And she is going to be the Superior. ....

24 June 1993

I have just heard one of the funniest things. We are supposed to write a paper on Chastity for Mother Regina. We have been studying this Vow for the past five weeks. Well, Sister Lucy just went to Mother and said, "Oh no, I don't know what I was thinking, but I wrote my paper on the Vow of Poverty. Mother Regina laughed. "Well, I can't wait to read it." She is such a good sport.

Sister Francis Mary is off to the store to look for garters. She said to me, "Now don't you tell anyone." She is thinking if we get sleeves for our outer sleeve on the habit, she can use them as opposed to metal bands. She said she would even get me a pair. (Winning........)

She also said to me, "Be sure and have the kitchen looking good because I don't want you to be getting any guff. There will be some people who have something to say about that, and you let me know if they do. I will straighten them out." I am not worried about that. I have a good rapport with the current proculator.

Sister Francis Mary was looking for me last night to say good night. We have a buddy system. We are sure to say good night to each other before retiring. I enjoy her so much.

Last week, during the readings when I read, there were some humorous and unplanned accounts that I would relay: "like the mattresses having fleas in them in Mother Seton's first convent, and how the Sisters all got to itching." Well, Maura hates any mention of any sort of insect – particularly while eating. It was smooth reading but intermittedly, I broke up laughing. Mother Regina even got laughing. There was an excerpt in The Sunday Visitor that I was reading about the 'Carny Priest'. Turns out, he is from the North Country and my natural emphasis on towns that I was familiar with: Potsdam, St. Lawrence, and Watertown, made this evident provoking a stir at the breakfast table. In general, my discipline has improved.

28 June 1993

Today is my brother Thomas's birthday. It was also the birthday of my late Cousin Marion. I used to help her get up in the morning and get her breakfast. I would section her grapefruit for her and remove all the membrane. When that was finished, I would give her dog Tiffany one dog biscuit and then let her out. Tiffany was a beautiful dog – the exact breed slips my minds. But she looks like she could be a hunting dog, though not a beagle. I then had to vacuum up all the dog hairs in the house.

It is raining out right now. Something is going on with Sister Aquinas. She has not been herself.

Right now I am on retreat at St. John Neuman House in Riverdale. I love it here. It is like coming home. It is my fourth or fifth time here that I have been on retreat. The first time I came here was when I had to take my "Psychologicals" as they say. Maura is here now. She can not get to sleep. She is in here snacking and telling me how she got hollared at after Holy Hour. Meanwhile, Mother Regina has just come upstairs and caught her in my room. So what does Maura do, she immediately picks up one of my books to make it look like she is borrowing a book or something constructive. Then, Sister Margaret brings all the snacks in my room which has turned into Grand Central Station. All I was trying to do was jot down a few thoughts before I forget. The weird thing is, I have the biggest room in the whole house. It used to be the "party room" on previous retreats. My last room was the size of a match box. I felt so claustraphobic that I let out a war hoop in my sleep.

Patti, Sister Lucy, Maura, and Sister Margaret are all wondering what I am doing with a type writer in my room, or should I say 'suite'. They are also wondering how I got it. My friend Peter from Vietnam loaned it to me. I feel like Sister Francis Mary making use of my connections. The truth is, there is no correction tape n this typewriter and I am making more mistakes than ever. Perhaps I would be better off writing by hand.

Oddly enough, Sister Agatha has that match box of a room (poetic justice). Mother Regina just handed out the keys at random. I was the very last person to receive a key and this is where I landed. The Lord sure takes care of the secret desires of my heart. Incidentally, the last time when I was in that very small room, and I had a nightmare, Sister Aquinas tried to get me to admit it in front of all the retreatants in an effort to make me look foolish. Ironically, Sister Lucy owned up to it – she thought it was she who had that nightmare.

The only clencher, is that Mother Regina has the other large room which happens to be right across the hall from me!

There is an unusual gal on the retreat whom I am anxious to write about. She has made an impression on me. When she arrived yesterday, I was going to bring her up some pink lemonade. Sister Agatha quashed that. She said, "She is much too natural for pink lemonade. At least if she is like me as that was sort of my reaction to it. I don't know why we even have it in the house." Horror of Horrors, I brought her up the regular lemonade.

Although this is an electric type writer, it is portable. Hence, the keys are much harder to press than the model back at the convent which I have grown accustomed. Good Night!

July 1st, 1993

From Thomas's birthday to my late brother Karl's birthday, it is July 1st, 1993. Karl would have been 38 years of age. My Mass and Holy Communion were for him this morning. The gal who flew in from Montana offered her Mass intentions for Karl too. Her name is, Virginia, just like me. She is called "Gigi". I got to pick one of the retreatants to bring the Gifts up with me, so I picked Gigi.

Gigi is a very capable gal – a few years older than myself. She hails from Montana. She has blonde short hair and blue eyes. She is lean and strong – an athletic look about her. She and her sister live in the mountains. They do not have electricity. They are very independent. They split their own wood, fish for their food, hunt and they have their garden. Virginia's sister's name is Marnell. Marnell is a gifted artist. Her work can bring in a fair amount which helps sustain their lifestyle. Recently, they lost their mother. They kept vigil while the mother offered her life to the Lord. They even built their mother's coffin and buried her themselves; gives new meaning to a low cost funeral. Anyway, Gigi had written to the Cardinal and here she was on retreat. The Cardinal was very impressed with her letter.

I look forward to visiting with an older Monsignor when I come to St. John Neuman. His name is Monsignor Green. He has a lot of wisdom. He gave me a prayer card of St. Anne with Mother Mary as a little girl. He also blessed my veil for me. I have two, one was blessed by the Cardinal. I asked Father Halligan to bless my habit.

XVII. Fourth of July

It is our letter writing day today. I am typing up something to send Grampa. Am also listening for the phone and manning the door for Rosario. Rosario was cute when she received the habit. She took the name 'John' for St. John the Evangelist. She was rather emphatic about this as Patti was taking the name John for the Cardinal. She would be Sister Gabriel John because she was born on the Feast of Guardian Angels.

I really like Gigi, though, some of her stories are unbelievable. She has a good sense of humor too. I asked her if she liked 'pink lemonade' and she said, "Bring it on." I was reassured. She would like to stay without returning home because the ticket alone is $500. Mother Regina told her that she would have to go back home. She would need to take tests and so forth. "I'll sleep in the garden. I'll even do your gardening!" Mother was a bit reserved with her. She handed her over to the Cardinal. The Cardinal enjoyed her candor. He found her refreshing. He did want her to return home to say good-bye to her sister and father. There are the other preliminaries too. The Cardinal said he would get her flight ticket. Meanwhile, he has arranged for her to stay for a few days.

We watched the fire works from the high roof, my former dancing arena, and Wow! They were spectacular! The moon was nearly full and the bridges lit up, and the hot, hazy summer sky was sparkling all around the East River and Long Island Sound. Sparklers and fountains of color lit up the sky making lots of crackling noise.

Am recalling one of our classes on Poverty when Mother Regina illustrates how this man in the TV commercial goes behind a barn to eat, rather horde, his candy bar. He did not want to share it. Sister Francis Mary got a kick out of that. Hmmmm

A big catch word around here is "Share". Maura, often will say, "Oh, thank you for sharing." Usually it will be after an unsavory discussion during meal time when conversing is permitted. It might be medical talk or talk about creepy crawly things. Sometimes she will thow the adjective "profound" in there to make it more effective. It is kind of a spin on those group discussions they have at retreats or prayer meetings where the director will say, "Would you like to share your experience with us?"

Speaking of Maura. She is very fond of Mother Regina herself. She has taken the name of the foundress of Mother's Community in Nashville. That name is 'Cecilia'; hence Maura is now Sister Cecilia.

Sister Francis Mary is so enjoyable in her own way. I don't think anyone else appreciates her the way I do. The other day, she was sitting at the table finishing her lunch, and she says, "Sister James," pause, "I am waiting for the ice cream." I laugh. Sister Margaret overhears it, and she takes things literally. You need an interpreter to translate everything to her. She says, "Oh, is there ice cream?" which was kind of a dumb question. Then Sister Francis Mary says, "Well, I wouldn't want to be singular."

I was in the office copying the schedule since I had given mine to a retreatant. Peter from Vietnam was assisting me. Sister Francis Mary pops her head in the door, "Peter, do you know this sister, my renegade friend?" Sister Francis Mary looks both mischievous and very holy at once, and slowly, she says, "I am Sister Mary Pious." I thought I would die. Peter looked, and even though he is from another country, he knew she was up to something. He laughed too. Peter did get me a correction ribbon too.

Dring one of the Cardinal's talks at the retreat, he decides to read from a letter he had receivd the previous evening. He closes with, "And I think you are the greatest American. You are my hero." He prefaced it using that word "share" coincidentally. Humility is truth. Have to admire that which he was keeping anonymous. One of the inquiring retreatants spoke out, "Where does your mother live!" That was kind of funny, but he rebuffed in saying, "Isn't it interesting what one will say when one decides not to enter The Sisters of Hope.

His Eminence came for the Fourth of July cookout, only we had it on the fifth of July. Today is the anniversary of Gramma LaPointe. It was 1976 and it is vivid to me still. I enjoyed seeing the Cardinal. I feel more relaxed around him. I also try to maintain a proper reserve. He came towards me and for the first time in about six months, he asked, "How is Grand Pop?" I was astonished. Nearly couldn't speak, 'Uh, good -" says I , then he says, "Is he happy you are here?" "Yes, Your Eminence. He is. Thank you for asking." That was very nice and personable of him to ask. I get the impression that, somehow, I have proved myself to him. He must be getting a favorable report on me or something as the vibes are better. He even called me "Heidi" again on this retreat. He had not called me that since I was a postulant. The poor man, he seemed like he felt dizzy. He suffers so much persecution for The Church. He is a good man and he is a holy man. He also knows my neighbor back home – Brigadier General Jim King. They served in the Navy together. He knows Father Salmon too.

I am such a klutz or just a lousy morning person. Was coming out o fthe Blessed Sacrament Chapel at St. John Neumann first thing in the morning. As I approached Mother Regina, all my books fell at her feet. "G'Morning." She said in her Southern drawl smiling. Then, today, I went to sit in my chair at the barbeque. It was on a hill, or a slope rather, and I tip over in the chair. Before I hit the ground, I manage to catch myself. Monsignor McDonald looks and then decides to make like he did not notice, a real diplomat. The Cardinal did the same thing. "Oh, hello…." I said.

Speaking of falling off chairs, I had Monsignor O'Rourke falling off his chair during Confession of all places. It was not the intent. I told him one of the retreatants was feeling a little put out on account she being older and all. I did not know what advice to give her though I tried to buffer her and make her feel better. "Pehaps she could go to the Cardinal." Monsignor suggested. "Well, yeah, she did that," I interjected, "only the Cardinal fell asleep on her." Well that sent the good Monsignor roaring which in turn provoked me to laugh. He tried to compose himself, "Yes, laughter is a gift of the Holy Spirit. It is good to have joy….." Then, he would lose it again, and I would too.

The other day as I was going out to see I could hear the bagpipes. I ran into a lady who was half Italian and half Puerto Rican. Her name is Lillian, her last name slips my mind. She wanted to go to the church but I knew it was locked. So I brought her into our chapel. I asked Mother Regina if I could show her and she said, "Sure." Lillian was very grateful. Tears came streaming down her face. It was very hot out so I got her some iced tea and cookies. She kept thanking the Lord. It was beautiful. I know how it feels to be at the right place at the right time and how it is a real answer to prayer. I asked Sister Lucy to assist with directions to the bus depot for Lillian. Then I went down to the kitchen to get the financial consultants some refreshments. When I came back, she was gone. I ran down to the bus stop to see if I could find her. "Lillian! Lillian!" She gave me a big hug. That made my day.

The Struggle

I don't know. It must be me, or maybe there is a full moon. If I could only accept things better. I suppose I am mad at myself for not being more accepting of things or welcoming misunderstandings than the actual reprimands. I can not continue my story until I at least get this off my chest. I can not tell anyone here because that is just leaving oneself open for more misunderstanding and judgment. Then one regrets that he was stupid in a vulnerable moment or that he sought consolation or worse yet – trusted somebody! How weak I am! The worst is when the Superior puts guilt in where there is no guilt. I guess it is to make one question his actions. I don't understand. Blessed Scrupulosity! Today after Mass, I no sooner get to the house, and I turned right back around to go back to the church to pick up a paper for my new friend Gigi. I hear a voice behind me, "Sister James Mariah, I need to know where you are going." "Oh, I just went to the church to pick up a paper for Virginia." Then Mother Regina says, "No, I need to see you." She pulls me in the front parlor, and says, "You know, you want to be sure and set a good example for her." I said, "Yes…." But I really do not know in which way I had erred. Most of the Sisters were still at the church or just coming out. Getting the paper would have taken all of sixty seconds. Perhaps she finds me too social and she was trying to squelch me. I do say hello to the parishioners on Sunday. I noticed Mother staring at me when I said hello to some folks. I kept my place, but her look was reproving. I then walked over towards her and Monsignor Devlin. Another Sister was there too but Mother said nothing to me. I suffer from "Superior-Clash" Syndrome; also, "Superior-elect Clash Syndrome". I was not permitted to go over and get the paper. I might be able to go after lunch in the 1:30 to 2:30 block of time, but then the church may be locked, and the paper may be gone. I guess I will just have to photo copy the articles for Gigi.

My other chastisements of the week include getting the kebosh on going to Carvel's with Peter Nyung. Last Thursday, after lunch, he asked if I wanted to go for ice cream. He asked Sister Francis Mary and Sister Aquinas too. Sister Francis lives for ice cream. She was all set to go until she heard Father Des say, "I hear you are going to Carvel's." Then she came to me and said, "The word is out. Count me out." Then she says, you may get in trouble. This Vietnamese seminarian merely wanted to share his story about how he escaped a Communist regime. He also wanted to take picture by Mount St. Vincent's. I thought, I will do the right thing and get permission from Mother. "No that is out of the question. I think you know why." She flatly said. "It would be different if he were going to take everyone." Seriously? A Vietnamese refugee is going to treat a dozen and a half Sisters to Carvel's and the retreatants too? I dreaded telling Peter. There would have been two others with us, so how could it be wrong? This made me mad. The poor guy is trying to make money to send to his family back home – a family he is unlikely to ever see again. They are poor beyond our comprehension. He is only 23 years old but he has been through the worst kind of living Hell imaginable. His story was compelling. I can learn from him – his interesting and heart wrenching story. I was permitted to talk to him on the property. Peter gave me his story which he had written. I read it later. It was better than any kind of spiritual reading that I could have done. It made me realize how fortunate I am. I should not complain or be homesick when I look on the sacrifice he has made. His reward is exponentially greater. Oh that I could give more. I do not accept 'No's' very well. I was a wreck over it, though exteriorly, I appeared to be the obedient novice. I still do not see anything wrong in this. I walk past this ice cream shop every day. This was going to be the day to stop. Nope.

Then, last night, what video to watch for the Fourth of July. Sister Aquinas suggest '1776' which was appropriate. I suggested 'Mr. Smith Goes to Washington' with Jimmy Stewart, or Sargent York. Yankee Doodle Dandy would have been good, or any movie with John Wayne. But no, Sister Agatha has a crush on Gregory Peck so she was bound and determined that we would be watching 'To Kill a Mockingbird'. I used to like Gregory Peck myself, but I have since soured on him since he loused thing up for Judge Bork. There was probably another motive – to appeal to our Southern Superior. The movie is depressing too. Michelle mentioned a film called "Blossoms in the Dust". It sounds nice though I never heard of it. I even suggested the video of 'The Tattoo at the Fort' but Patti who is now Sister John Gabriel emphatically says, "You are not going to drive that down our throats!" Michelle's recommendation actually won the vote. Sister Agatha glared at me. I don't think there are any real patriots in the group. I have to give Sister Aquinas her due here. Cornelia is adorable. She looks like the Anne of Green Gables type or the Little House on the Praire main character. She sweetly says, "In the movie '1776', everyone says 'Nay' or 'Yay'!" After this fedreal production, Sister Agatha came back with her choice of course. We could have asked our guest Gigi what she would have liked. I think that this is a foretaste of what lies ahead.

8 July 1993

Had some upsetting news from home. Mother Regina let me take my mail as it was marked "Important". Uncle Mike has been diagnosed with Cancer. He and Aunt Mary have been so good to me and the family. There was other sad news too. I used to take care of a family for a doctor in town. The doctor died of a heart attack on his birthday surrounded by his children and two of my nephews. He was the kind of a doctor who took poor patients without insurance that others would not take.
God rest Dr. Michael Shuhler and help his three young children.

Where there is no doubt, doubt is put in. Where there is no guilt, guilt is put in, and where there is confidence, it is taken away. Are we not Sisters of Hope? Is it not in God's Holy Plan that we reach out in human compassion? Maybe I let my heart rule too much. I

291

am trying to be obedient. Naturally, I would write a letter. It is second nature. Only when I ask, I feel misunderstood and I am told 'no'. It seems that it is loving Christ more when one reaches out with an encouraging or comforting word or letter. Only it is the opposite here. It is precisely in not doing so that I m doing "God's will." There is such unfairness. Sister Agatha sends out globs of letters on a regular basis. I try to take it to the Cross, only I have seen too many regrets in life where a person has said, " If only I had done something...."

9 July 1993

It was so nice to see Father Halligan again. We missed him last week on account of retreat. He stayed for supper.

It was 100 degrees Farenheit today!

Forgot to mention that Gigi has a squirt gun which she fills with Holy Water in which she then squirts her subjects. She said that she squirted a couple of "love birds" outside her window the other night. Then they left. Because of her unorthodox ways, a lot of people do not know quite how to take her.

Was thinking of a funny story Mrs. Keogh, a lady I used to take care of, told me. There was a lady, a school teacher like herself, named Jean Primmore. She was telling the priest, in Confession, that she had always wanted to try something daring. She got up in the middle of the night and proceded to paint her toe nails red! Mrs. Keogh said that he told her to paint the barn for penance.

Michelle has just shown me how to use the computer. Sister Francis Mary says that I will never go back to the typewriter. I find that hard to believe, but everyone says that. I am going to write about my birthday.
Grampa sent me roses. No one was around when I opened the card from Grampa. Then, out of nowhere, Mother Regina comes trailing through the community room catching me in this private moment. As I am in the basement office writing, Mother Regina comes in. She told me to go up and call my grandfather to thank him for the

bouquet of yellow roses. There was one red rose in the midst of the arrangement. My friend Chrissy, who is a florist back home, was sure to tell the florist here to put this particular hybrid of red rose in it. It is the "Life Rose" and we are all about respecting the sanctity of life. It was good to hear Grampa's voice. The heat was getting to him and he was still shook on Dr. Shuhler's death. Dr. Shuhler would make house calls for him. Grampa said the family tried to phone me yesterday but I was not here. Along with all the Sisters, I went to the Cardinal's Residence. Monsignor McDonald cooked hot dogs and hamburgers on the grill. The Cardinal said, "It is Sister James Mariah's Birthday..." Then, he led in the singing of one of my most favorite songs in the whole world - 'HAPPY BIRTHDAY'. There were two Cardinals, two Bishops, the good Monsignor along with the Sisters who serenaded me. It was very nice. I felt very calm perhaps in disbelief. "Thank you very much Your Eminence. That was very nice and unexpected." His Eminence put his arm around me and smiled. He looked really good – good coloring and like he was having a good time. It was sung to me no less than three times on this day. It evokes that strong sentiment in the way 'Auld Lang Syne' does. I love that song too! Monsignor McDonald presented me a muffin with a candle in it. His birthday is on the ninth.

We had our Vespers in the Cardinal's chapel. It was very nice to see. As I was coming downstairs, I saw Bishop Sheridan and His Eminence, Cardinal Cassidy, from Australia. They had just come back from Rome. I kissed their rings both respectively and respectfully. Bishop Manselle was also present but I did not kiss his ring because I feel that he is uncomfortable with that.

XVIII. Pressed Dinner Napkins

Sister Francis Mary is in here typing letters and thank you notes. For some strange reason, she is sticking her tongue out at me. Often she will chew at me, but I get a kick out of it. Yesterday at breakfast, she says to me, "How do you like the napkins?" "Yeah, very pretty." Then she adds, "I didn't even iron them." "Oh really," says

I, "You would never know." Then she confides, "Don't be telling anyone, but, I put them under my mattress last night."

Mother Regina stayed up late the night before making me an apron for my birthday. I guess I was making a nuisance of myself as I kept going in and out of the sewing room talking to her and showing her pictures. She had a peculiar expression on her face. Now I know why. She presented me with this apron prefacing it, "Sister James Mariah, I could have killed you!"

Sophia came in the office that night and asked me what kind of cake I liked. I told her that I like 'Devil's Food' cake but I just would get the regular chocolate because I did not like that name 'Devil' in the title. She smiled and said that I should have "Angel Food" cake. Later, I happened to go into the kitchen. I thought I would turn the stove off because it felt hot yet the lights were off in the kitchen. I noticed the temperature was 350 degrees. Then, it occurred to me – this might be my birthday cake baking! Now, I had to discreetly go upstairs undetected before Patti now Sister Gabriel John would discover I had been there. Made it! Whoosh! Incidentally, it was a lemon cake which was refreshing in this hot weather.
I found two bars of my favorite kind of soap on my bed. Sister Gabriel brought them back for me from her home visit. The soap is called "Magno'. It is a black glycerine soap from Spain. It makes a nice white lather and it has the cleanest scent to it. She is very good to me. She told me that she has two Guardian Angels. One is named Leonard, and I think the other one is Louis, but I am not positive.

I have a minute before supper to jot down a few thoughts before they escape me. The other day, after breakfast, Leila was primping and promping about – saying how beautiful she is in one of the blouses I had given her. It was strict silence. She was going on for three minutes. I was still finishing my breakfast because I was a server. I was trying hard to refrain from laughter especially because Mother Assumpta was behind her watching this whole performance. The more I would grimace, the more Leila would act up, "Lah di dah, aren't I beautiful..." Then, she swirled around only to see the Superior. She was so embarrassed. I thought I would die.

We were sitting outside for recreation the other night. Suddenly, one, then two little green apples came whirling over the wall followed by a raspy voice, "Will you people shut up over there!" It was none other than Monsignor Devlin. He is a character. Then, this morning, a huge moving truck was parked in front of the convent. Monsignor Devlin says, "Are we getting rid of you?" He was referring to the whole lot of us.

Recalling that story about Jean Primmore and the red nail polish, well, Leila presented me with a little wrapped gift which was Red Nail Polish! A sticker was affixed to it which said, "Give your toes a treat." Everyone laughed. Leila said this was one of the fruits of her morning meditation.

Mr. Gallagher had given us some fresh Boston Scrod from the market. Sister Gabriel cooked it to perfection. Then of course was that lemon cake which I spied the night before. There were 34 yellow candles on the cake. I blew each and every one of them out. Kind of hated to leave '33' as it is a significant number.

19 July 1993

I should know better than to sit beside Sister Francis Mary during meal time when it is supposed to be quiet, or during Holy Hour away from the convent as was the case in Larchmont. It was hot, and we had gone for long walks, and we were just lulling in the atmoshere. Father Groschel had Holy Hour outdoors with Exposition of The Blessed Sacrament. Sister Francis is sitting beside me. She had one of those expressions on her face like she could care if school keeps. Then it came time to say the Magnificant. We usually chant it so we break it up diffently than it was said here. Plus, we were all going by memory. We got hysterical. Sister Francis was making up the words. No one was saying the right words at the right time. It was awful trying to hold back laughter sitting beside her. The worst was when she turned sideways away from me. She grabbed a spiritual book in a desperate attempt to maintain composure. What makes it harder, is, you don't want to laugh when Father Groeschel is speaking.

Helene sent me a beautiful night dress from, of all places, "Victoria's Secret". It has roses on it and sweet tucking and little lace fringe. It is cotton. I almost wish she had not sent it as now I have to ask permission to keep it. It is lovely. Mother Regina is apt to see the "worldliness" in it. Was showing it to Sister Francis Mary, and she showed me a way to conceal the "frills". Then, she neatly laid the matching slippers on top. She told me to get a box. I suggested an old brown paper bag. It would look less frivolous. I am still waiting for my meeting with the Superior. Hopefully, it will be after a good meal and that she will feel rested – refreshed. I have to ask her a number of things. Gosh, I wish we weren't studying Obedience. I could plead ignorance then. Some would probably argue that – that would not be too hard anyway.

Letter from Grampa

Dear Sr. J.M. (Virginia),

Just great talking to you Saturday.

You would think that an Order that is supposed to offer "Hope' would be more accepting in these trivial
matters. They are going to turn people off. Just do not understand how thy want to separate you from family. But just keep on doing what you are doing. I am so proud of you. Remember to stand your ground too.

I sense your trials and tribulations in the order and I just want you to know that you are a credit to them. I pray for you all the time. I am so proud of you. Don't forget, God is on your side.

Sorry about your English friend. I am still shook over the good doctor's death.

I talked with Fr. Halligan and his sister last night (call me Betty). Fr. H. told me all about the surprise party you had for him and how you used the Fort Ti placemats. They both think so much of you. It made me feel good.

Father Garvin brought me Holy Communion. I really enjoy him.

The Kings are always asking about you.

Well my dear Virginia, I miss you and care for you so much.

God Bless you,
Love,
Gramp

Mid-July

Just came in from outdoors. We had to husk corn and take the stems off of the beans so Sister Gabriel can cook and freeze them. Mr. Gallagher sent over a whole load of them.

Yesterday, after our class on Poverty, Sister Francis Mary went up to Mother Assumpta, 'Mother, is it stealing to take a piece of cake or get something to eat in-between meals?" She had guilt written all over her face. Mother Assumpta looked in Sister's Irish blue eyes that take on a childlike quality, and she replies, "No, of course it is alright if you feel the need to have something." I had to laugh because when I was proculator, Sister Francis Mary was making Ice cream sodas left and right besides pilfering chocolate bars. I often would get snacks myself. Now I am getting general permission to take something at eleven a.m. as I get low sugar then.

July 18th, 1993

Yesterday, Sister Francis Mary wanted to go to the five and dime store otherwise known as "Frank Bees". She wanted to get some towels fr her bathroom in her area of duty. She said that she was going to walk, but that is a hike – a good one and a half miles each way. I offered to take her. Lately, she has been talking about death a lot. She figured, "What the hay, I will live dangerously." Then she told Monsignor Devlin to be prepared to give 'The Last Rites'. She is something else as a passenger: " We have a stop sign up ahead, the light is red, and someone is going to cross in front of

you." All this backseat driving contiued to and from Frank Bees.
"Be careful! Don't get in an accident! Just keep your eyes on the
road!" When I got back in the car, after picking up Sophia's photos
at the Quick Photo Shop, Sister Francis Mary had this mischievous
expression on her face. She says, "How daring are you?" I am
thinking that I just drove in the Bronx with her in the car. The
"Golden Arches" were right in front of us, and it was on our way to
the Post Office. She feels as strongly about McDonald's as I do
about Post Offices. She has an affinity for writing letters too, but
she can mask it better as letter writing is one of her duties. She does
write beautiful thank you notes. She also includes quite a few of her
own correspondence in with them. "Just go thorugh the "Drive –
Thru" she says excitedly. She is drooling for a hot fudge sundae and
I am not about to deprive her of one especially since she has herself
half buried.
"May I help you…." The voice came over the speaker.
"Uh, yeah, I'll take one of your hot fudge sundaes and one of your
hot butterscotch sundaes."
"We don't have butterscotch. It is hot carmel."
"That is fine. I will take that."
"Do you want nuts?" "Sister Francis Mary, do you want nuts?" She
says no.
"Okay, that will be $2.14." Sister Francis Mary, do you want a
receipt?" She was nervously fumbling for her change. Then she
shouts at me, "Turn that radio off! We are supposed to be silent!" If
that doesn't beat all! I was trying to find a spot by the Saint Jean de
Baptiste Nursing Home near the water as it is a pretty spot. We
figured no one would scout us out there. Meanwhile, the ice cream
is melting and Sister Francis hollars, "Whatever you do, don't get us
in an accident! That is all we need to be caught with our sundaes!" I
never did find that spot because Sister Francis was getting too
nervous. I went over by the marina. "Quick, get rid of the
evidence!" She says. I put the empties in the trash.

One time we were heading to class in Monroe and Father Anthony
came over to the van. Sister Francis Mary said, "You got to bed late
last night."
"How do you know?" He annunciates clearly.

"Because I saw your lights on. I went out on the porch." Sister Francis Mary used to watch the comings and goings of Father Paul at the rectory from the upstairs porch. She is so funny. I don't know what I would do without her. Just tonight while doing dishes, she whacks me with the dish towel. The next night, she splashes me with dish water.

About Sophia – as I stated before, she is a very striking beauty. She is nice too. However, when the brochures were in the process of being made, she had a secret desire to see or have her picture on the front of them. It would certainly attract people. It was just the measures that she took to carry this out that left me unsettled. Sophia wanted me to place a phone call to the Cardinal's office where likely his secretary or attorney would answer. Sophia wanted me to relay that unless they used her picture, she was considering leaving the community. It must be a cultural thing for her or her desire to make her family proud. She went so far as to scan the corridor while I was to be inside the office on the second floor placing this unusual phone call/request. I was uncomfortable about it. I did not make the phone call. I pretended that I did and that I left a message.

Another person who wanted to be featured in a publication, this time the New York Catholic paper, was Sister Josephat. She would go out of her wayto push me aside explaining, "They are mainly interested in the original first group of novices." She tried to get in as many pictures as possible. The weird thing is, when the paper came out, it was my picture that was featured on the front of the article. God sure has a sense of humor.

20 July 1993

Today I am portress. During recreation time, I take the phone up to the third floor and plug it in the jack there. I then try to catch a few "z's". Well, I can not catch them with my habit on, so I am barefoot, without my veil, and just a slip and tee shirt. Meanwhile, Sister Francis Mary has just awakened. She uses Sister Immaculata's old room and sprawls out on the bed in there. There are two reasons for this: one, her bed remains neat and made up, and two, the fact that

299

she is napping goes unnoticed. Only today I happened to notice th edoor closed which it normally is not. I peered in to see "the slain Saint". The phone rings, so naturally, I answer it.

"Hello, Sisters of Hope....."

The lady on the other end is a Mary Ellen Gibbard of Dunwoodie. She is asking about the new habits. "Are they hot?"

"Oh yes, they are warm. But I don't mind. I am a romantic so it is worth it for this nice habit."

Then she says, "Well, it is a penance."

"That's right. And isn't that what life is all about - "

At this point, Sister Francis Mary emerges in the hall, and I continue my conversation. "You know, a life of prayer, fasting mortification, penance...."

Suddenly, I notice that Sister Francis Mary is bent over in hysterics. She was bellowing in laughter with tears streaming down her face. Mary Ellen could even hear her through the phone. Here in our supposed silent cloister, Sister could be heard throughout the whole convent. Meanwhile, Sister Cecilia, formerly Maura, is going down to get the Superior as the phone is really for her. Sister Francis said here I was very relaxed and carefree with cookies and a cup of tea going in my room. I was anything but roasting in the habit while talking about mortifications. Yes, she did relay this episode to the Superior.

Phone rings later, "Hello, Sisters of Hope...."

"Is Sister Ascension there?" It was the electrician. I assumed he meant Mother Regina so I went to get her.

27 July 1993

At lunch, Mother Regina was discussing the guests who would be arriving the next day. "They are French Sisters." Then Sister Agatha chimed in, "The daughter of Hope and John Carter recommended that they come to us. John Carter is of course the President of Time-Life."

300

"Whoa!" says me. "You mean Hope and John Carter?!" Everyone at the table stopped eating. "I don't believe this, but I know them." It was funny because no one expected this. "Yeah, I waited on them when I worked at The Basin Harbor Club in Vermont. They have twelve children just like my family. In fact, they have a son named Henry same as I have a brother Henry. Henry loved "Shirley Temples". He was slightly mentally challenged. I used to load up on the cherries for him. When I was off duty, I would swim with the children. They were real nice and I felt very comfortable with them."

The Carters did something else for me which I did not share with the Sisters. It is something that I will never forget. I had just lost my dear friend Mark Day who was on a Heifer Project in Tanzania. I don't know what propelled Mr. Carter, but before he left, he presented me with a check for $100.00. He said to me, "Virginia, this is for you to do something special with that you have been wanting to do." How could he do this? How would he know? I was befumbled. I had wanted to do something for Mark. I sent it to Mark's mother and father in Monroe, Connecticut. A weeping cherry tree was planted in front of the church where Mark use to go. There is a bronze plaque beneath it. Mark's parents sent me a photograph of it. I hope to see it someday. I also received a beautiful letter of consolation from Mark's Pastor",Reverend Pierce.

The world is indeed small. I was sorry to learn that Mr. Carter has since died. I sent a note to his family by way of the French Sisters and Leigh Dupont who brought them over. Leigh used my Rosary beads to pray the Rosary. I liked her very much. I nedd a concluding sentence as the bell is ringing – does this count?!

XIX. Silent Retreat

We went to Wrentham for a 'Silent Retreat'. It seems Sister Agatha knows this priest and it was on her recommendation that we got him. He is going to be leading us in spiritual direction. The priest is young albeit very ascetic from New England. He belongs to a Religious Order. I was very impressed with his talks – so much so, that I disregarded the fact he might be a family friend of Sister

Agatha's. I opened up to him and told him my travails. I confided to him that I felt there was a jealousy of one having more 'crosses', sufferings than the other. With a large family, there is exponentially greater joys in the same way that there are many more sorrows and sufferings. Sister Agatha is from a fairly large family, but lately it seems I have had more in which to contend. It has been easier for me to accept these crosses of illness and death with those close to me, than it has been to accept the petty foolishness of those here trying to act like the voice of authority. This priest, who shall remain nameless, only to say he is renown today, helped me tremendously. He prays and fasts a lot. He has such a clear grasp of matters. This was such an unexpected and welcome consolation and affirmation to me. God Bless this holy man of God.

It was hard driving through Attleboro knowing Grampa's first cousin lives there. I would have given anything if we could have stopped by Morin's Diner just to say hello. Likely there would have been a piece of pie in it for everyone. Paul gave Karl a bunch of lobsters when he stopped on his way back fro Cape Cod. I mentioned this to the Superior, but she dismissed the idea.

Frank and Barbara are the care takers of the McMahon estate opposite the Cistercian Abbey where group two and three of the novices stayed along with the postulants. The first group of Sisters stayed at the Trappistine Abbey. Mother Regina stayed with us. Once again, she had the room opposite me. I had a nice big room This place was gorgeous! I love the old "Standard" fixtures – the old fashioned sinks and shower heads. I guess this mansion was built in the twenties. It features Georgian architecture throughout. It also has a real Yankee or New England feel to it.
Frank and Barbara are characters. Frank Pariseau is a little French man with a hearing aid. He is likely in his early seventies. He is real loud and here we are supposed to keep strict silence. He would be helpful with non - incidentals or he would just like to shoot the breeze. Sister Gabriel was telling him how the milk pitcher was broken or got chipped near the spout.
"Heck, accidents happen. They happen to the best of us." Frank says. Then he goes on to say, "We can pick them up a dime a dozen," he enjoyed being helpful in this mundane situation. He has

seven children and I forget how many grandchildren. He says he prays for the life of the unborn. "Yep, I am a real pro-lifer". When I asked him for a mop, his wife Barbara says, "I thought I heard a bang." It just so happened Sophia broke one of those old fashion window blinds. It was made out of wood. Sister Cecilia wanted me to get the mop for the kitchen. We would be in there cleaning and you could hear Frank and Barbara talking loudly back and forth watching 'Wheel of Fortune'. They are happy as clams with their "Genny's" and cigarettes. When we were leaving, Frank says, "Hey, any of you got a camera? What I generally do for our guest is, I take their picture so they have a little memento of the McMahon estate – you know. And I can work an instamatic no problem." "Sure," says I. Mother Regina's patience is running thin especially since I first took Frank's picture as I felt he would like that. He was patting his two dogs and you know, I think he hated to see us leave. Oh, he said one other thing, "We haven't had any complaints from our guests. We even have had them come as far away as France." Good people making an honest living.

31 July 1993

Did you know that on the Feast of Saint James, if you look up into the sky, you can see the pilgrim making their way – that is, the 'Sacra Way' to Santiago de Compostella. This year marks a Holy Year on the Church calendar as Saint James's Feast falls on a Sunday. It is the third most popular place of pilgrimage in the world followed by The Holy Land, and Rome. I have been fortunate enough to visit this shrine on two occasions. I witnessed the swinging o fthe great "Botufumeiro" which swings from the Cathedral vaulted ceiling with incense burning within. A good friend of mine back home has made "The Way" several times and his family has even accompanied him. Hello Pat Devaney! I did not realize that one day, I would be taking the name of 'James' in religious life. Father Halligan was my inspiration for that though. If it was not enough for His Eminence to come on my birthday two weeks ago, he came on my feast day too. We sat outdoors with a simple lunch of soup brought by Mr. Honerkamp. We also had a nice salad and a fruit cup for dessert. The Cardinal came over to me, and put his arm around my shoulders and wished me a Happy Feast

Day. I just soaked it in. Afterward, we got our picture taken. He celebrated Mass earlier in the church. It was very special.

The Sisters had a nice breakfast prepared for me. Sister Francis Mary was sure to see that nice linens were put on the tables. She is quite proud of herself these days as she is getting away without ironing the napkins. She continues to put them under her mattress. Sister Mary Pio cut up fresh mangos from Florida which came from Sophia's family. Sister Gabriel arranged flowers in a vase which was set beside Mother Regina. Usually, this is the "hot seat" but today it would be marked as an honor to sit next to the Superior.

Then, she picks up my sleeve, which appeared ever so slightly soiled, and she asked in front of everyone on my feast day, "Did you put on a clean habit today?" I was mortified. I answered, "Since we cleaned on Friday, I put my fresh habit on yesterday as opposed to today so that I could wash my other one before Sunday." She was not please with my answer. She felt she had made her point. Immediately after breakfast, I went into the laundry room, and Sister Cecilia dipped a brush in some bleach. She helped me scrub my sleeves and cuffs. Just like the commercial, "We tried scrubbing them, we tried soaking them, and we still couldn't get them entirely clean."

There were gifts at my place setting – the assorted prayer cards with Holy picture. Mother Regina gave me a cassette of The Poor Clares from Alabama singing Marian hymns. She also gave me a tiny medal of Mother Mary which she got in Rome. She wrapped up note paper too. Hmmm – could this be a presumed permission? She also gave me a little Scriptural Rosary bookle with black and white woodcut images of Our Lady in it. Sister Francis Mary was very thoughtful. She had asked me for a picture of Grampa the previous night. The next day, I received back – framed! She is so cute. She also gave me some Scripture verses in a little arylic rose box which has been recycled as a feast day gift several times now. She gave me a feast day card which she had in her private stock. Plus, she gave me a miniature book to write down my prayers in. Brother Ray had given her the book and I appreciate how she parted with it for me.

She has been taking me under her wing a lot lately. Sister Margaret was most generous in her Spiritual Bouquet for me. It included one month of Rosaries, plus the daily recitation of The Seven Scourges

of Our Lord for 33 days. She also stayed up late the night before making me a special dessert for dinner. She made three layer grasshopper bars. She outdid herself. I was very impressed.
We had the lively community of The Sister Servants of Mary come over to help celebrate. They serenaded me with their vibrant Spanish cheer clapping their hands and singing loudly. I love the Spanish culture. We got to have soda with dinner. Sister Gabriel manned the grill and we enjoyed a nice cookout. We did not have any wine though. Mr. Gallagher had given us a case of wine. Mother Regina gave it to these Sisters. I can not squawk though we had been having wine on all the other Sisters' feast day celebrations. To top it off, Mother Regina let me ride along with her to the Cardinal's residence to bring him a wrought iron patio chair. He had been sitting in it earlier in the day and he found it very much to his liking. It is one Sister Gabriel sent up from Kentucky. She had a whole truck load. It was a big truck too as it was the day that Monsignor Devlin joked about getting rid of us. Anyway, this chair is the next best thing to sitting on air. It has a rocking effect. If you invert it sideways, it is shaped like a "U". Sister Cecilia put a big bow on it – made from excess of funeral home ribbon.
When we arrived at the residence, there was a man sitting on the steps. He looked like he might be homeless. He was eating a bag of pop corn. "Mmm, that pop corn sure smells good." Mother Regina said to set the tone that would bespeak that she was not afraid or intimidated by this person's presence on the steps here. Then, the man looked up. He had bright brown eyes – even as the evening was getting dark. "You want some Sister?" He held his bag up. It probably would have been the ultimate compliment to him to have accepted his offer. The man was very thin and today there has been a lot of talk about the street people being HIV-positive. Mother said, "No thank you." As we were awaiting the bell, he said, "Sisters, do you know what a skull and two cross bones mean?" Then he mumbled something about a 'black mass' - I hate to even write about that which is why I did not capitalize it. He went on to say that his mother wore that on a black uniform or something. "I don't know ….." Then he said that he would look it up in an encyclopedia. He seemed sincere in his question as unexpected as it was. He was like a child in the way he asked it. Now Mother was sorry that she even made mention of the pop corn. Pop corn always smells good though.

Moira answered the bell. We both managed to get the chair in the foyer. The carpets were rolled up and off to the side. The Grandfather clock, the marble top tables and the fancy benches were all covered with sheets. The floor looked like it had just been polished. Certainly work was being done as His Eminence would not have receptions after the High Mass during the summer. I thanked the Cardinal again for coming though he happened to be in the neighborhood.

I believe that the skull and bones beneath the Cross has to do with Adam prefiguring Christ's triump over sin and death on the Cross. I think there is a place in the Holy Land where the bones of Adam are buried. Our Lord died on the Cross above that spot. I have to look into it more.

On the way home, Mother Regina said that she was going to treat me to an ice cream cone. I assured her that I could not eat another bite but the thought meant a lot to me.

I witnessed another funny scene tonight. The Sisters were cleaning up as I was leaving, and Sister Margaret was giving Sister Francis a hard time about taking a gingerale. She was saying that she had to have permission. Sister Francis Mary said rather loudly, "I do have permission! From God!" Then, as she was leaving the kitchen, she stopped at the big crate of green peppers brought by Mr. Gallagher. This was all she needed to see. Sister Margaret is very healthy in her eating habits. She enjoys her vegetables. Indeed she has the reputation of being a 'Eull Gibbons'. Sister Francis hurls a green pepper at her saying, "Here, why don't you take a green pepper to bed with you!"

2 August 1993

Monsignor Devlin is in the hospital now. He has been very sick for over ten days before he was even admitted. He has not looked well the last time I have seen him. Please God he will get better.

My heart went out to Sister Rosario (John). I know she suffers from allergies as I have been giving her my hankie every day up until July

25th. Then, when the Cardinal came, I noticed that she broke down when she approached him. She never breaks down. The Cardinal tried to comfort her but she put up a barrier. I suppose it is part of her culture. Sister Gabriel went up to hug her but Sister Rosario did not want any part of that. Sister Rosario is a private person and she probably would rather not have the matter expressed openly. Then Mother Regina informed us that Sister Rosario did not pass her Medical Boards. I could feel her pain most keenly, but I feigned to act natural – even goofy so as to put her at ease. The previous day, put some Holy cards and some candy on her bed whichfor she thanked me. Then, the next day, I found some more powerful prayers which I gave to her. She is aross the hall from me. I was coming out of my room and with complete resignation, Sister Rosario says to me, "Sister James, did you know I did not pass my boards." It was a declaration more than a question. "Oh Sister Rosario, I guess I did hear that. I am so sorry." I put my arms around her. She managed a smile. She has gotten up extra early and made many sacrifices driving in heavy traffic in the heat, giving up outings and picnic, and retreats. I would make her a lunch every day to take with her on these long days of study. Her main concern was getting to Mass, and then, being here for Spiritual direction with our confessor. She is good and she never complains. The other day as she walked in the door, she said to me exasperatedly, "Sister James? Are you praying for me?" She looked at me and waited for a reply. I looked at her, "Oh yes, I am Sister Rosario, but it is good to keep after me. Tomorrow, my Mass and Holy Communion are for you...all my prayers are." There was something desperate in her plea.

Was reading bumper stickers on the way to Wrentham. One says, "You are too damn close." This reminded me of the time Sister Francis Mary's sister, who is also a religious, was studying for the third summer in a row at Notre Dame. She always had the same room. She had always seen some tiny writing on the ceiling. This time, she would get a chair, get up on it, and find out what it said. And she did, "What the hell are you doing up here?" read the small print.

Mother Regina received a small package in the mail the other day. I am always intrigued when it comes to mail. "Hey look Mother Regina, six stamps and they are not even canceled." They came off ever so easily from the Jiffy envelope. "Good grief." She says. Then, I got thinking, maybe I shouldn't have said anything because that might be like copying a cassette or something. The next thing I noticed was that these stamps were in the stamp drawer.

The other night I went up on the roof to dance. The trees were so full. Their branches seem to reach out and touch me like Michaelangelo's "Hand of God". It was wonderful dancing in the midst of the treetops.

I made a visit to the Sisters of Saint Chretienne. This is a community that I had written to and spoke with on the telephone a couple of years ago though I never got to visit them. It was interesting to discover their Provincial house righ across from the Cistercian Abbey in Wrentham. One morning, during my meditative walk, I made my way to the front entrance of this convent. One of the Sisters was sitting at the breakfast nook in the kitchen. She was wearing a house dress and slippers. "Hello," I called out. A Sister Louisa, have always loved that name, came to the door, her hazel eyes smiling. Sister Jacqueline came down the stairs at the same time. She reminded me so much of the school nurse back home. She was on her way to a funeral for a man who worked in the hospital. He had helped out with her father for the past thirteen years. Her father is a stroke victim. She also lost a brother who was 55 years of age. Her eyes welled with tears as she recounted this. "I will pray for him." I offered. She seemed pleased. I told her that I understood that she had a funeral to get to. I just wanted to say Hi, as I had contacted you a couple of years ago. Then Sister Louisa held out a big bear-shaped jar filled with animal cookies. "Sister James, have animal cookies." She has a lovely childlike innocence. "Oh, thank you." I was not about to say no as Sister Gabriel is running a pretty tight rein in the kitchen these days. I have received a general permission from Mother to have a snack but Sister Gabriel is holding out on me. She says that I need to have a dispensation from Father Halligan. Anyway, Sister Louisa gave me two pieces of

fudge in addition to the animal cookies. I put a piece outside Sister Gabriel's door with a note that read: "Sweet Dreams from Saint Chretienne." She liked that and only because I let her in on my little secret visit earlier in the day. Sister Louisa gave me the grand tour. She told me about a Sister Joanne who recently died of Cancer at age 72. She was showing me her room with her pretty curtains and bedspread which were given to her by the dying Sister. Then she showed me her room – rather proudly. Wht I liked the most, was seeing her family picture blown up big enough to cover her bedroom wall. She has seventeen in her family. She has a sister who is in the same Order. She is in Marlborough, Massachusetts. I took delight in how Sister Louisa showed me a poster of a kitten, and "How do you like my oven?" She was so proud of everything and she took such good care of everything. She is in charge of the kitchen. She really made me feel welcome – almost, like she was expecting me. They have been preparing for eighty of their Sisters to come this weekend for a big Provincial meeting. Many would be coming as far away as France. Sister Louisa showed me the huge tray of fudge she had made fo their picnic lunch the next day.
It is the details like the fine bone china cup and saucer with pretty painted violets on it that I remember. This was in the room of Sister Joanne. Was also thinking how proud Sister Louisa is of her sister whose name is "Louise'. She said that she is a real clown. I was looking at her smiling picture. She also showed me her plant growing on top of the hi-boy in the dining room. She was very pleased that she had not over watered it. The vine, and how I wish that Sister Immaculata were here to tell me what kind it is because she has one just like it. Surely Sister Gabriel would know. The vine was flowing all over, and it hung pretty on the new china cupboard. The dining room table was also brand new. Sister Louisa proudly displayed it, lifting aside the table cloth.

August 1st, 1993

Today is my very good friend Chrissy's birthday. Tomorrow is Virginia Miller's birthday and she will be arriving on my brother Henry's birthday which is also Monsignor Smith's birthday.

309

On our way home from Wrentham yesterday, we stopped in Newport, Rhode Island. We said Midday Prayer with the Sisters of Jesus Christ Crucified. The first Sister I met, was Sister Mary Gertrude. She is from Singapore. She has a British accent. This particular accent sounds more refined than the accents of the mainland England. If I closed my eyes, it was like listening to my friend Wanda who is from a British Colony in the West Indies. Her pinafore is buttoned to her tunic which I think is a neat idea a we use a zillion safety pins on ours. Sister Gertrude got this particular habit in Japan which is only natural as they are into uniforms. I recall a plane stop on my way to China and I can still see all these uniformed children getting out of a bus. They are always so crisp and neat; tidy with their shiny black hair cut evenly. They like their hats too – that which I can appreciate.

Anyway, we were sitting in the chapel, one by one, the Sisters filed in. First, you could hear someone hobbling on crutches followed by two electric wheel chairs zooming in and taking their places.

"Certainly this can't get any worse." I thought to myself. I was either going to laugh or cry. It reminded me of that movie with Roddie McDowell as a young boy - "The Boy With Green Hair".

One of the last scenes in it that I recall is that of a group of handicapped people all gatherd round full of joy, love and peace.

They were deemed "Society's Misfits", but they were God's chosen ones. This scene here evoked that same kind of feeling. The most heart-tugging one, was this tiny, frail little elderly nun with knotted up hands wearing one shoe bigger than the other. They all were wearing braces or orthopedic shoes – one shoe being a couple of inches taller than the other. Sister Xavier projected very well as she spoke and sang. Something about her reminded me of my sister Lizzy. She had blue eyes and I am sure she must have had blonde hair at one time though it is white now. Her gestures were sharp albeit slightly spastic. I looked at the faces of these Sisters. They helped each other. They may have appeared helpless at first sight, but they were the most capable, loving, joyful Religious I have ever met. I felt spoiled – having such good health, but really, they have more. I believe all the Sisters were edified. It brought us out of ourselves. There was a nice simplicity. They took time for each other.

Mother Regina tried to tell Sister Alice that she could go ahead and start 'Office'. Sister Alice told her that she had told her Sisters it would be at noon in the event we got held up in traffic. Some of our Sisters did get caught in traffic too. I think Mother Regina was also taken aback upon seeing these Sisters, truly, of Jesus Crucified.
All twelve of these Sister pitched in providing us with a nice picnic lunch. They are amazing. They sang "Ubi Caritas" their voices blending beautifully. I love Taize. I sat with sister Mary Joanna and Sister Margaret Mary, two very intelligent nuns. Sister Joanna had a twin sister named Matilda who died some years ago. I told her I would pray fo her. She is probably about my mother's age. Both of these nuns are in a wheelchair. Sister Joanna says to me, "Sister James, tell me about yourself…." Then she chuckled, "That is, in between bites." She made me think of my Latin teacher with her expressive eyes. That little tiny nun with the gnarled hands is Sister Beatrice. She told me that she used to be Sister James until she went back to her Baptismal name.
After lunch, Mother Regina seemed anxious to get to the water, and she was tooting the horn for my benefit. I thought we were going to walk to the water. Besides, I wanted to thank each and everyone of these exemplary Sisters. Sister Gertrude came up to me, and said, "I want to give you a big hug." I looked up and I noticed Mother Regina left without me. The other van was still there. She thinks I am too social, but to me, this was the better part.

First Week of August 1993

XX. Virginia from Montana

Virginia, Gigi, from Montana arrived back on August 4th which is my brother Henry's birthday around 5:30 in the evening. It was good to see her. We never really said good-bye. The weird thing is, the Superior told me that Virginia was looking for me to see her off when in fact she had been trying to keep us separate the whole time. Sophia accompanied her to the airport and she said that Gigi was asking for me but there was no mention made of getting me.
Virginia herself told me that she felt we were being separated. She

was reluctant to send me a post card. She sent one to everyone but it had a picture of "Mariah's Pass" which is where she is from in addition to being part of my religious name.

She was put to work the instant she got here. Four days later and she is just finished unpacking. GiGi had been washing dishes and setting up the porch for a reception for Sister Agatha. Mother Regina has already finished plans for Gigi to finish laying down the parquet/parkay in the basement.

It was not enough that she built a bookshelf in the kitchen, she also had to build one for the classroom. The poor thing had just flown in, her bags were heavy and she had to have been exhausted. It seemed unfair to put all this on her.

All day on Thursday, which was Virginia's entrance day, Mother Regina gave her a huge stack of papers – another psychological exam. The questions were ridiculous. Gigi had a terrible head cold as she had cared for a battered wife and her sick children before she got here. It was not enough for her to have gone to a stupid psychologist or psychiatrist the last time she was here. The woman ried to intimidate Gigi. She refused to believe that someone her age could be so pure, innocent, simple and real. To compound things, Gigi was lead to believe that she could join us on retreat in Wrentham but then it was decided that it was too expensive for her to come. That is crazy. There were several extra beds. She actually sleeps on the floor. Food donations pour in from Mr. Gallagher and The Little Sisters of the Poor, so that is not a valid factor. Sister Francis Mary even tried to dissuade her in their conversation on the phone. After the Cardinal told her not to worry about her plane ticket, she was now being told that the flight was awful expensive. That is why she suggested staying on in the first place. Now she was told that she would have to agree to take more psychological testing and that it was conditional as to whether or not she would be accepted if she were to "fail" these tests. The psychologist in the group, the very one who was exempt from taking any of these tests, was telling her this. The problem, Sister Agatha stated, was, "Could this girl live in community?". The very one who keeps to herself, who is the most distant and aloof in the community, was saying this. I think she is crazy. Of course Sister Agatha has to mind her 'p's' and 'q's' and carry out what the acting Superior may be recommending in the name of Obedience. It is injustice and judging beyond discernment.

Gigi also eats like a bird so she hardly could have put a dent in the food. Now she has been taking those Psychological exams for over five hours straight on her entrance day with a miserable cold and fever not to mention jetlag.

Gigi had over 150 friends come to see her off back home in Olney, Montana. They came as far away as Washington, California and Oregon. These are folks Virginia met from housing people in need; many poor people but they can be counted on where it matters. Gigi holds firm to the adage, "Where there is a will, there is a way." Thus it was another humiliation to attend Church again after having said good-bye to everyone previously thinking she was returning the end of July. Since she could not be put off entirely, though I believe every effort was made to thwart her, she did come the following week. She even received letters from certain people telling her not to come. Mrs. Dechame always said that I was idealistic and give people the benefit of the doubt.

Virginia Miller is one who prefers to receive the Blessed Sacrament on her knees. It is very natural and reverential for her to do so. I admire this, however, the Superior has told her that it is spiritual pride. She also asked her to remove her head covering. Gigi has always worn a bandana on her head in the Presence of The Blessed Sacrament.

I overheard the Cardinal ask Virginia how she was feeling when he greeted her. Then I heard Mother Regina say, "Don't tell him that you're sick!" I could not believe my ears. I can not help but think that she has made her mind up a long time ago that Virginia Miller does not belong here and that she has told the Cardinal so much. It is as though the Superior is trying to do everything in her power to dissuade this aspirant. The Cardinal seems to be half going along with it as Virginia is to be subjected to yet further testing. He is, however, taken with her – fascinated by her. I showed him a picture of Gigi on her horse making a mail run and he said, "Here's a picture for our future brochure."

It was interesting the talk the Cardinal gave during the new postulant's entrance ceremony. He talked about Blessed Margaret de Costello. She was rejected from religious life because the community thought she was too holy.

313

On this night, the Superior came to Virginia's room to tell her that she had an appointment on Tuesday to see the psychiatrist. Gigi is so strong, but now, she lost it. She was already trying to finish questions on the written exam and now she was told this. She did not sleep well the night before because there were these tiny spiders or something that came in ther window through the air conditioner. This was Sister Gabriel's former room so there was an air conditioner in it and Gigi was unfamiliar with it. We sprayed 'Raid' and tried everything to fumigate the room. Then, I helped her pull the air conditioner out of the window. There was a whole swarm of these little critters on her. There was a nest on the corner of the unit where she had hold of the unit. It was dark and this was the part that was hanging on the outside of the window so there would be no way of knowing. Sophia came in the room on hearing the commotion. She suggested that Gigi ask Mother Superior for a different room. The awful thing was that Gigi referred to these critters as "lice". I knew this would not bade well with the Superior. The Superior would really think that she was crazy and disbelieve her. I tried to discourage her from going to Mother, but Gigi said, "I know lice when I see it. That's animal lice." I tried to air the room out but it still smelled strong of chemicals. Another room would be preferable but I can only imagine Mother's reaction.

"Well, you lived in poverty, you should be able to handle it."

"Yeah, but I'm not up to lice. There is a difference between poverty and cleanliness."

In the end, she did go up and sleep in Sister Immaculata's old room which is next to Sister Francis's room, the latter to whom she gave quite a fright. Sister Francis has taken over the room to store her linen napkins and table cloths and assorted "contraband" in her spare suitcases.

Mother Regina had upset Virginia in regard to finishing the written tests on the night of her entrance ceremony. She did say that she could go to bed and finish them in the morning.

Next day

Gigi is in Manhattan seeing a shrink. They should all just shrink and shrivel up away and stop trying to get in people's heads, heart and souls. Even Monsignor Smith infers it is a business and he looks down on that "profession". When Monsignor came for class, it was "overlooked" that the new postulant was not introduced to him. Last night, Mother Superior told Gigi that she would go to a different pshychaitrist. Virginia responded, "Good, I have been invoking St. Joan of Arc." Mother just looked at her and Gigi continued, "She was burned at the stake."

They are trying to convince her that she can not live in community where she has lived with us and the retreatants for over two weeks. Everyone sought her out. People are drawn to her goodness.

I did ask Gigi about how it was that she was not using the poker in her woodstove back home when she was miraculously spared from getting burned. She replied, "Because I am stupid. I do dumb things like that without even thinking. Then my mother stopped me."

Instead, she has come here to get "burned". Virginia has reconciled herself to offer up all the crosses that come her way for The Holy Father and the Church.

Excerpts from a letter from Leon Prior:

Dear Sister James Mariah,

We were so pleased ro receive your interesting letter. Congratulations on your selection of The Sisters of Hope for your life's work.

Adjustment to a new way of life always requires self-discipline. Your jolly sense of humor can only help make it easier. Do not ever lose your sense of humor Mildred Virginia – remember when I used to call you that?! We remember all the laughs we had in China with the assorted personalities in our group.

Remember when "Dirty Gertie" was the only one to eat the ugly "black chicken" served at Dazu and thereafter suffered a severe case of the Chinese trots. Can still see that thing lying in watery soup complete with head and feet!

It will require our concentration to adjust to your new name after years of calling you "Mildred Virginia".

Keep us advised of your progress in your "canonical year". Don't lose your sense of humor. Remember, laughter and jocularity are also important factors in coping with life's problems.

Best of luck to you Sister James Mariah. We love you. You will be a wonderful Sister for the Sisters of Hope.

All our love,
Dione and Leon

****

I met Dione and Leon back in 1982 on a month long tour we took to China. Leon was a news correspondent for the Miami Herald. He was one of the funniest people who I have ever met in my life. It is interesting that he mentioned, no less than three times, to not loses my sense of humor.

9 August 1993

It is my neighbor's birthday back home. Happy Birthday Timmy.

I just owned up to breaking a bowl. It was an accident, and probably would not have happened if Gigi had not reached up for it at the same time. I feared she would take the blame and since breaking dishes was brought up in class again, I confessed. I also had to ask forgiveness for being two minute tardy. Mother said, "Good." It is easier for me than it I for Sister Francis. Sister Francis could look on the bright side as there would be a trip to "Frank Bees" - all inclusive taking in "the Golden Arches"!

Our number is up to nineteen with the four new postulants, twenty if you count Mother Regina, but she will soon be leaving us. Sister Agatha was professed on Friday and she is home now with her family for a week.

One of the entrants resembles Carol Burnette. She has these big eyes. I have always loved Carol Burnett. In fact, I have her autograph back home in one of my scrap books. This lady whose name is Louann, does not like to be compared to Carol Burnette. Anyway, I was getting overtired and silly. I told Leila to give her some tooth picks to hold her eyes open. Louann's sister and brother-in-law came for her entrance. Sister Francis asked if they were her mother and father. Her sister has white hair same as Louann does. Her sister is quite attractive. I thanked them for giving us Louann. Her brother-in-law said, "No, thank you." It struck me funny. We both chuckled.

10 August 1993

Today is the Baptismal date of Blessed Brother Andre Bessette. Have always had a special devotion to him. I like Brother Solanus Casey too; and , St. Joseph Cupertino, St. Francis of Paola, and St. Jean Marie Vianney. I seem to gravitate toward the humble porters.

My heart goes out to Sister Francis Mary. Her sister is in the hospital – dying at this very moment. She is 72 years of age. Sister Francis has gone to be with her. She has asked me to iron some table cloths (she did not suggest that I put them under my mattress). Saint Joseph, grant her sister a happy death. Mother Mary, comfort Sister Francis.

Speaking of suffering, I worry about Grampa. He said something that made quite an impact on me. I do not think he was aware of it. I said, "Grampa, how are you feeling?" He said, "I am as good as I will ever be." Then he added, "Little Virginia, the way the world is, somebody has got to suffer… it might as well be me." Blessed Atonement -

Father Dennis came to Mass on Sunday rather than Saturday. He got up at 4 a.m.! He did not want us to know that only I happened to casually ask him what time he left. He came from Newburgh. He brought us some delicious coffee cake. What annoyed me, was that, when he called, I got the distinct impression that he was being put off. Sister Rosario told me later that he specifically asked for me,

that which I did not know nor was I supposed to be made aware.
When the Superior announced that he was coming for Mass, she said, "I don't remember his name as though he were insignificant. She looked directly at me. "Oh, Father Dennis Dinan. How nice." He chanted a good deal of the Mass and he gave a beautiful homily. The part about "unending praise" struck me funny because the chanting seemed to go on. I saw Mother Regina looking at her watch. Everyone enjoyed Father at breakfast. He is very open and refreshing. You can not help but like him. Sister Francis Mary told Mother Regina later in the day that he gave his whole life story. Why did she have to say that! Mother was not with us for breakfast as she brought Leila and the other three new postulants to the Sisters of the Renewal . Leila would catch the bus there to go to Denver for her home visit. Sophia added, "Yes, but he was very interesting." Michelle said, "He has quite a vocation story." He had called off his wedding. I was misconstrued here with certain ones whom I trusted, people whom I thought were women of God because I had called off an engagement. Now, they did not know quite how to react. Previously they lamb basted me and assaulted my integrity. Now, I shared as openly as Father Dennis did. Am so grateful and edified for the people the Good Lord has put in my path.

Was thinking about how Sister Rosario lives for the Sacrament of Confession. On the day when she needed consolation the most, the Superior was running our Confessor out the door. Sister Rosario had just arrived home. Father Henchey was giving a retreat while Sister Rosario had to attend classes all day. I knew she would welcome the chance to see him. She is low-keyed and often gets overlooked. I broached the Superior on this. She said that Sister Rosario could see him; she just never told Sister Rosario that. Sister Rosario was not going to pursue it even after I told her. She was feeling kind of low. Finally, and before the priest left, I nabbed Father Henchey and she got to see him. Thank you Lord.

18 August 1993

Oh, I have missed my "Frances Parkinson" - that is my "keys/keyes"!

Anywho, yesterday was my dear mother's 61st birthday. I wish that I could have bi-located and been up to the lake at Gramma Burleigh's camp to help celebrate. I did have a good day, unlike today.

I have always enjoyed being portress – answering the telephone and the door. Lately, they have become times of dread. Usually, the person on the other end just wants someone to listen to him. More than often, the callers ask for me. Today, Mother Regina has asked me to keep the phone off the answering machine during Holy Hour as she was expecting two very important phone calls. A woman named Louise called and she was so happy when I answered the phone. I was not at ease to talk with her under the circumstances. Then, of all things, someone was banging wildly at the door. "Could Sister Rosario have forgotten her keys?" I thought to myself. She was due to return from class about this time. Nope. I unlocked the door, my mouth fell wide open as I gazed on John Cardinal O'Malley. I certainly was not expecting him. He had only returned from Denver the day before. Monsignor Sullivan was with him. He seemed to thoroughly enjoy my being caught off guard. It was a funny instant, because I held the door for a solid sixty seconds that which His Eminence permitted as he delighted in throwing yours truly for a loop. Meanwhile, that lady Louise is still on the phone. She can't contain her excitement over the new brochure. "Why Your Eminence, I was not expecting you." His and the Monsignor's expressions were priceless.
"Do come in." I reached for his hand to venerate his ring. He smiled pleasingly and put his arm around me. Then he said, "Sister James Mariah, this is Monsignor Sullivan."
"How do you do Monsignor Sullivan."
Then the Cardinal told me to return to the phone unaware of my difficulty curtailing this phone call. I did brief him on what was going on at the moment. He and Monsignor made their way into the chapel. I had managed to get off the phone in time to see Mother Regina's surprised face.

Then, I was in a pickle because Monsignor Smith called. He is all business though I believe he is very compassionate underneath. I knew this must be one of the calls that Mother was expecting. The Cardinal was clearly blocking the way out from her pew. I returned

319

to the phone to explain the situation to Monsignor. He was modest enough to say that he could not be one of the important calls. He is also wise enough to deflect it if indeed he is one of the calls. He then asked what time Holy Hour would be over. "5:15" I told him. I wrote this down on the back of my Community Prayer booklet, and I was going downstairs during the Rosary, as I am cook today, I handed the message to Mother Regina. She looked at me like she was going to scold me, "Why didn't you give me this message earlier?" I looked at her in the eyes, and calmly said, "Because you were talking with the Cardinal."
"Oh." No argument there.

This morning, The Little Sisters of the Poor, called about having someone pick up some maps for Auriesville. She called back to say that her driver has not returned so she was unable to send someone over with them. By the time the driver would be back, we would be gone on a picnic. I told her that we could probably swing by with the maps if we were going out anyway. Plus, I have some extra literature on the early Jesuit martyrs I would like to give her. They do so much for us, it seemed little enough we could do for them and yet this humble Sister would not ask this of us. I relayed the second conversation to the Superior who said to me, in front of the entire breakfast table including Father Michael Morris, who is a beautiful young priest, "You should not have done this. You should have gotten me."
"I am sorry."
I would do it all over again too. If someone else had done that, it would have been fine. I seem to irk her as of late. She neither likes it if I appear too meek, nor if I appear too confident. As a result, I appear very awkward and self-conscious. She is not relaxed with me. I guess I make people uncomfortable. The future Superior is very tense with me also. The former one, Sister Rita, whom I hold in very high esteem, was ill at ease with me in the beginning, but later that dissipated. I miss her. She has a brother who has a birthay the same day as mine. He served in Vietnam. Sister Rita was always going to tell me the story which I imagine is pretty gruesome as she could not tell it in the refectory. I never did hear it. Poor Sister Rita. She just lost her father recently. He reminded me a little of Grampa from some of the stories Sister told me about him. As far

as Superiors go, Sister Mary from the Parish Visitors was extraordinary. She was great. I just received a lovely card from her. I am fond of my North Country ally Sister Carol Marie too. But, I digress...........
I went into the pantry to compose myself, trying to overcome my humiliation, and return to the table as though all were well.

At lunch time, the Superior came into the kitchen to tell me that I was too loud. Then, during class, I did not have time to put the answering machine on and my greatest fear was confirmed when the phone rang during one of Mother Regina's lectures. It should not be surprising that I then burnt the peanut butter cookies which I made for the picnic we were supposed to go on today. We didn't go on account of the weather. I can not help but think Mother Regina wanted to teach me a lesson about dropping off the maps for the Little Sisters of the Poor.
Last night, I made oatmeal cookies with raisins and walnuts. I served them today at lunch.

Back home if I was having a day like this, I would visit the sick or elderly. I always felt better afterward.

23 August 1993

XXI. The Agony and the Agatha

It would seem that we got drilled by a German warden today. Sister Agatha used her reverse psychology in telling us that it depends on us and not her if this community is to survive. She is so afraid of it reflecting on her should someone decide to leave. Her tactics are untimely and have put some in tears while leaving others ill at ease. Myself, I thought I would be sick. It was like receiving some tragic news. She has made out new schedules which she calls "Transition Tasks". The great organizer in authority has every minute of the day blocked saying that we can not take any breaks. If one deems it desperately necessary to take a drink or eat a cracker, she must do so standing up and then do it quickly. Her approach is rigid and austere and has since earned her the moniker of "Attila the Nun". She goes on to discuss the birthing pains of the community. I am tired of

321

hearing about them. There is no joy in anything she does. She is unoriginal, and very predictable. She is also a control freak. She has been calling all the different groups of postulants and novices together for these meetings. She looks like the wrath of God in her haste to set things accordingly and at a rapid pace. She might have a few good thoughts which she speaks about in a condescending manner pointing her finger and addressing all the Sisters as: "You Folks" and "You People" and what are you doing these days.............ad nauseum. When our group was called upon, she said that we would not be taking vows in February with the first group, as it is written up in the Constitution to go the full two years for novitiate, "We can not count the Postulancy". Of course it was different for her, having a six month Canonical Two Year. She is quick to justify herself in saying, "Well, I console myself with the fact that I had four months at Marycrest in Monroe." That would have been like a vacation or a retreat. She would not have been forced to give up her will. That is all fine and well, but she contines, "The novitiate is a special time which you people will grow to appreciate and I think it is better for you." I think it is better for her because if any in our group were professed, it would threaten her position in the future. It has nothing to do with being ready for the Vows. In one sense, no one will ever really truly be ready and yet, in another, one could be ready yesterday. It is all relative, as far as the realm of it is concerned, so a suggested time frame is put into place. The interesting thing is, Mother Regina indicated to me that our group would indeed be taking our first Vows in February. Mother's Community in Nashville take the vows after a one year Novitiate. There is not a more solid and traditional community there. I think it would be special for our group to take them among ourselves. Perhaps I am not ready. Perhaps I never will be. I know that I want to serve the Lord. I know that I love Our Lord and I do believe that I love The Lord. To serve this one put in charge poses a great obstacle for me.

I am also finding it extremely difficult not knowing when and if I can go home and see my grandfather again.

It was painstaking for me to watch her "Expose the Blessed Sacrament". I have only seen a priest do this. I would almost prefer It to remain hidden in the Tabernacle in this case. Maybe she is not comfortable doing it either but she is doing it.

This calling her "Mother" and seeing her write up on the "Transition Tasks" for two postulants to move her into "Mother Superior's Quarter" was just a bit too much for me. I overheard her say at lunch how being called "Mother" is a mark of respect, and how when you love someone you call her that like how some people call Sister Regina 'Mother Regina'. I have no trouble calling Mother Regina that, but I do not love this one, and she still refuses to address me in my religious name.

I feel like I am the poison in the community for feeling this way. I don't want to be. I wish I didn't have feelings sometimes. God help me.

24 August 1993

Last night during recreation, we were playing a card game called 'Killer'. The one who gets the 'Ace' is supposed to wink at everyone – hence "killing" them. The last survivor, or the person who guesses who the killer is, is the winner. The game went on and on and nobody was getting killed or winked at. So everyone started guessing who the killer was and they all got dead. Funny enough, Sister Rosario had the Ace but she did not know what an Ace looked like. Then Sister Gabriel said, "That's okay, it took her one hour to crush a dozen egg shells for the garden." Sister Rosario and I are on afternoon garden duty.

I am so exhausted. I am bell ringer this week. We usually can rise at 6 o'clock on Tuesdays, but no, 5 o'clock this morning because the priest could not get here to say Mass this morning. Even Mother Regina would let us get up at 6 and do our private prayers after Mass at the big church.

I had a post card from Father Salmon. I thought I would lay the ground work for when he comes. I said, "Sister Agatha, I had a post card from Father Salmon today. He hopes to come and celebrate Mass here on September 1st or 2nd. Anyway, he will call."

"Okay," She said abruptly. Then she said, "Did you get the mail today?"

"No, this went to the rectory, and the secretary gave it to me on my walk."

Mother Regina always gave me the post cards from Father or mail from any religious person. She never withheld mail like that.

Yesterday, as I was standing on the spade; I seem to go from aces to spades, and I even call a spade a spade, I looked like I was on a pogo stick. I used to have a pogo stick. I got one for Christmas when I was little. I would bounce up and down like a kangaroo. It was so much fun. Suddenly, I heard this voice, "Do you know what you are doing?" I looked up and it was Monsignor Devlin. "Oh, Hi Monsignor Devlin! Well, it is the first time I have ever used one." "Yeah, I could tell." He said. "Don't ruin your shoes."
It was so good seeing that once familiar face raoming around here again. He is still quite thin though he says he is gaining. I like him. Then Father Keehan passed by to say how pretty the garden looks but it sure is a lot of work isn't it. It was nice to work in front of The Blessed Mother statue. This is the same Blessed Mother statue that Helene and I cleaned up. We washed the lichen and black mold (stachbotrys) that had grown on the statue the first Spring that we were here. We had drawn names to see who who would crown our Blessed Mother. Ironically, and much to everyone's chagrin, my name was drawn and Helene's was next. She carried the floral wreath in procession for our May Crowning while I got to place the crown of Mother Mary.

Poor Father Keehan. He came by last Saturday as we were finishing lunch and he wanted to get our reaction to a story he was thinking of using in his homily. Mother Regina invited him into the refectory. He proceded to tell about this woman who sustained an injury on a cracked toilet seat in the Burdine's Department store. I think it was in Florida, and she was suing. His point was that this took real humility to seek justice. He wove in a few other details, and then came the reaction. Some of the Sisters put their thumbs down; others did not say anything. Mother Regina did not react favorably. Sister Gabriel and I laughed. Then Father went on to say that he tried it on Monsignor Devlin. Monsignor Devlin said that he could not do it personally, but he figured Father Keehan could. I looked at Father Keehan, and his eyes looked glassy. His feelings were hurt. It was one of the few times that I noticed he might break. He continued to talk in an effort to conceal his feelings. "So I can tell my parishioners that I have the Sisters of Hope's approval. It was as though he was trying to convince himself that his idea had not been rejected. The parishioners have grown to love and accept their pastor. I think they would get a kick out of this. He makes a good point too. I have come to appreciate him. He is generous to the Sisters too. God love him.

25 August 1993

Last night, during our class with Monsignor Smith, I noticed Sister Gabriel behind the pillar. She minds the heat being a little on the round side. She resorts to all measures to make herself comfortable. Next thing I know, she has her two stocking feet pressed against the pillar. She was sitting in the back so she was able to get away with this. I was sitting beside her and it made me chuckle. She likes to make me laugh. I looked over at Sister Rosario. She was nodding off appearing like a Siamese cat with her eys slitting open and shut.

Monsignor McDonald came for lunch with the Cardinal recently. He enjoyed himself immensely. He loves telling jokes. He was asking us if we heard about the crisis in Heaven. God sneezed and no one knew what to say to Him. He was telling us about the time he went to the Holy Land with Father Matt." "Can you imagine of all the places, he picks the hottest place on earth. Even Our Lord went to Galilee in the summer." Then Monsignor continues, "There are some Sisters up North and they have an ideal place. There aren't very many of them.
"You wouldn't be trying to bump them off would you?"
"No, but I would pray for their early demise."
"Yeah, and I bet you would do their funeral too." says I in jest.

There was this other priest who came in on the train from Boston. He wanted to see Mother Regina and meet the Sisters of Hope. His name was Father Russell. He appeared very somber. At lunch, he talked about the Capuchin 'Monastery of All the Bones' in Italy.
"Excuse me, I have a bone to pick with you Father."
Well, we got on a roll. "Two heads are better than one." and "I got to hand it to you." That was when he spoke of Saint Catherine's

Hand on display there. "Yeah, and they had a 'skeleton' crew working."
I served apple pie for dessert, and the plates were hot as I warmed them in the oven. I asked him not to touch the plates. Mother Regina made a joke about "Do Not Touch". Then of course, Eve in the garden came up and wouldn't you know, this was apple pie.

We went to Auriesville the other day to Saint Isaac Jogues Shrine and the shrine of the Jesuit Martyrs. We also visited the place whre Blessed Kateri Tekawith died. My friend Mark Day died on her anniversary of April 17th. Talk came up about lunch and Sister Gabriel announces, "Well, we will be having "Finger" sandwiches, and 'Ladyfingers' for dessert."

25 August 1993

XXII. Angels Around Us

One day last week, we went up to Cedarhurst to have a picnic lunch with some elderly Sparkhill Dominican nuns. We got caught in a traffic jam a mile before the exit. When we did arrive, it was so nice. It was an overcast day much like that one in that famous painting "On the Road to Emmaeus". It is one that every convent I have ever visited seems to have. This one was no exception.
I helped bring out the food. A Deacon and his wife in the parish catered it not accepting any recompense, instead suggesting that any contribution for their efforts be given to The Sisters of Hope. These kindly nuns presented us with a check for fifty dollars in addition to putting on this nice feed. They also gave Mother Regina a check to show their appreciation to her for upholding orthodoxy.
Sister Stephen Gerard had tears in her eyes as she thanked everyone. It seems they had been given the brush-off and we were their last link to where they could draw unity; where some semblance of tradition remained. What is remarkable about Sister Stephen Gerard, is that she is recuperating from treatments for colon Cancer. She suffers in silence. I know this through Father Matt as he used to serve in that parish. They loved him there. He was very good – relating to all age groups and instructing them accordingly. Father Matt was speaking of her nobleness. She is only sixty years of age.

These lovely Sisters gave us a tour of their convent and school. They did not leave a stone unturned as far as that meal was concerned. Since it was a Friday, we had a tuna platter with fresh tomatoes and cucumbers; honey dew melon and fresh fruit. There was bakd ziti, rolls and butter, soda, coffee and New York cheesecake with fresh stawberries. It was delicious. Oh, and I almost forgot, Sister Stephen Gerard's lime jello with pineapple in it. It was relaxing and enjoyable. I felt right at home bringing the food to the porch. We had a small gift of clay angels for them. I could not wait for Sister Josephine Marie to see this as she has an angel collection in her bedroom. She showed it to me. She wound up one music box and it played "When You Wish Upon a Star" (That has special significance to me as Grampa gave me a music box figurine of an angel that plays that). Sister went on to tell me that she was dusting yesterday and just as she was dusting her framed Vows, her Blessed Mother music box began to play 'Ave Maria'. Sister Helena Marie says she now sleeps with her lights on and the door closed.

Sister Josephine Marie says that the reason for her angel music boxes is that she is the last one left in her family. She wants to go join them, but until then, she has the angels to remind her of them.

That is very sweet. God Bless Sister Josephine Marie and God Bless Sister Helena Marie. God Bless them all. Poor Sister Theresa Agnes could not be there as she went to visit her sick sister up in Monroe. I had spoken with her initially on the phone. She told me to be sure and come with Mother Regina when she comes. Well, we all got to go. It looked like there should have been a rainbow after it poured rain. It was like being in another world sitting on the screened-in porch – just lulling and listening to the rain on that vinyl roof.

Sister Josephine has been a religious for 53 years. She enjoyed showing me her sterling napkin ring which she received upon her profession. I like that idea. It reminds me of those wooden ones they have in Bretagne, France with French names carved in them.

I must not to forget that there is a Sister Genevieve too.

Then we had to go.

We stopped in Sparkhill to see the The Saint Thomas Aquinas College. Sister Aquinas was in her glory.

There appeared to be a remnant of old nuns in habit who stayed close together, and then another sect of middle-aged liberal Sisters.

327

It was sad to feel this unity broken; an unfortunate commentary on the state of religious life.

As we were preparing to leave, after the tour, an old Superior, Sister Joseph Francis, came out with a box of fruit (produce) for Mother Regina to take to her Dominican Sisters in Nashville. She kept talking with her arms expanded telling us how glad she was to see us, that is, a fairly young community in habit. I went right into those expanded arms as this seemed to be the motion she was waiting for. She says, "I was hoping somebody would do that." and she did not want to let go. It was beautiful. It is a funny thing, but a print of a painting of and Indian sitting in a winter snow scene struck me. That very same painting manifested itself to me three days late in Auriesville. I had never seen it before. It had a dreamy quality about it.

XXIII. DEPARTURE

Oh God! Help me! What is to become of me? I wish I could die. Yet it is myshortcoming that I react this way. It is true, I feel I have been treated unfairly that which wounds me. If I were supernatural, I would forget the things and the people who have afflicted such. It is difficult for me to do the latter. I am suppose to call the very source of so much pain, "Mother". Is it pride to not want to do this? Truly, I would rather die. It is not in my heart one iota. It was hard enough to survive her First Profession Ceremony. It is not anger, or jealousy so much as it is injustice. It makes one ponder though. What is both amazing and strange, is that when one professes publicly, or in the eyes of Holy Mother Church, her Vows, every trace of sin from her past life is wiped away. It is as though she were newly baptized. Yet it seems one could have a baptism of desire and if she were to die tomorrow she too might receive the same grace. It is baffling because what I am having a hard time forgiving and forgetting has already been blotted out. She is good to go, but I am suffering the consequences. If it had not been The Feast of The Transfiguration, I don't think that I could have gotten through the day. I tried desperately hard to let that seep through my warped being.

I do not like myself for feeling this way. If I can only overcome it. I believe that she has come about it in a political fashion. I find it hard to accept because I do not believe that it is authentic. That is a sin on my part to undermine a grace given by the Church for one who chooses to respond. For that alone, she even deserves better. Intellectually, I know this. This has been her goal. She comes from a competitive family. I like Sister Rita's theory, the one best suited for the job is the one who does not want it. Have also heard that one can grow into the position. One can be one way in the beginning and then end up being a wonderful Superior. Of course, it could go the opposite way too.

Mother Regina has left us today. I was sorry to see her go and more sorry for what lies ahead. Am minded of LBJ moving into JFK's office on the same day he died. Sister Agatha gives a speech at supper on why she should be called 'Mother'. God, I beg you to help me.

Ironically, some of us performed a skit for the Cardinal last night. I took the part of Mother Regina. I must say that I kept character and I had her Southern accent down to a 'T'. The Cardinal was both surprised and impressed with my impersonation. Mother Regina was thrown for a loop too. She was amazed at all I had taken in of her. She enjoyed it because imitation is the most sincere form of flattery.

His Eminence said, "Well, this sheds new light on things. If we can't have Mother Regina, we should have Sister James Mariah be the new Superior as she could act like a Superior." I could not believe my ears. Immediately, almost before he could get his last wrods out, Sister Agatha said, "Great!" emphatically, to cover up any possible show of being threatened or insecure about the mere thought or suggestion of it – that which everyone secretly enjoyed. She could not look at me in the eyes. I enjoyed this little prestige at the moment. Of course, he was kidding , but it made doing that play all the more worthwhile. I do not mean to harp on this subject any longer, but pray tell me, how am I going to call her 'Mother' when I have been blessed with a real mother who is without compare.

Was sitting in the middle seat of the van the other day heading over to the Jeanne Jugan residence. Sister Gabriel was sitting beside me., and Sister Josephat was on the other side telling us to put our seatbelts on. Sister Gabriel was clearly put out. At first, she said no, and then, in the spirit of trying to give up her will, she obliged with much adieu. I assisted her. Then Sister Gabriel says, "After all this fussing, we better get in a wreck."

Sister Josephat is famous for being an "Indian Chief". She is overly scrupulous always saying, "I think you had better re-think that." She is very irksome. I take pleasure in knowing that I grate the heck out of her. She told me that in fraternal correction one day. She told me that I try her patience. I do it by merely existing. She got on my case the other day about getting books accessioned when we were all going around like madmen trying to get things in order for Mother Regina. It wasn't like I was goofing off or anything. She loves to take the upper hand with me and undermine me. I find her repugnant the table – burping and blowing her nose, and picking the sleepy sand off her glasses at the table. God forgive me. I am not being very Christian, but I am going to get this off my chest in writing rather than talk aloud to the wrong person. When Mother Regina was leaving, I said, 'Oh, we should have done that cheer for Mother that she likes..." To which she says, "Have a little respect, Mass is going on across the street.". I thought, "You big jerk. Everyone is in tears and you can not see a moment of levity to bring cheer to everyone. Who the heck is thinking straight at a time like this." I did not say anything. I would not give her the satisfaction. The fact of the matter is, Mother Regina's car has already pulled out so there would be no cheer. She should have kept her big Michigonion mouth shut! Everyone around here is tense and moody. I guess I am absorbed in my own travail. I don't think anyone here can understand.

Poor Cornelia. Someone upset her at the table tonight. I talked to her to make her feel better. I did not ask any names, but I believe it was a novice – someone who should have known better. That burns me. I like Cornelia. She is such a sweet gal. She has a brother named Karl same as me, but his might be spelled with a "C". In fact, something about her reminds me of Karl's daughter, my niece Mary Evelyn.

Sister Francis Mary was well-composed saying good-bye to Mother Regina. She says, "Honey, life is a series of good-byes." Then she beat it out to the telephone right after lunch and once she saw that Sister Agatha had gone for a bike ride.

The Little Sisters of the Poor donate tons of food to us. Mother Regina said to us the other night during dinner, "Sisters, it is not prudent to tell people where we get our food." The very next day, at the Cardinal's Mass, His Eminence himself, announced to the whole parish that the Little Sisters of the Poor give us all our food. I thought that was pretty funny.'

We also have a little garden where we grow tomatoes and cucumbers. Mr. Gallagher in his kindness brought over all these plants and vegetables. In his ambition, he had a couple of fellows put up a fence for us. It was a riot – as it is a real eyesore in the neighborhood. Anne, the crossguard lady told me that everyone was complaining about it. I think Sister Gabriel said it best when asked what she thought about the fence, "I think I would have to travel to Haiti to find one uglier."

The other morning, during breakfast, I am the reader in the refectory. Chose Father Rinaldi's book 'In Verdant Pastures'. Was reading about Father Alfonso who happened to be born on December 20th. Spontaneously, I interjected, "Hey, that's Grampa's Birthday!" Everyone looked up from their corn flakes.....and, I continued reading. But, in the beginning, I was reading the part about how Father Alfonso would invite people to his Jubilee celebration and have them bring money gifts to the church. Father Rinaldi was questioning this. I guess I was not expecting to read this ploy –but all for the greater glory of God – so I shouldn't call it a ploy - only it sent me into a bout of uncontrollable laughter at 6:30 a.m. which is odd because I am like a zombie until noon typically. I tried not to look for fear I would lose it worse. With my head down, I begged pardon from all the Sisters. Then, I noticed Mother Regina was trying to hold back laughter. Fortunately, a humorous account did follow which acted as a release valve for everyone. Then, I stumbled over the part where Father Alfonso left instructions that he did not want any "new clothes to be buried in". I omitted the word 'new'. I felt my face redden as I tried in vain to cover up hoping no one noticed. I did get a repercusssion later on that, but not from the Superior.

331

When Our Holy Father arrived in the states, we went over to The Little Sisters of The Poor to watch it on their big TV screen as they get EWTN. Well, as we were waiting, it seems the station put in a "filler". It was a priest teachng about The Visitation. I was fine, and then every now and again, I would hear Sister Cecila let out a burst of laughter. Then, I heard Sister Paula of The Holy Face laugh. She is so cute and tiny with this unexpected raspy voice. This priest on the screen was very animated and annuciated every word emphatically. His dynamics were over the top as we were all waiting and trying to be gracious. Then sister Mary Pio lost it. I was in hysterics. It was the best laugh I had in a long time. Mother Regina enjoyed it too. I wish I knew what his name was. I would like to see him again. He certainly captures one's attention in the most unexpected of ways. Mother Regina had given us a lecture beforehand to all act like ladies.

Othe day in the refectory for lunch there were no spoons to be had for the soup. Sister Francis Mary rebutts, "What's the matter, can't you use forks?" She of course is in charge of the dining room.

I heard that Monsignor Powers is leaving Dunwoodie to go to a parish. Boy, St.Joseph's is sure going to miss him. I got such a kick out of him. He would come across as some kind of a curmudgeon, and then greet you in the morning, "Peace and Joy, Peace and Joy, ….." without cracking a smile. He loved doing this. His favorite devotional statue is Our Lady of Joy – Laetare. That should tell you right there that he is a joyful and good person. In fact, he did something very special for me – something I will never forget. It was when were on the Cardinal's retreat at Dunwoodie. It was New Year's Day. I was eyeing the corridors to see where the "radar Nun", aka Mother Regina, was. Monsignor Powers was observing this unbeknowt to me. He asked me if I wanted to go with the others to the ping pong room. I hesitated, and said, "No…." He looked at me, and then I said, "Well, you see, my grandfather is supposed to call me today back at our convent – only I won't be there. I was going to try to call him, only I must be "discreet". He picked right up on that, and he showed me into his office. Monsignor Powers connected me to an outside line and he insisted that I dial direct. He closed the door behind him, and the next thing I knew, I was wishing

Grampa a Happy New Year. I was so happy. I really appreciated this gesture of the kindly rector. God love him.

Today at lunch, Sister Margaret was allowing herself one slice of alfalfa bread. I asked her if she ever had difficulty keeping her weight down. She answered, "Oh yes, I was tipping the scales in college at a good forty pounds over what I should have been." "Oh Wow, you would never know it to look at you now. Do you have a picture of yourself then?" Sister Francis Mary chimes in, "She wouldn't fit in the lens."

Last night Sister Gabriel was cutting my hair in the laundry room. "She does a good job." I was telling Gigi as she passed through. "Oh, you wanna do mine?" "Sure," says Sister Gabriel. So she is cutting her hair and she says, "You need a hot oil treatment on your hair. What do you use – brown soap?" I thought I would die. Virginia laughed too. She did not take offense. She does break down and use shampoo.

Virginia Miller got the final affirmation that she is now part of the community – thanks be to God.

We were listening to the tapes on 'The Story of a Soul – Saint Theresa, The Little Flower'. We are having our dinner, and come all the explicit details surrounding the Saint's death. Looking around the table at everyone's faces was something else.

26 August 1993

Father Keehan came and celebrated Mass this morning. He was telling us about an elderly Sister, a Sister Stanislaus who use to attend every wedding and every funeral. She would be sitting up in the front row at each ceremony. Father Keehan would say, "Gee Sister Stanislaus, I did not know you knew "so and so"?" She would reply that she had taught him, the 93 year old man in this case, in the eighth grade. He said it became her standard answer. Everyone in my family are famous for attending wakes and funerals. I come by it naturally.

I can not wait to tell Grampa that Boopa's Inverness cape is being used as a model for our winter coat. It is also referred to as an "Ulster". This is what Laura and her sister Susan are working on. Susan plans to enter in February. Her sister is a costume designer but both are excellent seamstresses. Susan's father served with the Cardinal in the Navy. The Cardinal has known her family for most of Susan's life. She also has a brother who is a priest. I understand that he is a wonderful mimic. Like me, they both sisters love "thistle". I love that symbol. It means "earthly sorrow". I had some in my room and I applied some on contact paper and a note card and made them each notes telling them of the meaning. I always see them by Mount Hope cemetery back home. My dear Mrs. Dechame has just returned from Scotland and thistle is the flower of Scotland.

Something very special happened to me on my mother's birthday (August 17th). When Father Keehan came to me, he switched Chalices. He gave me some of the Broken Consecrated Host - the Big One. This meant so much to me. Just today, nine days later, like a Novena of the Soul, he repeated this Communion in the exact fashion. I was in a different spot for reception of This Most Sublime Sacrament. Thank you Sweet Jesus.

Sister Gabriel has this huge statue of Mary at The Foot of The Cross along with St. John and St. Mary Magdalene. It was on the sideboard in the refectory beside the coffee maker of all things. Now it is moved to the second floor landing. I overheard Sister Aquinas say she didn't feel right about making coffee at the Foot of the Cross.

About that shipment of statues and garden furniture that Sister Gabriel had shipped from Louisville – there is a very large statue of Mother Mary. It is lifelike, and towering. I call her, "Our Lady of the Amazon". No disrespect meant, but she looks like the one they would have down there. The young Black man who drove her up said, "You know, I am gonna miss her. I kinda got use to riding with her." Interestingly enough, he is a Baptist. Sister Gabriel assured him that Mother Mary would always be with him and for him to pray to her. When he was bringing her into the house, it meant leaving another statue on the sidewalk. So, Calvin came to the door to say he did not feel right leaving her on the sidewalk while he brought in the other statue. He grew very protective of her. He was bringing Mary at the Foot of The Cross in first. Mary go to sweet Calvin always.

28 August 1993

XXIV. Parlor Vous

I am portress and bell ringer today. I sprinkle the rooms with Holy Water and say "Ave Maria". I enjoy this ritual especially when I come to Sister Margaret's room. I can always count on the response, "Deo Gratias". She is usually facing the wall on her futon or Chinese bed. Whether it is late and the lights are out, or very early, I still hear her squeaky voice.

"Parlor" - This is an old convent term used to describe visiting day for Religious. That is what Sister Helena Marie of The Sparkhill Dominicans told me. She also showed me th speical bathroom they had installed directly off the closet for this purpose. She would say, "This comes in handy for when we would have "Parlor". I got a kick out of that. Forgot to finish about the napkin rings. Theirs has the Dominican Coat of Arms on them. Some have their religious names engraved on them. Sister Stephen Gerard had a small Blessed Mother on hers. I kissed it to honor her absence, and, Our Blessed Mother.

The new Superior was determined to meet with me, following suit of Mother Regina, right before my Confession with Father Halligan. She seemed to be primed as she was asking the same sort of questions that Mother Regina would ask. I was courteous. It was nice, and wise, that she began with a prayer. However, I did resent some of the questions regarding my spiritual life s I feel that is very private – sacred. I gave her general answers. Then she would ask, "How do you plan to get closer to God?" I thanked her for her time. I know she is trying, though I do not feel she is sincerely interested in me. She told me not to let feelings get in the way of approaching the one God has designated to be in charge. Then she said, "Isn't it easier being away from your grandfather now?"

"No, it isn't."

Then she gave me this line about how it is a gift and I just agreed for her sake. Then, she told me how freeing it is not to write letters. I said, "Not for me. It can be too late. I am a firm believer in the present tense. I would prefer to express my condolencess or well-wishes to a person while he is still alive."

Sister Francis warned me not to buck her. It has not been my intention. I am not going to have her dictate my feelings though. Sister Francis also said that she would not call her "Mother", "She is no mother to me."

One thing I forgot to mention about that dear elderly nun called Sister Stanislaus. Father Keehan had an alarm system put in on account of her. She was in the laundry room one day, and there was this big Black man. He not only scared her, but she scared him. So Father Keehan had a system put in promptly. The only problem was that Sister Stansilaus would quite often forget to turn it off as she made her way over to Mass. The Police Department would call, and say, "Is it real?" or, "Is it Sister Stanislaus?" They would reply, "It is Sister Stanislaus." (Yes Virginia, there is a 'Stanis – Laus).

How about twenty nuns on The Circle Line cruise last Saturday. We took a picnic lunch and we stopped by the Elizabeth Ann Seton Shrine afterward. The best was our tickets, compliments of Mr. Peter Grace. They have "Nun" typed right on there. We were just as much of an attraction as the five boroughs of New York. Mother Regina, our last outing with her, was at the helm and we in our full habits were close behind. We had to turn in those tickets. It would have been fun to keep one for my scrap book. I was expressing this to Gigi who produces two tickets from her pocket. "How did you get these?"

"I have my ways." She said. She wanted to send one to her sister. She is funny.

I came across a book about Elisabeth Hesselblad who started the resurgence of the Brigittine Order. I was particularly excited because I relayed an excerpt one time to the Sisters about how Mother Elisabeth was a nurse in a hospital in New York. She got locked in the morgue one night. So what did she do..........she went around praying for each of the souls. Well, didn't one start to kick. It seemed she revived the poor soul. Well, I got the feeling that not everyone believed me. Now I have the book to prove it. Only Sister Josephat was adamant telling me to put the book back as we would be giving it away to a poor person as donor requested. Couldn't even share my excitement. Sisters of Hope – Sisters of Kill Joy ....

Gigi just came in, "You wanna hear the bagpipes?" They were from my friend across the way. Only the Silence bell has rung, so I opened the door to listen to a few ballads – or whatever they are called.

Sister Mary Pio came to get me to assist her with carrying a mattress from one room in her area of duty to another. She wanted to put a bed skirt underneath. I was wondering why she just couldn't set the mattress on the floor but she said she did not want to get the sheet dirty. So why not take off the sheet? She did not want to get it wrinkled as she had just ironed it. So, a few minutes later, after I had helped her move the mattress, she calls me back as she has put the bed skirt on the wrong side. I insisted we take the sheet off right there and we could do it without getting it terribly wrinkled. We do that. Then, she goes back down to the laundry room to re-iron the sheet. We put it on but the irises are upside down on the sheets so we switch it. Then, she calls me a third time to remove the mattress as she needs to dust the headboards. Whoa, I keep telling myself this will make good writing material.

Speaking of mattresses – our little Cornelia, the postulant from Saint Louis, has a head of hair which likens her to "Sister Mary Medusa". She brushed it all out and it was at least ten times the size. She wore it like that for our play the other evening. The Cardinal got a big kick out of it. He said she could make a couple of mattresses out of it. She is so cute. She laughed. She has a great sense of humor. I like people who love to laugh and who are sensitive.

29 August 1993

The Cardinal came yesterday and said Mass on the Feast of Saint Augustine. He and Father Matt stayed for dinner. I served along with Gigi and Sister Josephat. We had a delicious meat cooked on the grill that had beenmarinated. We had to move everything inside at the last minute as a storm came up.

Then it came, right before everyone was about to eat, "How do you feel about 'Mother Agatha'?" Silence, followed by a pause and then a half-hearted clapping of hands. I was glad I was serving because I lost any appetite I had. The irony is, I was the first one to address her in her new title. That is because I prefer to address people using their name, title, etc. It came out like "M-O-T-H-E-R A-A-gatha..... Then I said, "I am sorry, it is going to take some getting used to." If nothing else, I was sincere, painfully sincere. Her face grew contorted. She wants all this but she does not expect it to be difficult for anyone. I gave her – her due on Friday. I asked her permission for a graham cracker. She pulled me aside, "Is there a medical reason for this?"

"No, I just get the hankering for something sweet about this time every day." I told her that Mother Regina had given me General Permission for this. She says, "Every time you feel the need, you must ask me for permission." She did ask if I was hypoglycemic which my sister Annie, a nurse, suspects I might be.

Then, I had to report a juice glass that I broke while drying dishes. The new Superior told me to change my shoes as I was not wearing my black ones as I was cleaning my area of duty. Oh well, life is great in the convent. Keep it coming Lord!

Sister Josephat was her usual annoying self yesterday. It started when I asked the Sisters if they wanted to hear what happened to me in the morning. "Well, I was blessing myself as I was leaving my room. I got a real wake-up call. Why there was a fuzzy critter in my font – that is, my Beleek Font of The Sacred Heart which Georgie and Loretta gave me. This centipede died a holy death. I did not want to throw it down the drain being holy water and all; so I waterd my brother's plant with it. It got a little extra nourishment this morning." Well, there were mixed reactions. There are always a couple who get grossed out. Sister Josephat says, "Let's move on to more pleasant conversation." She is always calling the shots instead of just stting back and hanging lose. Then, later that evening, when the Cardinal was leaving, I said, "Oh, we should have given him that Spanish cheer."

Sister Josephat glared at me, "No, we aren't doing that!" She was perturbed about something. I don't know but I can surmise. I asked her if she was feeling alright. She was embarrassed that I had noticed she was "out of character". The truth is, she always acts that way. I don't think her health is the best. There is something kind of pathetic about her. Helene even felt sorry for her. But boy, is she passive – aggressive.

Incidentally, when I broke that juice glass, there was dead silence. Everyone was waiting for Sister Francis Mary's reaction. She stopped a few seconds after everyone else, and she raised her eyebrows. She looked at me with those owl eyes. If she were not a person, she would be an owl. She actually resembles one. She pursed her lips. She secretly enjoyed the power she has with nuns who break the refectory wares. Then, she told me not to worry about it. I told her that I can probably get some more juice glasses from home. Anyway, I don't get upset over stuff like that. The other Sisters were picking on me for my poker face as I stood with my mouth wide open. A Laurel and Hardy performance ensued as I go one way to get the broom and dust pan and Sister Lucy goes the other way. Only, we both miss each other and come out on opposite sides with our brooms. Sister Cecilia and Sophia are in hysterics.

Sister Josephat does not like it whenI use the type writer in the office. Granted, she is in charge of the office, but everyone is privy to the computers and/or typewriter. I prefer the typewriter. I get the distinct feeling that she resents me writing when she is working about the office like right now with with books in her hands running to and fro. Well, this is my only free time, right before bed. Plus, I think it is driving her up the wall as she is wondering what the hoot and howling I could be writing about almost every night. She is wondering why she is not privy to my thoughts. Well, for one, she is very narrow-minded, and two, it is none of her business. She is only letting me stamp books when I work with her as she is afraid that I might get "in the know" on how to run a library. I happen to come by it naturally as my mother is a Remedial Library Specialist and Mrs. Dechame had me fill in for her at Saint Mary's School library. I do whatever Sister Josephat says and my willing compliance irks her as she is trying to break me, have me lose my cool which I refuse to do. She would feel threatened if I got my hnd into too much of the book work. Hence, I just stamp those books during my work period.

While I was stamping the books, I came across a holy card which is identical to the one we had for my brother Karl. I have never seen one like it before or since. It is the most beautiful picture of Mother Mary – so sweet, loving and gentle. I felt rewarded in this mundane task.

If it isn't centipedes, it is something else. I saved my candy bar that I got from the Little Sisters when we went to watch the Pope on their TV. I ate a piece of it, but the next day when we went to Auriesville, Sister Cecilia was craving some chocolate. So I shared my chocolate bar with her. We were making The Way of The Cross, and Sister Cecilia shouts, "Ugh! Sister James Mariah, there are worms in this!" "You're kidding.... I just had some last night."

Gosh, I am going to have to improve my hoarding techniques – like get a small refrigerator in my room, or send out for fresh chocolate.
Actually, I was a little embarrassed. I was trying to do a good thing.

Another embarrassing thing happened was the other night when I was typing, Sophia wanted to use the type writer to type an address on an envelope. So I interrupt my writing and let her. She presses a memory code button which starts printing out my most personal thoughts. I heard her laughing. I was mortified. I always learn the hard way.

I am blessed though. Sister Mary Kaiser, a Poor Clare Sister who lives the on the next block, is praying especially for me. She is small and cute – like a leprechaun.

30 August 1993

Every night, for the past week, without fail, Sophia interrupts me to use the typewriter. I should not monopolize it, but her timing is questionable. I have also noticed that she gets what she sets out to get.

I think I figured out why Sister Josephat had a bee in her bonnet onSaturday. I have a hunch that she had a secret desire to be the Superior on acount of her "apparent humility". She is reacting peculiarly because she was not chosen coupled with having to call the one who was, "Mother". The other contributing factor is, that she spilled marinated cucumbers on the Cardinal. She dwelled on this for hours. It would have been par for the course for me, and we all would have had a good laugh about it. Because she is so darn scrupulous, she views it as a great fault which she will probably confess. Woops! Gotta be careful, she is right over my shoulder with "Mother".

I don't know. Certainly it is not me, but some other voice that comes out and gives her the title that she laps up. She loves being in charge. She loves authority. When I accord her this, she is much more tolerable. I try to concede and not fight it. Then I run to the chapel and contemplate Our Lord's Passion. That is the only way I can get through it. I will be a contemplative. I will have no time to dance. Strangely, everyone is having trouble getting that word "Mother" out. I don't think she realizes it. She likes the idea of it too much. What is it they say about ignorance? I have called her "Mother" more than anyone else here. Who am I to stand in the way of her happiness, especially if God is using her as an instrument to sanctify me. I even went to tell her that I acted presumptiously in giving some children holy cards. She said that was alright.

"Let the little children come unto me." My little friend Nancy and her two young cousins, Michael aged about seven, and Lauren, about six, came to visit me today. Sister Agatha allowed me to see them. They make me feel like a child. I like what Father Dennis Dinan's Ordination card says, "Rather, imitate little children walking with their father. They keep one hand in his and with the other they pick strawberries and currants along the way," St. Frances de Sales. I love that. I read it to the children.

I am finishing a French translation, copyright 1938 on Blessed Brother Andre. Boy, is it good. He shares the same birthday as Saint Jean Marie Vianney. He also bears an uncanny resemblance both physically and spiritually to him.

I wish to express that Our Holy Father is ineffably beautiful.

I must retire now, but first I promised Gigi I would go up on the roof and shoot the bull with her.

31 August 1993

Oh, to be misunderstood and then have someone give you a lecture as though that certain someone has been infused with divine understanding when she doesn't have the foggiest idea where you are coming from. I hate that. Yet, I always make the ignoramus feel like she has given me some great words of wisdom. She walks away feeling pretty special while I walk away feeling bruised and misunderstood. Then, the next day, there is a note in my mailboxwith some advice which only further proves my point that she does not know what she is talking about and she really should not bud in. If such a one truly understood, she would have a little clout. For me, the test of good manners is putting up with bad ones.

Gigi went out to pick granny Smith apples from the tree beside the rectory. She said she was going to climb it. "Well, I have a friend who is a Poor Clare nun and she climbed the peach tree in her monastery garden. We met a Sister the other day who likes to climb trees."
Then Sister Scrupulous buds in, I told her, nuns do not climb trees, monkeys do." I felt like telling her they eat bananas too and that never stopped you from eating them. There is no room for spontaneity here.

I should be more upbeat. I will tell a story that Mother Regina told about one of her novices from her community who was bringing beans upstairs. She was told to carry them in a certain way only, she thought she knew a better way. Well, the beans spilled. Mother Regina saw the whole thing right before her eyes. She pretended that she did not notice so as not to embarrass the flustered novice.
Then the novice started scooping up those beans off the floor and shoveling them back into the dish. It was too much. Mother Regina said that she had to retreat to her room as she was having fits of

342

laughter. Soon after, the novice went to her to ask permission to go to her room and take a rest. Mother said, "Sure." I got a kick out of that story. I can certainly relate to it.

Black shoes on the window sill. If you are the bell ringer, and you go around splashing Holy water on the rooms, or, if you are up on the roof, and you happen to peer in the lit windows of St. Francis de Paola Convent, you will see black nun shoes on all the window sills.

Sister Rosario's Baptismal name is in honor of the Rosary. But, have you ever heard her pray it aloud as hebdomadarian? Her volume goes up I don't know how many decibals. Mother Regina did not know what to do about it. Sister Rosario is not aware of the strength she puts into it. She might be little, but she sure is powerful. The contrast is so sharp that it took every ounce of my control to get through it.

1 September 1993

The other night, I went up on the roof to hang my laundry. It was a bright night, so I could see fine. Gigi came up to help me. We rehash the day. Well, what do you know. There is a concert going on in the nearby park. Yours truly is dancing up a storm to 'Amore' and 'La Bamba'. It was so much fun. We had a blast. You could see the lights and hear the music as clear as could be. It was a great release. Then, Sister Cecilia came up and joined in the fun.

A man by the name of Sean Ryan came the other day to do an interview on The Sisters of Hope for The Sunday Visitor. Sister Gabriel was funny when she met him. "Sean Ryan, you don't say. Now I used to date a fellow by the name of Sean Ryan. My, how you have changed!" This man was balding and a little on the paunchy side. Toward the end of the interview, Mr. Ryan asked if he could see one of the cells or rooms – always a point of intrigue to the outsider. Since this was not permitted, I offered to describe it to him in full detail. This of course included the enjoining bathroom though some use a dormitorystyle bathroom. Siser Agatha came in on the tail end, "You are not telling him about our bathrooms, are you?"

343

Getting back to Sister Gabriel. It really has been eventful the last few times that she has asked me to bake. She did try to make me feel better about it and blame it on those expired cake mixes donated by the Little Sisters. The truth is, the cakes were either soggy in the center, and then flat; or the brownies were all gooey. I follow directions and cook them the required length of time. But she buds in and makes me put a cookie sheet underneath them and then one underneath the brownies too. I do that for pies, but not cakes and brownies. It is no wonder they did not bake through properly. When she sees the results, her expression is too much – nothing short of disgusted.

The Brownie Bang-Out

It happened like this: last night, during Monsignor Smith's class, that is, during the break, I ran down to the kitchen to get a drink of water. It was 8:30. I noticed the oven was still on. I knew that Sister Gabriel had put it on at 6:30 to finish cooking the brownies I had baked earlier because as the chocolate had not cooked thoroughly. I opened the oven. I did happen to see a few brownies in there. Just at that moment, Gigi came downstairs. She and I nibbled a couple of corners. You might say, we were cutting corners. Then she says, "We better turn off the oven." "Yeah, you're right. No telling how long Monsignor's class will go 'til, and shoot, I think Sister Gabriel has had this oven on since 6:30. The weird thing is, the brownies are still gooey in the center." So I thought nothing further of it. Returned to class, and all of a sudden, it hit me. Three separate times I had to refrain from laughter. It dawned on me that Sister Gabriel might not be too happy. In fact, she may fly off the handle. I tried to put it out of my mind. I locked up after Compline. It was close to ten o'clock. I happened to notice the courtyard door open, so I went to lock it. On my way, didn't I see, as big as life, Sister Gabriel fully animated over the oven. Oh no, I can just imagine what she is saying. I am not going near there. I checked in with Gigi before bed. She seems to be the only person who I can talk to. She told me that Sister Gabriel was madder than a hornet over the oven being turned off. She said also that she was hot to trot to find out who exactly turned it off. "What did you do Gigi?

344

You didn't tell her did you?" "Heck no, I wasn't about to tell her. I just acted like nothing happened." Then Gigi went on to say how ridiculous it was to get mad over that. I asked her, "Did she notice any of the brownies missing?

"No, she was too mad to say." Suddenly we both burst into laughter. Today I have been avoiding Sister Gabriel like a hot cake -woe, did I say "Hot cake"? That was Gigi's advice. There is this huge note on the kitchen door which says for people not to turn off the oven as it causes great problems. I thought I would die.

First Week of September

This has been a week of crosses. A week and a half ago I put up Father Salmon's post card and I told Sister Agatha that Father would be calling the following week on either the first or second. He called tonight. In the interim, Sister Agatha has planned for us to be away. I was sorely disappointed when the announcement came today. I was really looking forward to seeing him. He embraces our charism. He offers Mass for the success of the community and he comes to support me in my vocation. I had heard the phone ring. I asked Sister Mary Pio, the portress, if it was Father Salmon. She hedged, and then said, "You would have to ask Sister Agatha." I know it was he just by her reaction and the fact that he said he would call at this time. He is punctilious besides. Plus, when I asked Sister Mary Pio earlier, the first time the phone rang, she said no. If it had not been he, she would have said no again. I am humiliated, embarrassed and very upset. Am thinking of Saint Margaret Mary and am trying to rejoice that I have something to bring to my Crucified Jesus.

4 September 1993
XXV. St. Elizabeth Ann Seton Shrine

Today is Mrs. Dechame's birthday. I remembered her in a special way at Mass and in my prayers. I also remembered her, fittingly enough, as we visited the Shrine of Saint Elizabeth Ann Seton. Mrs. Dechame is a descendant of hers. It pleased me to no end to receive Holy Communion at the tomb of this first American Saint for dear Mrs. Dechame in Emmitsurgh, Maryland. I like what Elisabeth Bayley said, of 'Innocent Pleasures':

As a teenager, Elizabeth Bayley enjoyed dancing and listening to music.

Years later, Elizabeth Seton advised one of her daughters that "I never found

any effect from dancing but the most innocent cheerfulness both in public

and private."

"The Cotillion Dance, England – 1771"

Alone On The Beach

When Elizabeth was 15, her father was once again studying in England. Alone at the seashore in New Rochelle she said, "I once thought my father didn't like me. Well, my God was my father after all."

On this day, there were those in one car who were keeping their eyes open for a picnic area. We ended up pulling into a parking lot of a shopping plaza. At the entrance, was a man holding some sign. He looked unkempt, and tired; hungry too. We pulled into a parking spacee, and got our lunch out of the trunk. Really, we were just having a snack as we would eat after Mass at the Shrine. I didn't have much appetite seeing that poor man. I suggested we take him a sandwich. He could have mine. Sister Luy said that we had to save them for supper, and Sister Cecilia made fun of me saying, "Why don't you give him this apple." She had bitten into it and it was very puny in siz. Sister Francis Mary said that I would not have a sandwich for tonight. "I don't care." I said, "He looks hungry, and we are going to have a big lunch. He can have mine." Sister Lucy was reluctant to let me open the supper sandwich bag. I went ahead and did it.

"You don't even know what his sign said." Sister Lucy admonished me.

"That's irrelevant." I kept fixing a small bag – embarrassingly little to offer: a peanut butter and jelly sandwich, a small apple and a cheese & cracker pak. They agreed to drive over and let me give it to him though I was ready to walk over. It was 93 degrees out. I was in the back seat. I handed Sister Lucy the bag. It only mattered that he get it. We slowed down. All read the sign: "Hungry man with three children – willing to work for food." It grew real quiet in

the car. Sister Lucy said, "Excuse me, do you want a sandwich?"
The man came over. He was very surprised. He had only a few
teeth. He looked like he was around 47 years old, but a very worn
and weathered 47. Humbly, he thanked her. I could not refrain my
tears. Then, Sister Cornelia and Sister Francis were commending me
which I could not stand. I felt ashamed. We could have given him
more. I thought about him the rest of the day. Saint Joseph, help
him find work to feed his family.

At 5:00 p.m. while still at the Shrine, the incumbent Superior told
me, "By the way, Father Salmon called. He will be in touch with
you."
"Did you talk to him?" I asked.
"Well, that was the message given to me."
"Thank you." I mumbled under my breath. I believe she had primed
Sister Mary Pio on how to take his all when he would call and tell
him that we would be out of town. That would be easier than she
telling him.

On our way home, at one of the rest stops there were a couple of
people walking in front of our car in the crowded parking lot, "Never
mind her, hit the one with the ice cream cone, and then I can get it."
Sister Francis Mary says.

Today, Sister Francis Mary took my head off as I was vacuuming
during the 1st two minutes of Meditation. I was helping cook in the
kitchen on account of the freezer door being left ajar and we had to
cook up the food lest it spoil. Therefore, I could not go into
Meditation a the regular time. Rather than interrupt, I figured I
would try to finish up my chores before going in. Besides the air
conditioner would be on in the chapel and the door would be closed,
what harm could there be. Wrong. Sister Francis came out and she
lit into me. I said, "I have only been vacuuming for two minutes."
"And why aren't you in meditating?" Well, I couldn't win today.

The minute I stepped foot out of the Poor Clare Monastery, Sister
Josephat gets on my case about not sitting with the Sisters. The
Monastery chapel is so small and there were four empty pews on the
right hand side. I did not give it another thought. It was first thing

in the morning and it made perfect sense to sit where there was more room. In fact, Sister Gabriel joined me. As it was, the Postulants were all sitting up in the choir loft so what difference did it make. She says, "You know, in the spirit of community, I was thinking how nice it would be if we all sit together. You know, you should be a witness and show that you love us and not sit where you sat. Perhaps in the future you will do that." I couldn't believe my ears. I said, "Yes, I guess I didn't give it much thought, although Sister Gabriel did join me." Then she walked beside me back to our convent very proud of herself for giving me this fraternal "correction". I wanted to say, "You know, it is a funny thing, but I don't really love you."

Poor Louann, I feel for her. She is so self- conscious about her hair turning white that she approached the Superior about getting dye for it. She has prematurely turned white in her twenties so her hair is a very natural looking ash blonde. But no, Sister Agatha willnot let her continue to dye her hair. Louann is frantic as to what color her hair will come in as. Her circumstance would seem extenuating but Blessed be the letter of the law!!!

Then, at lunch, Sister Francis Mary says, "I know someone who is mad at me. She is not talking to me. She had to go to Chapel and ask The Lord for forgiveness." She couldn't stand it any longer and I was so embrrassed that I blushed. Yes, I was annoyed with her. Then Sister Francis Mary comes over to hug me and she says, "I know you love me."

5 September 1993

Mr. Al LaMario is an usher at the Sunday morning Masses. He is about five feet, four inches in height, and sort of barrel-shaped. He has hazel-colored eyes. He is a man of about 70 years from Italy. He fought in World War II in the South Pacific. He received some special medals for his service. Anyway, he wears a light blue suit and he greets me each Sunday before the 8 o'clock Mass. Today, when he saw me, he nervously fumbled for something he had in his pocket. It was a little pink display stand with a picture of Our Lord on His Way to Calvary. Mr. LaMario says he had a friend pick it up in Italy for him as he goes once a year. "I want you to have it Sister James. You are the only one who gives me a warm greeting out of the whole lot." I was taken aback. He told me to put it on my dresser. That is where it stands.

6 September 1993

Today is Father Wright's birthday. He is in his late 50's. He is a living miracle. He had a gall bladder opertion a few years ago which resulted in many more operations due to a massive infection. He is a trooper. He is also a character. He has a great sense of humor and he loves to live it up. He is very open about everything he enjoys too. He is similar to Father Keehan in the way he does things. Father Wright is a real 'P-R" man. He knows how to go about procuring large grants to help the parish. He was at Saint Mary's for several years as pastor. His favorite motto to live by "JOY". That is, J- for Jesus, O-for Others, and Y-for You. Have just learned that this likable priest has Cancer. I hope and pray he will be alright. He did Karl's funeral and he baptised Jane's little girl Alexandra. Dear Jesus, please make him well.

I made the Novena yesterday to the Infant of Prague. It is one that is done every hour on the hour for nine hours. I can not bear any longer not seeing Grampa. This was the favor I was seeking – to be able to go and see him. With this, courage was needed, great courage. It would be necessary to approach the new Superior. It would demand the utmost humility as I would have to address her accordingly while maintaining my composure, and make her understand my urgent request. Gigi was praying for me and Sophia said that she prayed for me as she noticed me go in her office. I had asked "Mother Agatha" that morning if I could meet with her. She throws her wrists up in the air, and she said it was inconvenient then, but perhaps something could be worked out later if I were going to be around; like, where was I going. Finally, it was agreed upon that she would see me at 9:00. When I asked her where, she said, "Wherever." I suggested her office, and she hemmed and hawed and agreed in the end. I had butterflies in my stomach the whole work period. Then, at one minute before nine, I went up to her office. She was not there. I waited. Then after ten minutes, I went looking

349

for her. She was in the basement on the computer. I made my presence known. "I'll meet you upstairs. She told me seeming put out that I would go look for her. Finally, closer to 9:30, she came upstairs. I tried to appear calm, but only moments earlier, I broke down in the storeroom just in anticipation. Now I was walking behind her in the office. I waited for the cue to sit down. I sat down on the little couch. Firstly, I said, "Mother Agatha, I would like to thank you for meeting with me." She was brisk, and was wondering what possibly could I have to say that would merit taking her away from her agenda. Then I began. I looked her straight in the eye and calmly stated, "There is something weighing heavy on me." She pursed her lips, as she often does, and she stuck her chin out. "I need to see my grandfather." Clearly, she was not expecting this. "Well, is he sick?" She asked.

"No, not really. I don't really know. I only know that he can not walk. He crawls up the stairs to go to bed. He does not eat well on account of his haital hernia."

Then, she looks at me trying to think what to say next. "What brought all this on?"

I prayed that I would not cry, "I can not bear it any longer." I lost it. "I asked Mother Regina a month ago and she was hoping to take me up but time got away from her. She told me not to lose hope and to just ask. Mother Agatha, I have come to ask you. I wanted to go through the proper channels. Therefore, I did not go to His Eminence." It was then that her conversation turned into a lecture. "You would have comitted a grave violation if you had done that. Besides, he would have to ask me."

"That is why I am asking you now....." Then she went on, and said this is a time for me to be tested, and "How are you going to be if you take vows?" She asked. "Are you going to be able to handle being away from him? You just can't go and see him."

"Can't we go home once a year?"

"Yes, but not for very long. Perhaps this is something you should ask yourself."

"I will not have him forever. I will take one day at a time – same as I am doing now." I had regained my composure.

She did most of the talking. She went on to say, "The novitiate is for two years. You can not go home until after that. The only reason I could visit my Aunt Loretta was because the doctors thought death was imminent. It is really a miracle that she is still alive and they give her another year."

I felt sick. Grampa may not have another year. I don't know. "I don't like to gamble with life. He is very lonely. He is not well. He could die of a broken heart the way he feels. He is the same age as Monsignor Devlin. His legs are not good. If he were to fall, he could break a hip and then it might be too late."

"Well, I am going to have to discuss it with the Cardinal. Even if he were to consider it, it would have to be on a visiting day."

"If my grandfather could come here, it would be different, but I have not seen him in over a year."

Then she asked he how come his legs are so bad and I told her "severe arthritis". Then she asked when was the last time you were home and how long have you been in habit. I wanted to leave. She is merciless. There was no compassion. She was somber the whole time though she cries at the drop of the hat when it concerns her own feelings. She has seen and called her family at least a dozen times during her six month canonical year. Then her cousin would just show up any time for a visit. Why can't she that?!

"Thank you for your time Mother Agatha."

She tried to prolong the agony. It was very humiliating. "I'll have to pray about it."

"Thank you for your prayers." I said, as I got up and left the room, and I hate to say it, in tears.

7 September 1993

Today, when Gigi and I took our walk, a silver Mercedes Benz pulled up. There were two middle-aged men in the car. The driver had silver hair like his car only he was balding at the crown. He had a mustache and wore reading glasses. He was looking at a map on his lap. He had on a nice plaid shirt and khaki trousers. The passenger seemed to be taller and a little more serious. He was well-dressed too. "Excuse me….." the driver said as he slowed up toward Gigi and myself. We walked over to the car figuring they were probably looking for directions. "Do you know where 'Providence Rest' is?"

"Is that the same as Saint John the Baptist?" I asked.

"Yes, that is right."

"Well, okay, let me see. Well, if you were to turn around, you would drive up and take a right. Well, not the first right because that is where the mailbox is. It would be the next right."

The men are just looking at us like they can't believe they asked two nuns for directions. This was only the beginning.

"Okay, then, you go down a couple – wait no, I think it would be about three blocks to 'Pennyfield", or do they call it 'Penny Lane'? I always get that mixed up with that song by the 'Beatles'." Then it came to me, "Well, perhaps it would be easier if I were to tell you that if you were to throw a boomerang in an exact diagonal that is where it would be. Wait no, that wouldn't be right. If it were a boomerang, it would come back here wouldn't it?"

Then, the driver, who was as nonplussed as ever said, "You know, it would be great if we were in a helicopter."

"Okay, I've got it. You see, it is right on the water. It is not too far from here. Oh, gosh, you will have to forgive me if these directions sond shoddy, but you see, I am from a small town."

Then the passenger suggests, "Could you just tell us which direction the water is Sister?"

Gigi points straight ahead and like the scarecrow on 'The Wizard of Oz', I point in the opposite direction.

The two men look at each other like they don't believe this and Where is 'Candid Camera'!

"Well, you see, there is water in front of us. I guess that's the East River, and then you have water over yonder. I guess that is the Long Island Sound, and that is where the Saint John the Baptist Nursing Home is I am sure. Sister Margaret always rides her bike over there. Gosh, I wish she were here. Oh, but wait, I thought of one other way to tell you. If you take a left at Pennyfield or Penny Lane, whatever they call it, you'll go over this bridge. Well, I guess I shouldn't say bridge, because it is really more of an over pass as there is traffic beneath it. Once you go over that, take a right -"

Gigi added, "Yeah, what you wanna do, is king of go zig zag. I remember that's how we got there."

"We did a lot of zig zagging didn't we Gigi – but all in a diagonal as I have said."

Then Gigi suggested, "You might want to stop and ask again along the way."

The passenger says, "We'll do that."

"Gosh, I am sorry if I was confusing. I know I can be at times. Good luck and God Bless you." Gigi and I walked away from the car. Then we noticed that they were not moving. We looked. Was the driver having a heart attack? His face was beat red and contorted. He and his passenger were doubled over in hysteria. We looked back and waved. Then we got to hysterical laughing. Maybe my directions weren't the best.

This morning we rode into the city with Sister Aquinas as she had to get new shoes. We went to 'Harry's", Jim Crawford, the one who sold us our shoes the last time, was not there. I told one of the shoe salesmen to be sure and tell him I said Hi. As we were waiting for Harry's to open, there was this little old man who was staring at Sister Aquinas and me. We went for a little walk and when we came back, we bumped into him again. He pulls out ten dollars from his pocket and hands it to Sister Aquinas, "Here's one for The Lord." He says. He kept right on walking like he did not want to be ackowledged. He looked like he had a little difficulty walking too. God love him.
Then, since it was taking longer than expected, I went back to the car to put more money in the meter. It was fun to watch the people and to look in the shop windows. I passed 'Ollie's' which is an Oriental restaurant. I watched an "Ollie" employee make homemade noodles. I waved to him and he looked up. I don't think he smiled. He comes from a very reserved culture.

Monday before Vespers, I found two freshly pressed handkerchieves outside my door. I love handkerchieves. I always thought if I had ever written a book, that "handkerchief" would some how figure into the title. I had mentioned that to Sister Aquinas one time quite a while ago. It was she who left them outside my door. That was very thoughtful of her since my day had gone a little awry. The Superior also suggested that, "It could pose violence, if you were to go home to make a quick visit to see your grandfather."

Mid to late September 1993

Sister Francis came into my room early today. She kidded, "You looked like you were packing ofr a moment!"

"Oh no, just have a lot of stuff to clear out."

Then Sister Cecilia was coming down the hall, "Look at Sister James," Sister Francis said to her, "She nearly gave me a heart attack. I thought she was leaving."

I was trying to hold my door closed, Sister Cecilia looks at me, "Sister James! You are leaving!"

"Promise me you don't tell a soul. I mean it. Have I got your word of honor? Sister Francis Mary?" Sister Francis Mary looked at me with those big pitiful eyes and she started to cry. "I promise, I won't tell anyone." Then she took my hands, "You go and take care of Grampa. We're going to miss you."

Sister Cecilia said, "Don't you dare leave without saying good-bye to me. Promise me that."

"Awww, come on. I am not saying good-bye to anyone. I am going to take French leave. I will leave like a thief in the night." Then Sister Cecilia said that she would help me pack which I appreciated as I knew I would need help with my stuff. My secret was out.

I had phoned Grampa the day before. He told me to hang on another day so that I could see my Confessor Father Halligan. I did. I did not want to tell the incumbent Superior of my plans. I had no intention of telling her. My Confessor urged me to tell her. He said I would only have to say three little words. When I told Grampa this, he said, "Were they, 'Go to Hell'". They were, "Mother, I'm leaving." The whole idea of it was utterly distasteful to me. If she were any kind of a human, she would have picked up on this a long time ago. I would have to educate her in the manner in which I was to leave. Only I had to be obedient to the last, one last time. I went in front of The Blessed Sacrament, and coupled with The Sacrament of Reconciliation, God gave me the grace to do it. I might even enjoy it. There was a certain sense of vicariousness in dropping the unexpected bomb. I scouted out the whole convent. Before finding her, Gigi and Sister Francis came to my room to find out if I had told the Superior and if so, what was her reaction. They also wondered if I would be telling the Cardinal. They were more anxious than I was, but I had no report at this time to give them. They told me to meet them down by the water.

XXVI. Guess Who's Comming to Dinner

354

It was shortly before Vespers that I found Mother Agnes on the third floor in the ironing room which happens to be next to my room.

"Oh, Mother Agatha, I have been looking all over for you." She looked up not even thinking that I could have anything worthwhile to say. "Mother, I'm leaving." Those fateful words rolled off my tongue. Then I simply left for my room. She followed behind me – her mouth open in complete astonishment.

"Do you always make such hasty decisions?"

"Not as a rule."

"Well, do you know what brought this on?"

"Yep." I was very flip. I could not be bothered with her questions. It was too late now.

"Well, do you want to talk to Sister Regina?" (She always referred to her as "Sister" not "Mother").

"Nope, that won't be necessary."

"Did you know that the Cardinal was coming for dinner tonight?"

"No, I didn't." (Actually, Sophia slipped this out to me but I did not let on.) "It is a funny thing, I am not one for good-byes, but it will be nice that I can say good-bye to the Cardinal." I picked up a laundry basket and I nonchalantly walked out of my room. I left Mother Agatha in my room completely baffled.

I went to Vespers and I watched dear Father Halligan repose The Blessed Sacrament and lead us in Benediction. To see him lift the Monstrance with that Crucifix above the altar which I had grown so familiar with was more than I could take. I put the idea out of my mind.

Mother Agatha wanted to meet with me in her office in five minutes. I felt weak, and emotionally drained. I have not had much of an appetite for a couple of months. I have not been able to sleep either. I went to the kitchen and grabbed a banana. Then, I proceded to my room. Sister Cecilia was already there waiting for me. She was upset. She said, "Look, you be sure and tell the Cardinal everything when you meet with him. And don't you tell Sister Agatha a thing."

"I won't." Well, wasn't she standing outside my door. I am not sure how much she heard, but Sister Cecilia grabbed some paper towels and began to blow her nose in them. She did not want to be seen as no one is supposed to be in the room of another Sister's.

I went into Mother Agatha's office. She said to me, "Well......, you seem to be at peace about your decision." I nodded. "Have you prayed about it?"

"Yes." I replied.

"What are you going to do when you get home?"

"Do you mean before the embarrassment, or after the embarrassment?"

She laughed nervously under her breath. That was a dumb question and a premature one to ask. She kept trying to drive answers out of me, but I could not be moved. Then she added, "The Cardinal will want to know why you are leaving."

"I am sure I can think of something." I said. Then I decided, this interrogation is over.

I got up and I said, "Well, you have a birthday coming up Mother Agatha."

"Oh, I would rather not think about them."

"And your sister's anniversary. I will keep her in my prayers. I will pray for you and I ask that you pray for me Mother Agatha." I left the room. The Cardinal was due to arrive shortly.

The bell rang. The Cardinal has arrived. We greeted him, he greeted us. I could not be sure that he knew of my leaving at this point. Then, I noticed Mother Agatha take him into the classroom where she wold tell him. Afterward, Sister Aquinas nabbed the Cardinal as she wanted to talk to him. Dinner was running late. It was closer to seven before we ate. In truth, I can not eat in the presence of Mother Agatha. I am repulsed. I just see such injustice when I look at her.

Sister Francis Mary had pulled Father Matt aside near the image of Our Lady of Guadalupe. She said, "Did you hear? Sister James is leaving." His face seemed to register shock. Then Sister Francis Mary added, "Attila the Nun." At that moment, "Attila" came over to break up whatever conversation was taking place.

We went down to the refectory. I would have to wait until after dinner before I could actually talk to the Cardinal. It was close to 8 o'clock now, and it appeared that no overture would be made about me speaking with him. I took this as a cue to broach him myself.

"Your Eminence, may I see you for a moment?"

"Yes," He looked at me searchingly. We made our way to the parlor on the main level.

I asked where he would be more comfortable and we took our seats.

"I suppose you have heard that I am leaving Your Eminence."

"I only heard this evening." He sort of implied that he wished he had known sooner.

"Well, I am sorry. I never thought it would come to this. I certainly don't want this to be a reflection on any of my references. I had hoped that I could have spoken with you before it came to this, but I have unequivocally been dissuaded on both counts."

He looked at me, both surprised and distressed. He listened to me very carefully, and he rubbed his chin with his hand – like he could not believe all that he was hearing.

"Your Eminence, it was the straw that broke the camel's back. I was told tht I probably did not have a vocation because I can not go two years without seeing my ailing grandfather. I have seen so much unfairness and met with very little mercy in the case of the new Superior." I was tired and I just spoke my feelings off the cuff. I feared I had nothing to lose at this point. Afterall, I was leaving.

Several of the Sisters had pleaded with me to be open and honest and tell the Cardinal like it is. On the Cardinal's coat of arms, his motto is: "There can be no greater love without justice." Now I would set the record straight. I proceded to tell the Cardianl of incidents in which I felt the neophyte had been most unfair and unreasonable. I then kissed my medalion as he himself had done once in bestowing it on me. "I do not deserve this." I handed it over to him. The chain broke when I took it off. "But Your Eminence, if I may keep the Office books? I will continue to pray for you every day." He nodded yes. Then I said, "I am sorry."

He said, "That is life, honey."

Previous to that, I had told him about my grandfather and I lost all composure.

He then said that I could go home and see Grampa if I did not stay for any extended length of time. I could still come back and finish the Canonical year. I thanked him, but he could see, that it made no difference now.

We both got up. To my great surprise, the Cardinal looked at me, and he said, "I love you." He embraced me. I managed, "I love you."

How could he possibly love me when I am walking out on him. Could he have respected my stance.

I met the Cardinal's attorney out in the hall. Alice was crying. I could not believe it. She cares for the Cardinal and his community. She hugged me. God love her. She is as beautiful on the inside as she is on the outside.

Mother Agatha was lurking in the hallway. I asked, "Do they know?" She nodded.

XXVII. Ironing Out Some Wrinkles

I went upstairs to finish getting my things together. Sister Cecilia came, followed by Gigi and Sophia. They were all wondering how I made out. I did not feel like talking. I only said, "I told him all he needed to know."

I believe the Cardinal was talking to Sister/Mother Agatha now. The Sisters went in the chapel for Compline. I did not go. I slipped over to the rectory to see if Monsignor Devlin was there. Maybe it was just as well that he wasn't. I told the young receptionist Christine just to tell the Monsignor that I stopped by. I returned to the convent. I noticed Father Matt in the front parlor. I went in and sat with him. I started to open up a little to him. He looked at me most compassionately. The door bell rang twice, but both times it was Hispanic women looking for the prayer meeting across the street.

Then Mother Agatha came to me and told me that I needed to take the habit off.
I always wore it with a spirit of detachment. It had, of course, been blessed by someone very special. That in itself, would make it difficult. Now I had been stripped. I was ready for the humiliations that would ensue. "I don't have anything to change into save that of a tee shirt."
"We will find something."

Sister Cecilia was nearby. She said that she would get me something. She is so good. I will really miss her. She helped put all my stuff on the "dumb waiter"

I thought it was a little late for Mother Agatha to be "ironing out wrinkles" as she was now doing on the blouse that Sister Cecilia had gotten for me. She was suddenly trying to be nice to me. For the first time, she even addressed me with the religious name that I no longer had, "My Sister James, you are full of surprises."
"Yep, I have been known to be." I said almost sarcastically. The last time I was in the ironing room I told her I was leaving. Tonight, she was wondering if I had called someone without her permission. I said, "Yes, but not to worry. I called 'Collect'." Then she was afraid that I superceded her and told the Cardinal before I told her. She gave me a lecture in this "eleventh" hour about how wrong it would have been had I gone to him before her. She was still afraid of losing authority.

Now, I was using the navy webbed belt from my habit to hold up this skirt which was three sizes too large. I felt bare without the veil.

My sister Annie had just arrived with her oldest son, my nephew Kenneth. I learned, after the fact, that she had been in the hospital. She is quiet and she does not tell anybody. She is very good. She would do anything for anybody. I was glad the Cardinal was still here so that he could meet them. He was waiting for whomever in my family was coming to get me.
I took pride in introducing Annie to His Eminence. She said that she felt as though he looked right into her soul. The sense of relief was evident in my voice when Annie came. I felt stronger. I was composed saying good-bye one final time very much aware of this tender moment. He looked at me one last time, then took me in his arms, gently hugging me. Then, he rested his hands on my shoulders and kissed my left cheek. He said, "Let us hear from you." It was very fatherly. I just looked at him and then I noticed the entourage in the corridor – all in tears. At that point, His Emininece said, "I am going to slip out." This was it.
Now all the Sisters knew and I had to face them. Here I was for the first time since the novitiate not wearing a habit. I was wearing

Sister Cecilia's oversized blouse and skirt. I felt a freedom; a repression lifted. "Gosh, I can even dance in this skirt."

This was the painful moment that I had hoped to avoid. I embraced it fully. I walked into the living room which took on the semblance of a funeral parlor. My voice cracked as I looked around at all the Sisters one last time. "Sisters, Thank you............" Then I went to each and everyone fully aware of each one as an individual. I said something to each that related to them specifically and to me regarding them. I spoke to each of the new postulants. I had a soft spot for Cornelia. Michelle reminded me of St. Faustina. Gosh, this was not easy. I went to Sister Francis Mary, Sister Aquinas, Sister Cecilia, and to Gigi. Then I approached Sister Gabriel. She ran up to her room to fetch the little book of Psalms which I had left on her bed earlier. She was sobbing uncontrollably. My heart ached. She was so much fun. Sister Rosario looked at me, "But Sister James, why, why didn't you tell me?" Her eyes pleading as she looked at me for answers. "I am sorry Sister Rosario. I just couldn't." Sister Mary Pio went to get some gingerale and some cookies from the pantry for my sister and my nephew Kenneth.

Now the car was loaded up thanks to Sister Cecilia, Sister Aquinas, Sophia and Gigi. The put my 'Heidi' doll in the front seat like a mascot.

All the Sisters came out to see me off. Sister Agatha pulled Annie aside, "Well, were you surprised at your sister's decision?" Annie, who is always right on the ball, said, "Nothing Virginia does surprises me." She was still at that response.

Everyone said good-bye to me again. Gigi gave me her little Mother Mary statue that she had always carried. I said to Sister Agatha, "I'll send you some 'Empire' apples." She laughed nervously. She was the only one who had dry eyes; well, she and Sister Josephat.

I was in Annie's car now. It was just starting to get dark. Sister Gabriel shouted, "You will always be my little Sister James Mariah."

"God Bless you all!" I was waving my hand out the window. I could hear many shout, "I love you!"

And a voice trailed in the wind, called 'Mariah', "I love you all..................